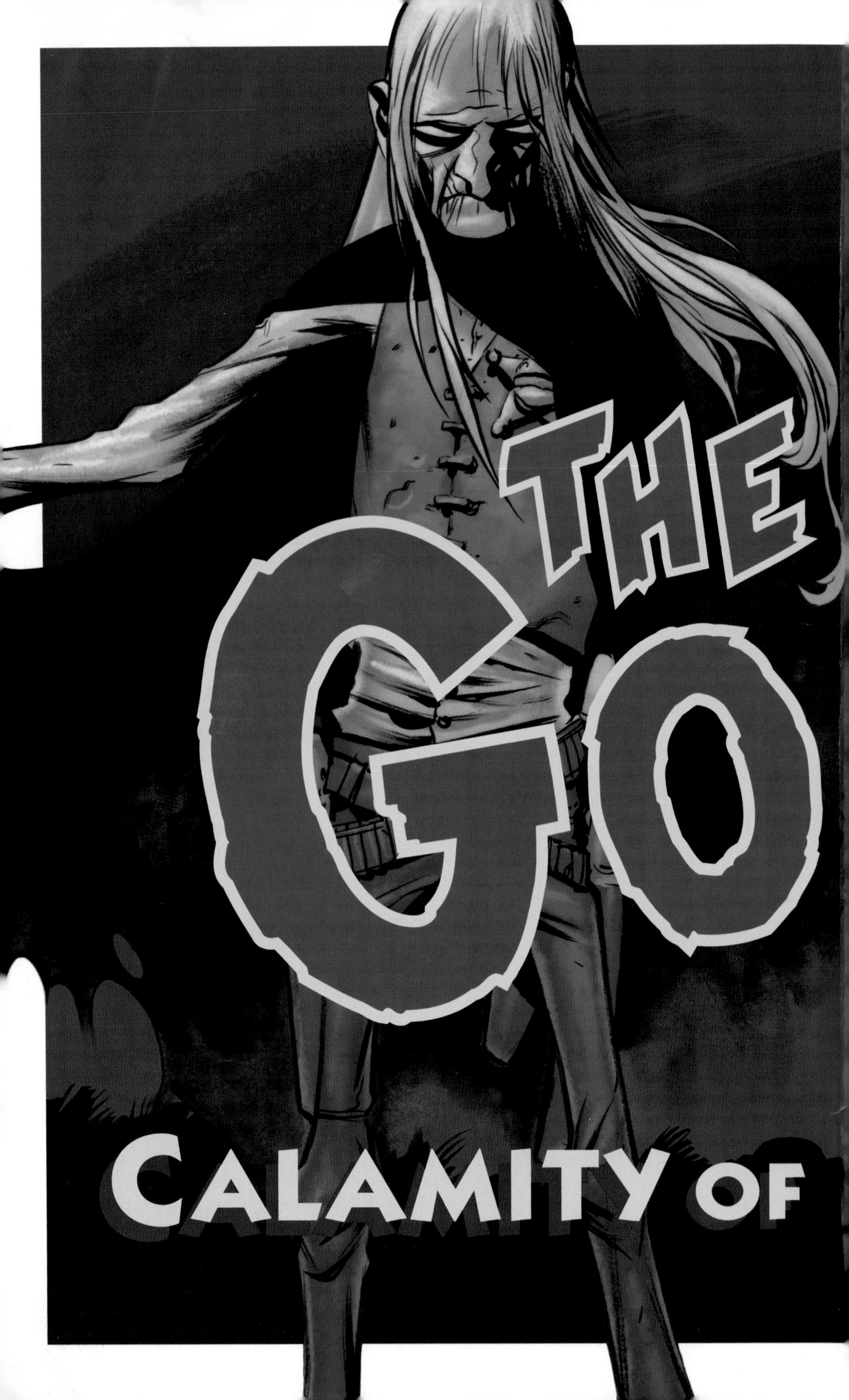
THE
GO
CALAMITY OF

Written and Illustrated by **ERIC POWELL**

With Colors by **DAVE STEWART**

GOON™ IN CONSCIENCE

 DARK HORSE BOOKS®
MILWAUKIE

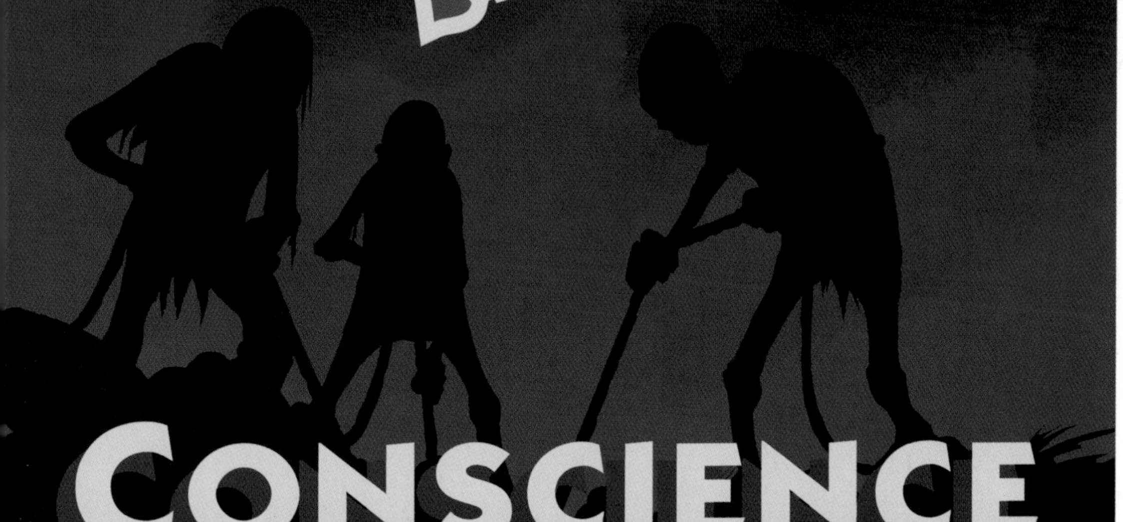

editor SCOTT ALLIE

associate editor SIERRA HAHN

assistant editor FREDDYE LINS

designer AMY ARENDTS

president & publisher MIKE RICHARDSON

Neil Hankerson *executive vice president* • Tom Weddle *chief financial officer* • Randy Stradley *vice president of publishing* • Michael Martens *vice president of business development* • Anita Nelson *vice president of marketing, sales, and licensing* • David Scroggy *vice president of product development* • Dale LaFountain *vice president of information technology* • Darlene Vogel *director of purchasing* • Ken Lizzi *general counsel* • Davey Estrada *editorial director* • Scott Allie *senior managing editor* • Chris Warner *senior books editor* • Diana Schutz *executive editor* • Cary Grazzini *director of design and production* • Lia Ribacchi *art director* • Cara Niece *director of scheduling*

THE GOON™: CALAMITY OF CONSCIENCE

This volume collects issues #28–#31 of the Dark Horse Comics ongoing series *The Goon*.

Published by
Dark Horse Books
A division of
Dark Horse Comics, Inc.
10956 SE Main Street
Milwaukie, OR 97222

darkhorse.com

To find a comics shop in your area,
call the Comic Shop Locator Service toll-free at (888) 266-4226.

First edition: October 2009
ISBN 978-1-59582-346-5

10 9 8 7 6 5 4 3 2

Printed at Midas Printing International, Ltd., Huizhou, China

HOW I MET POWELL AND LEARNED TO STOP WORRYING ABOUT THE COMICS

Introduction by STEVE NILES

When I met Powell he didn't hang out with fancy-pants cable-TV stars. Hell, he didn't even have cable or a TV (or as Powell called it, the electronic the-ater box). Eric and I met online, and no, it wasn't on match.com so ~~fuck~~ off.

I was on the ebays looking at art, wishing I could afford some, when I came across this amazing image of a cybernetic gorilla, beautifully drawn and selling for way too cheap, so I bid on it. I also dropped the artist a note saying I loved his stuff. It wound up being Eric Powell. We became immediate friends, and bitched and whined for days on end about how nobody would hire us in comics. We talked horror and shared a mutual love for '70s comics and we even came up with a Defenders pitch that was immediately shot down by Marvel. I think Powell has the pitch piece in one of those sketchbooks of his he sells at them funny-book conventions.

Anyway, that's how we met, and yes, I won the gorilla.

But we're here to talk about Powell's creation, *The Goon*. This is something that started out as a black-and-white indie comic and has grown into a multimedia empire, or as close as you can get to an empire in Kentucky, Tennessee, or wherever he lives. I think they filmed *Deliverance* there. Not sure.

The Goon is one of my favorite comics, and Powell is on the top of my list of best artist/writers out working today.

The Goon combines two of my favorite things: laughing and ~~shit~~ting my pants (comedy and horror), and the volume you hold in your hands is yet another example of just how good Powell is at what he does.

Sit back, put on a diaper if you're not already wearing one, enjoy the conclusion of the Labrazio saga, and see a true master at work.

Steve Niles
Los Angeles, 2009

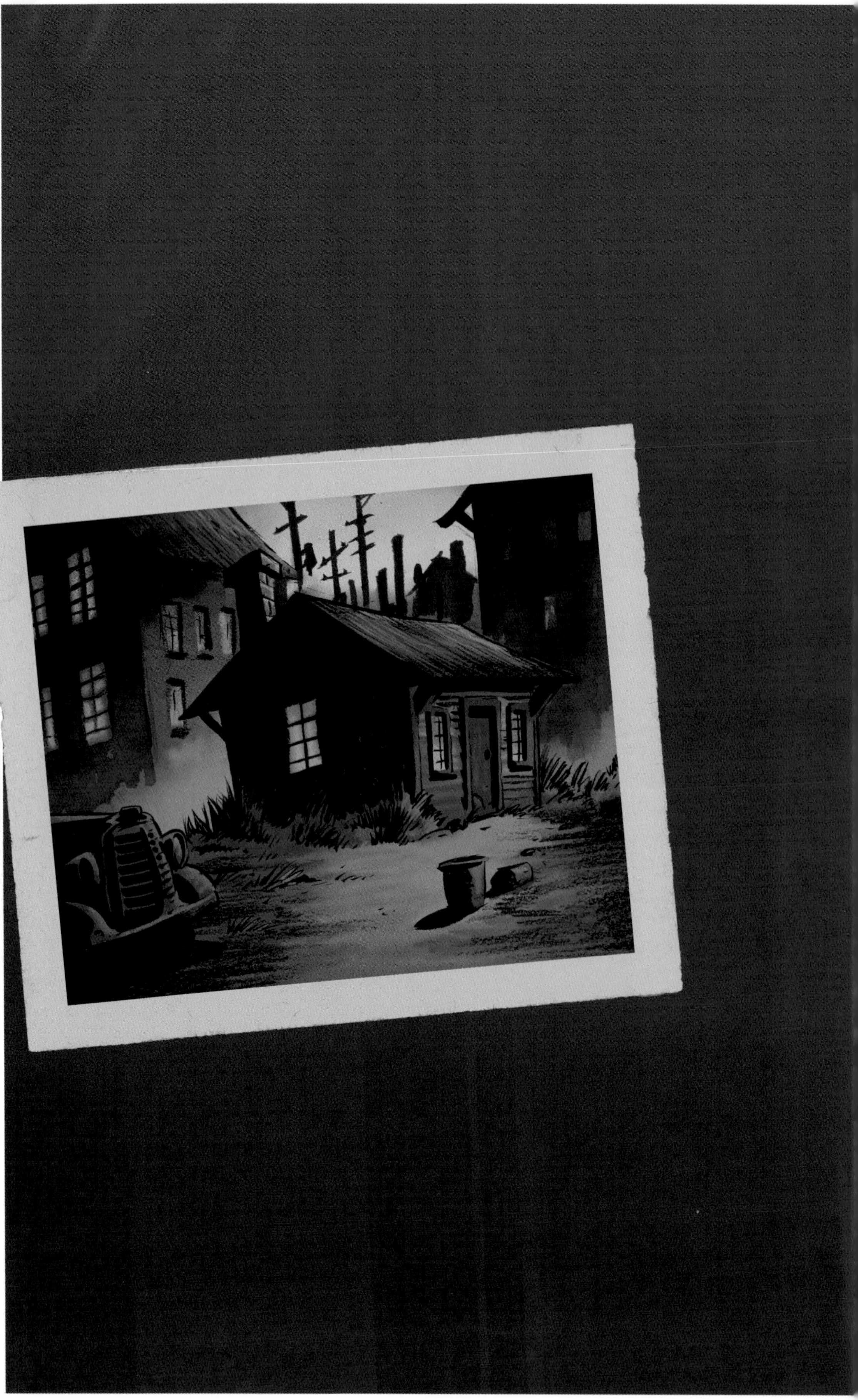

CHAPTER 1

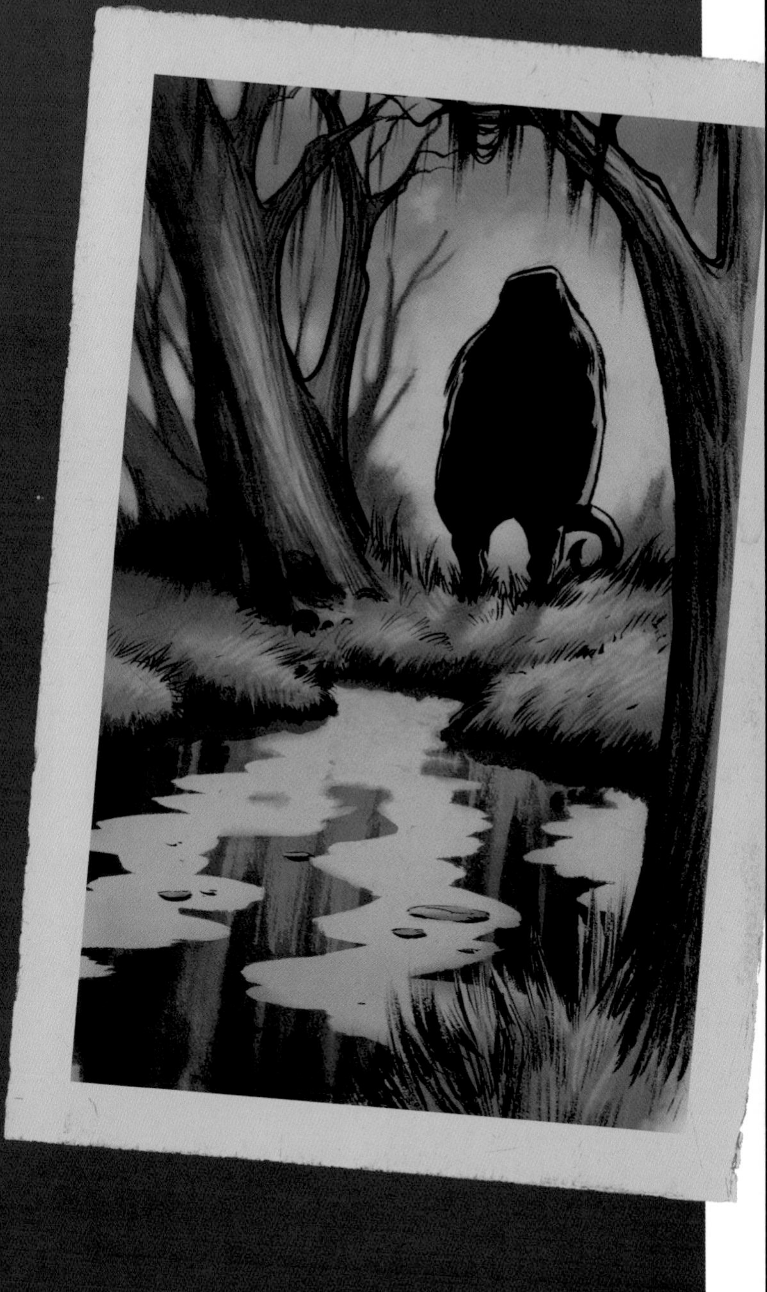

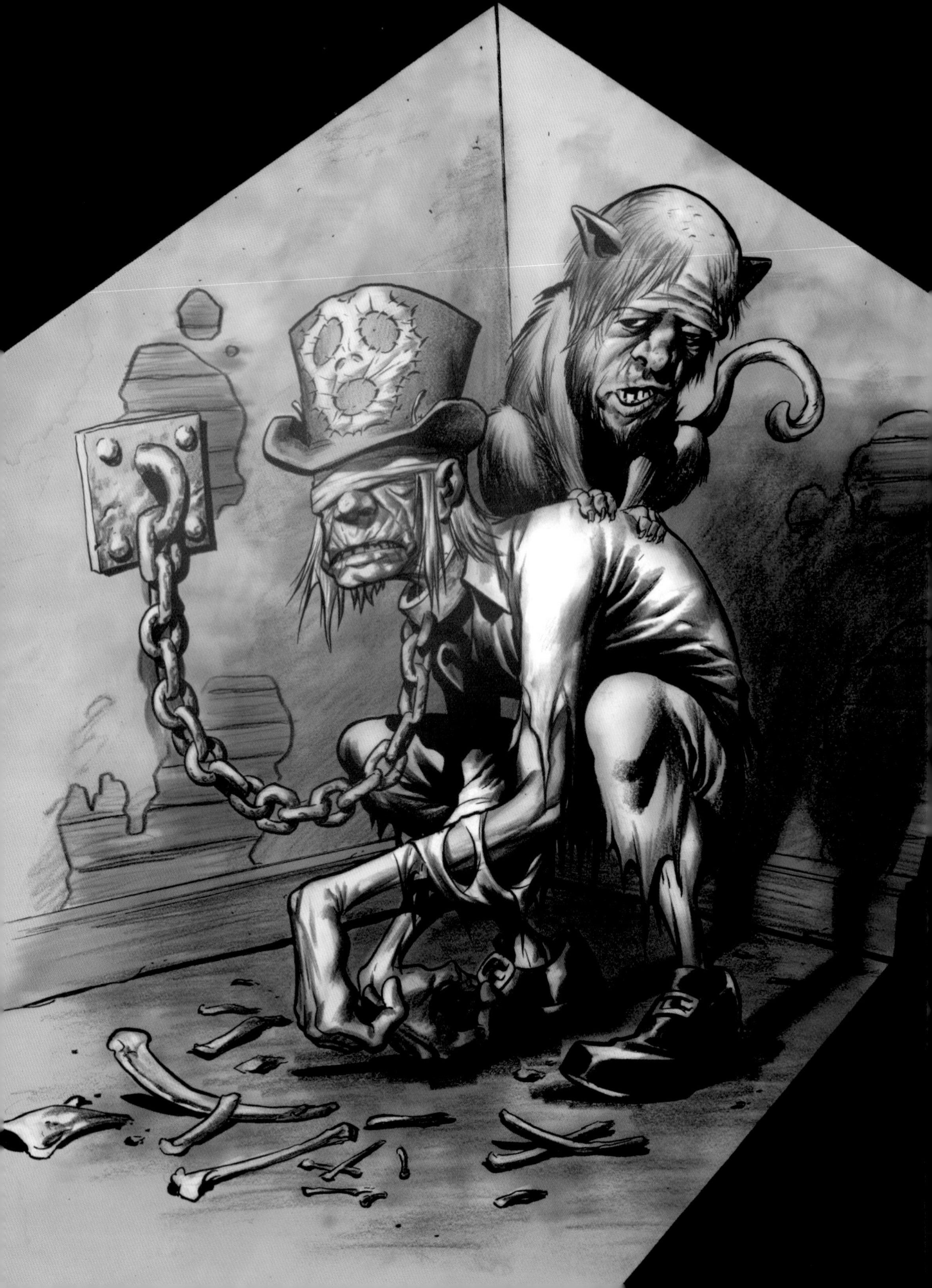

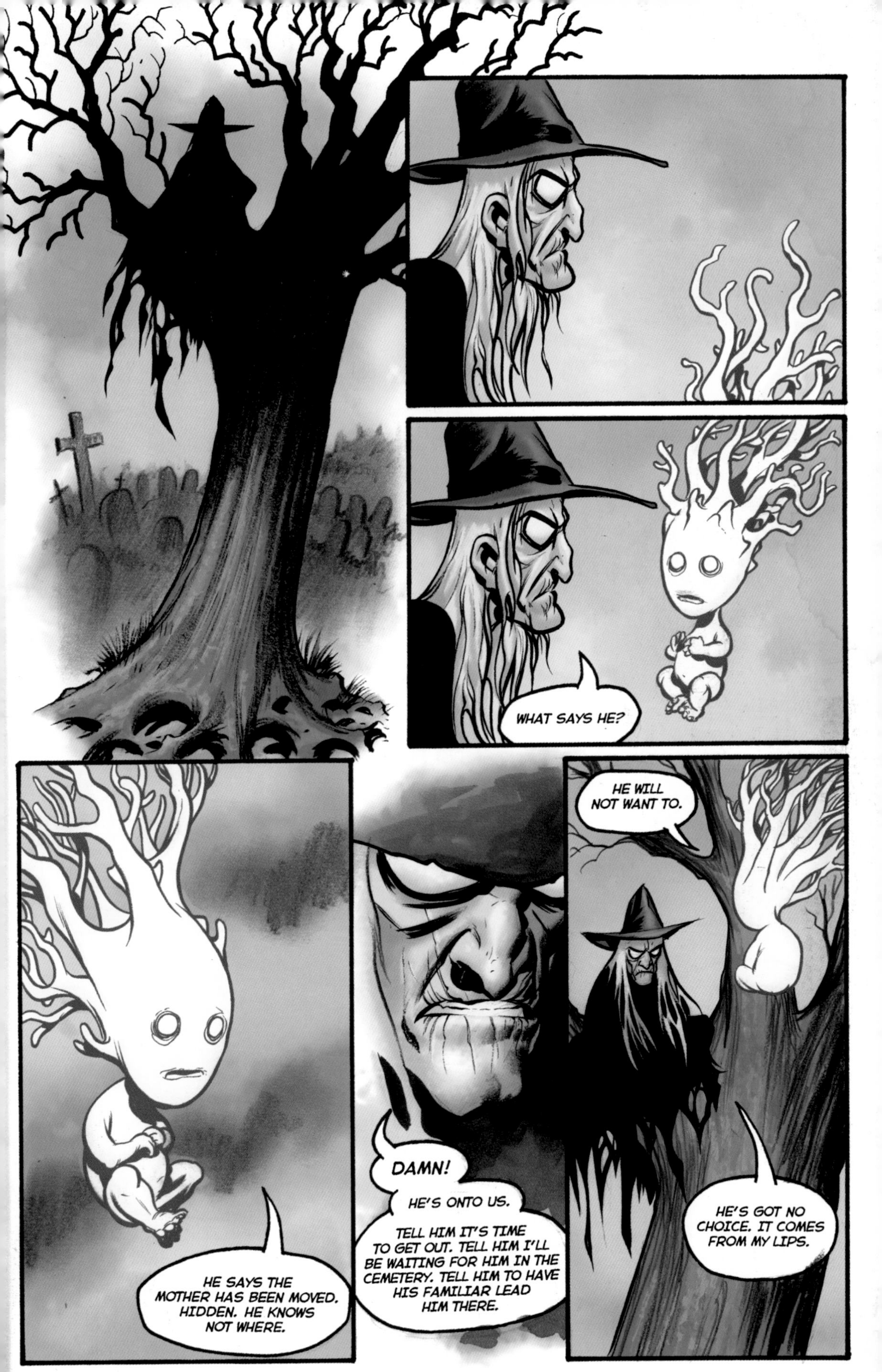
WHAT SAYS HE?
HE SAYS THE MOTHER HAS BEEN MOVED. HIDDEN. HE KNOWS NOT WHERE.
DAMN!
HE'S ONTO US.
TELL HIM IT'S TIME TO GET OUT. TELL HIM I'LL BE WAITING FOR HIM IN THE CEMETERY. TELL HIM TO HAVE HIS FAMILIAR LEAD HIM THERE.
HE WILL NOT WANT TO.
HE'S GOT NO CHOICE. IT COMES FROM MY LIPS.

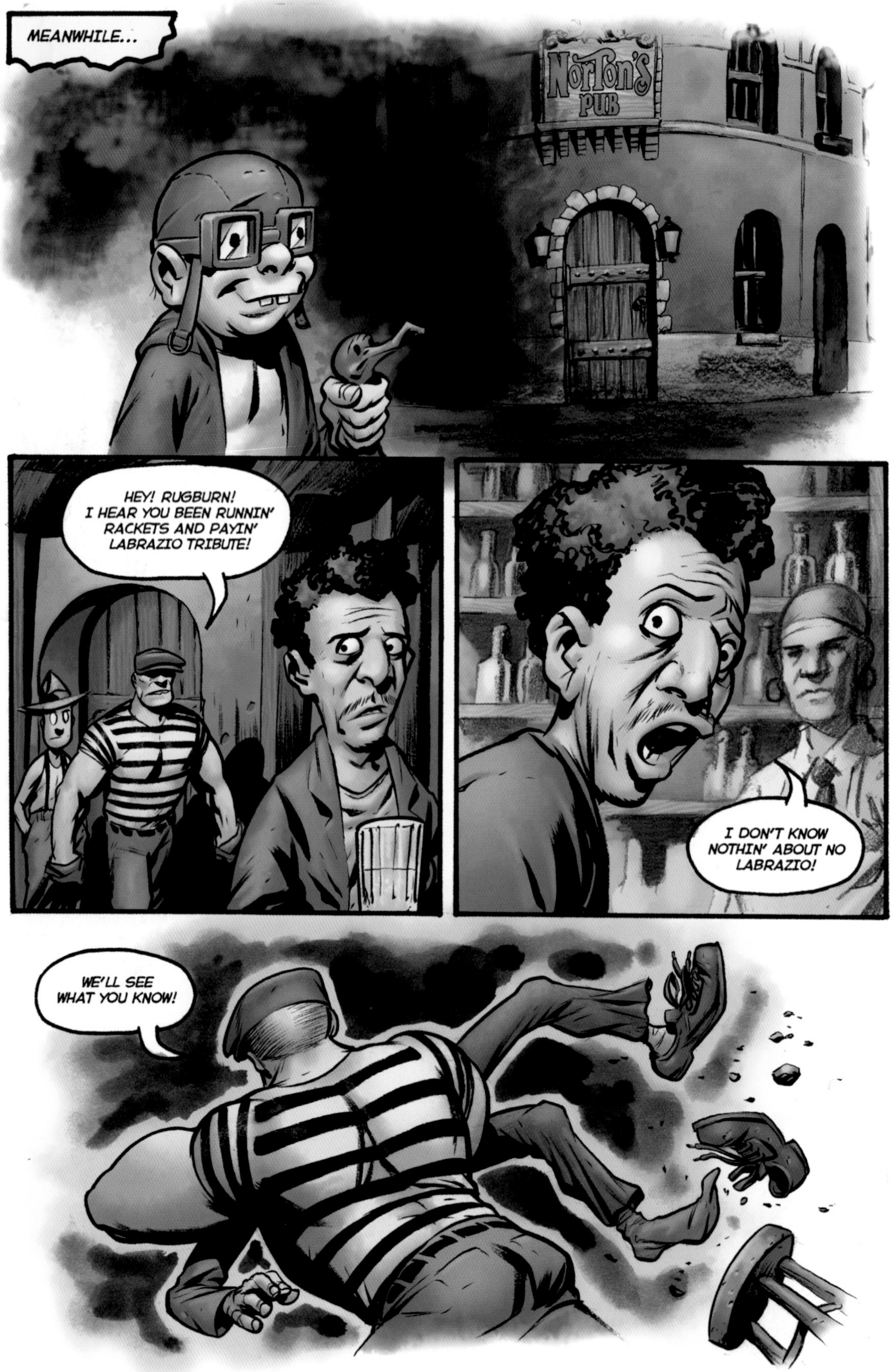
MEANWHILE...
NorTon's PUB
HEY! RUGBURN! I HEAR YOU BEEN RUNNIN' RACKETS AND PAYIN' LABRAZIO TRIBUTE!
I DON'T KNOW NOTHIN' ABOUT NO LABRAZIO!
WE'LL SEE WHAT YOU KNOW!

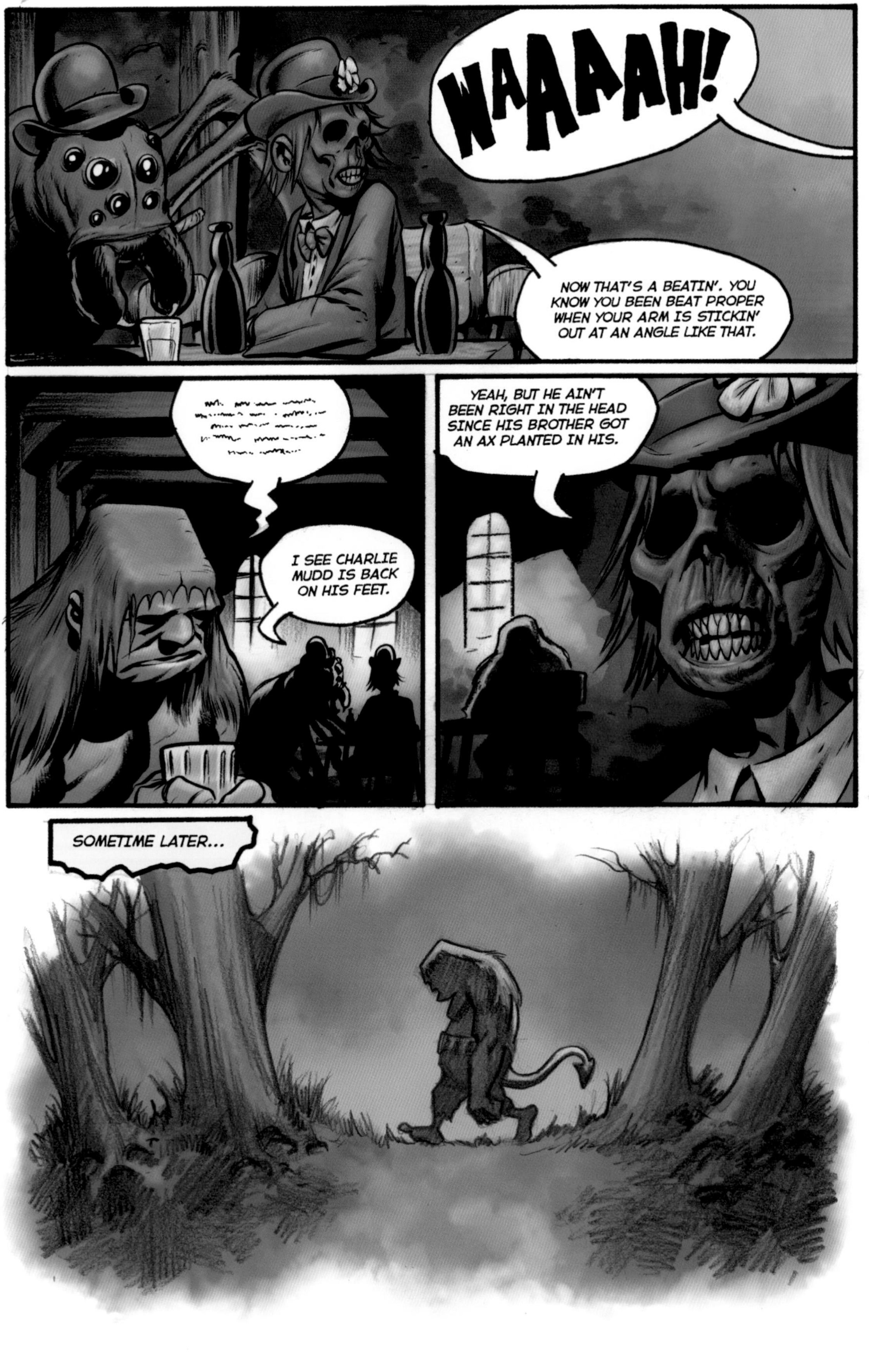
WAAAAH!
NOW THAT'S A BEATIN'. YOU KNOW YOU BEEN BEAT PROPER WHEN YOUR ARM IS STICKIN' OUT AT AN ANGLE LIKE THAT.
I SEE CHARLIE MUDD IS BACK ON HIS FEET.
YEAH, BUT HE AIN'T BEEN RIGHT IN THE HEAD SINCE HIS BROTHER GOT AN AX PLANTED IN HIS.
SOMETIME LATER...

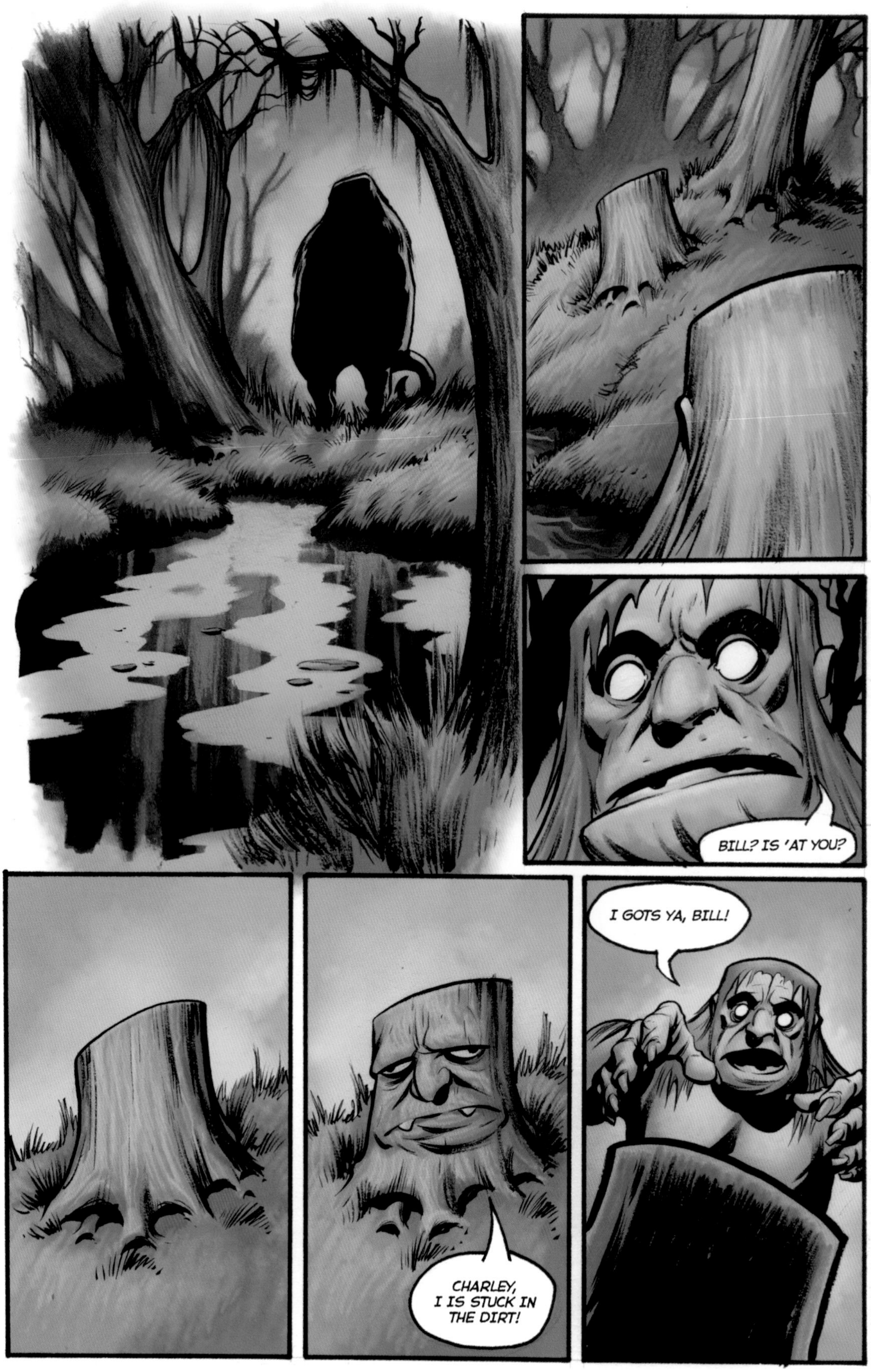
BILL? IS 'AT YOU?
CHARLEY, I IS STUCK IN THE DIRT!
I GOTS YA, BILL!

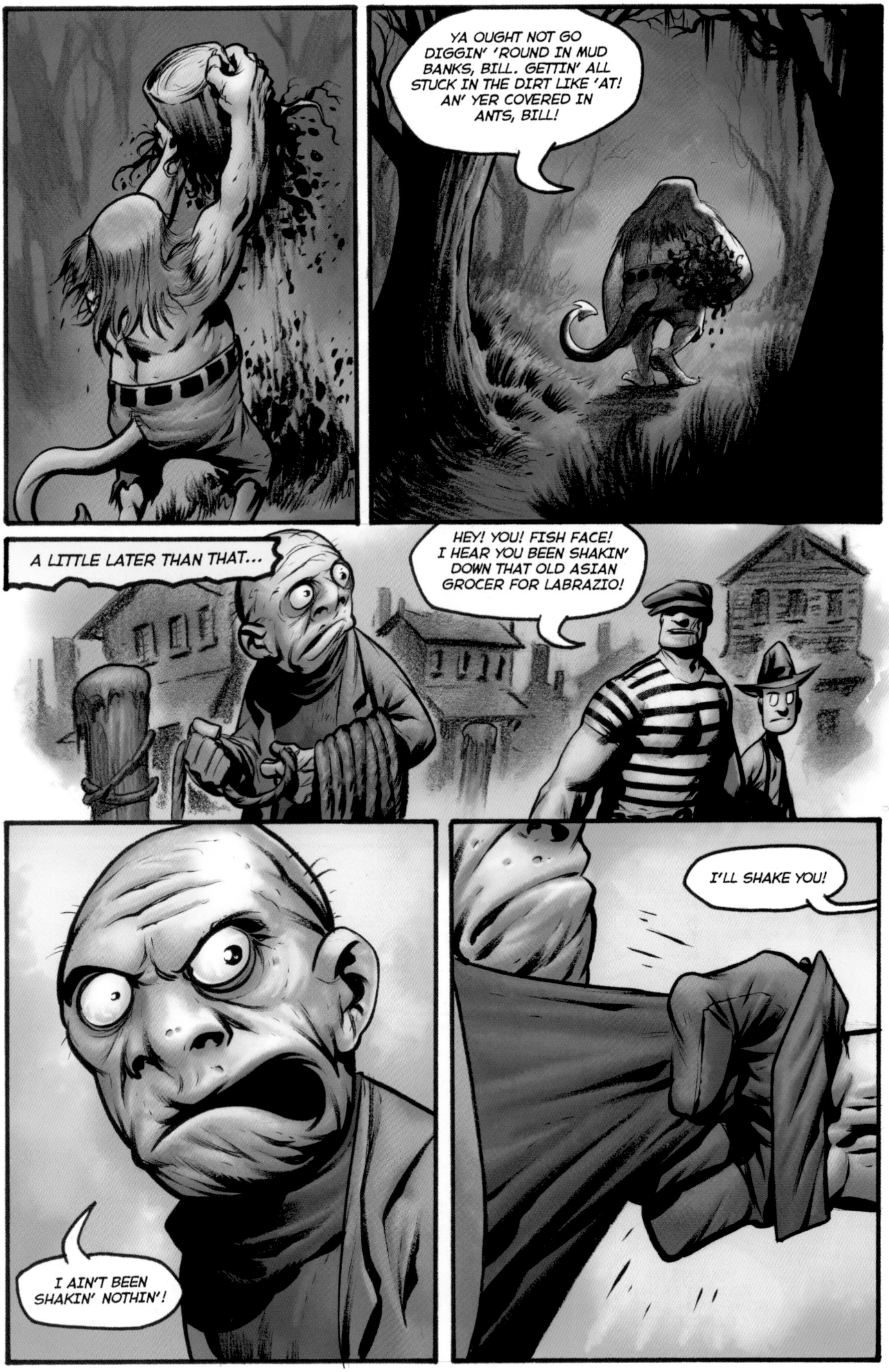
YA OUGHT NOT GO DIGGIN' 'ROUND IN MUD BANKS, BILL. GETTIN' ALL STUCK IN THE DIRT LIKE 'AT! AN' YER COVERED IN ANTS, BILL!
A LITTLE LATER THAN THAT...
HEY! YOU! FISH FACE! I HEAR YOU BEEN SHAKIN' DOWN THAT OLD ASIAN GROCER FOR LABRAZIO!
I AIN'T BEEN SHAKIN' NOTHIN'!
I'LL SHAKE YOU!

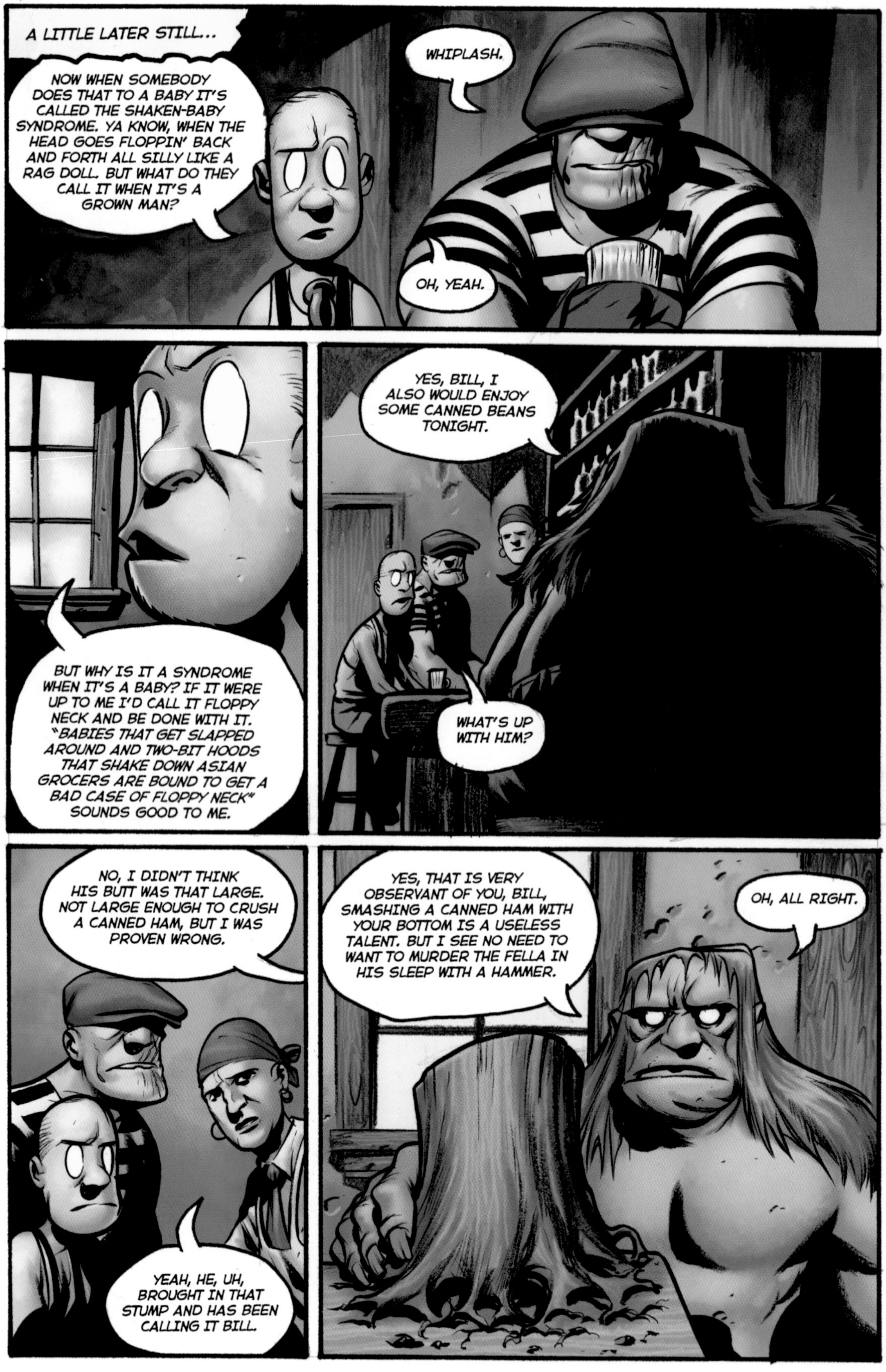
A LITTLE LATER STILL...
NOW WHEN SOMEBODY DOES THAT TO A BABY IT'S CALLED THE SHAKEN-BABY SYNDROME. YA KNOW, WHEN THE HEAD GOES FLOPPIN' BACK AND FORTH ALL SILLY LIKE A RAG DOLL. BUT WHAT DO THEY CALL IT WHEN IT'S A GROWN MAN?
WHIPLASH.
OH, YEAH.
BUT WHY IS IT A SYNDROME WHEN IT'S A BABY? IF IT WERE UP TO ME I'D CALL IT FLOPPY NECK AND BE DONE WITH IT. "BABIES THAT GET SLAPPED AROUND AND TWO-BIT HOODS THAT SHAKE DOWN ASIAN GROCERS ARE BOUND TO GET A BAD CASE OF FLOPPY NECK" SOUNDS GOOD TO ME.
YES, BILL, I ALSO WOULD ENJOY SOME CANNED BEANS TONIGHT.
WHAT'S UP WITH HIM?
NO, I DIDN'T THINK HIS BUTT WAS THAT LARGE. NOT LARGE ENOUGH TO CRUSH A CANNED HAM, BUT I WAS PROVEN WRONG.
YEAH, HE, UH, BROUGHT IN THAT STUMP AND HAS BEEN CALLING IT BILL.
YES, THAT IS VERY OBSERVANT OF YOU, BILL, SMASHING A CANNED HAM WITH YOUR BOTTOM IS A USELESS TALENT. BUT I SEE NO NEED TO WANT TO MURDER THE FELLA IN HIS SLEEP WITH A HAMMER.
OH, ALL RIGHT.

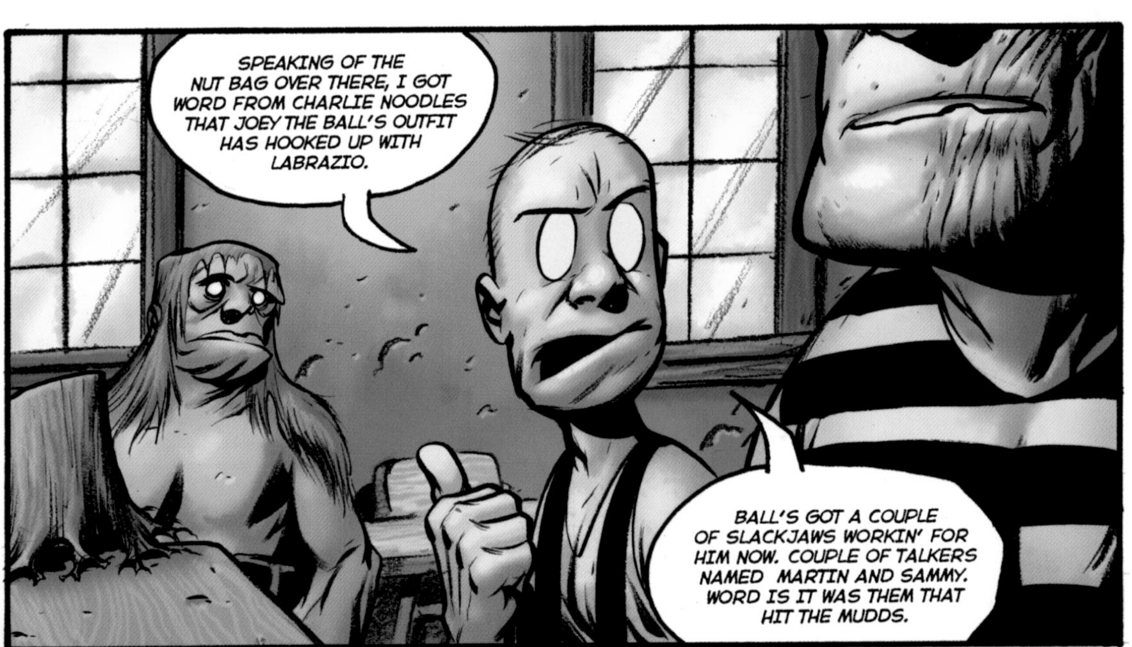
SPEAKING OF THE NUT BAG OVER THERE, I GOT WORD FROM CHARLIE NOODLES THAT JOEY THE BALL'S OUTFIT HAS HOOKED UP WITH LABRAZIO.
BALL'S GOT A COUPLE OF SLACKJAWS WORKIN' FOR HIM NOW. COUPLE OF TALKERS NAMED MARTIN AND SAMMY. WORD IS IT WAS THEM THAT HIT THE MUDDS.

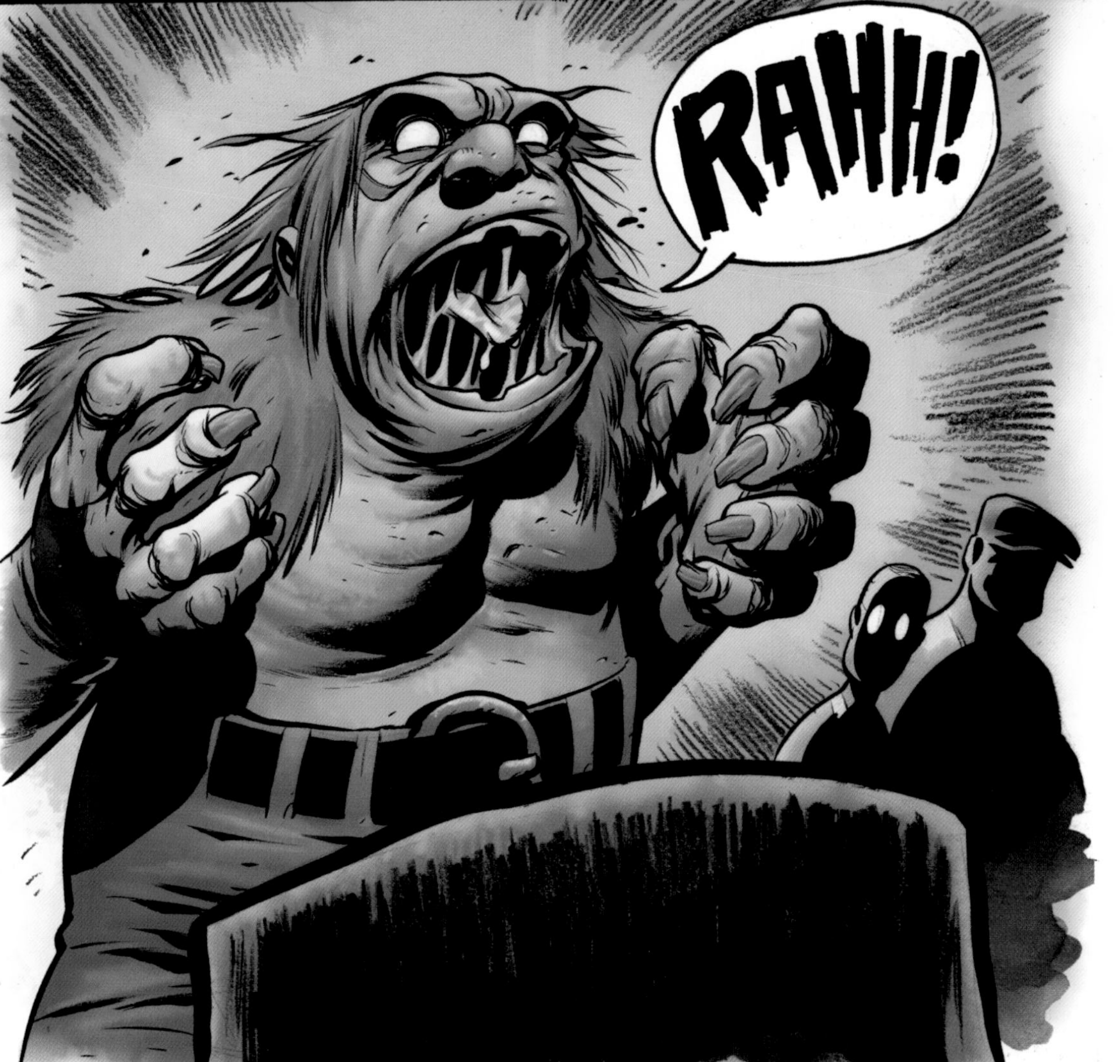
RAHH!

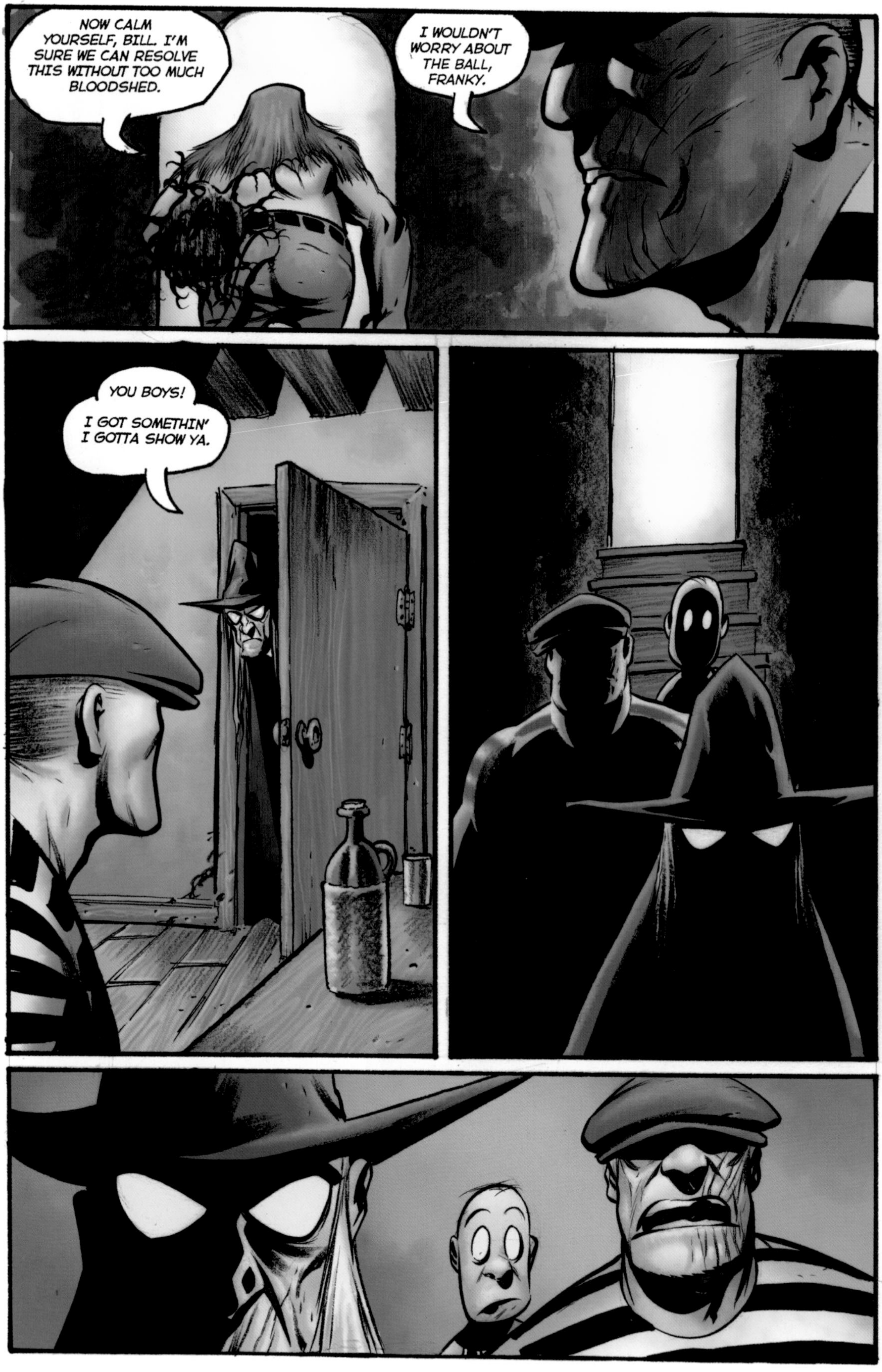
NOW CALM YOURSELF, BILL. I'M SURE WE CAN RESOLVE THIS WITHOUT TOO MUCH BLOODSHED.
I WOULDN'T WORRY ABOUT THE BALL, FRANKY.
YOU BOYS!
I GOT SOMETHIN' I GOTTA SHOW YA.

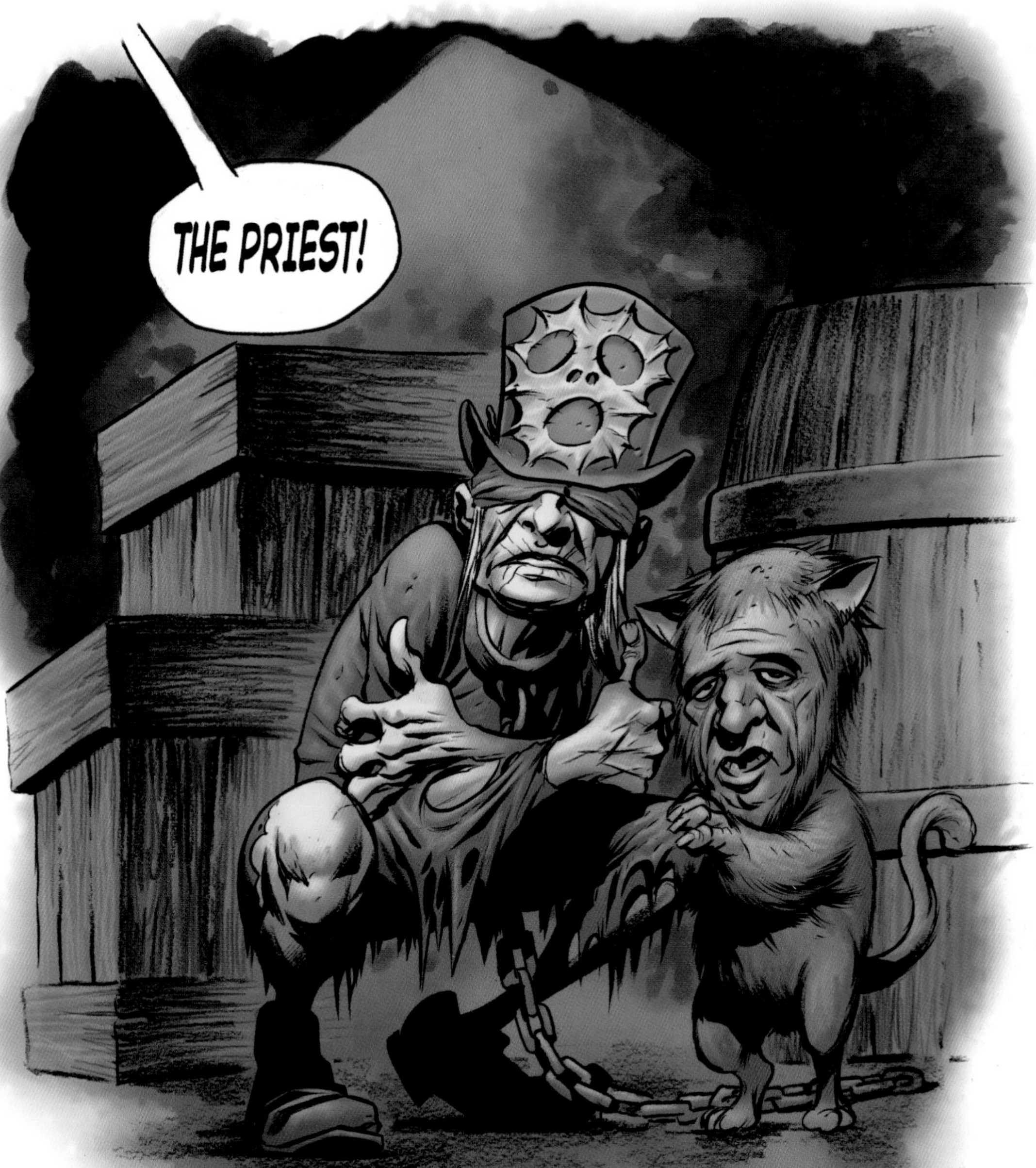
THE PRIEST!

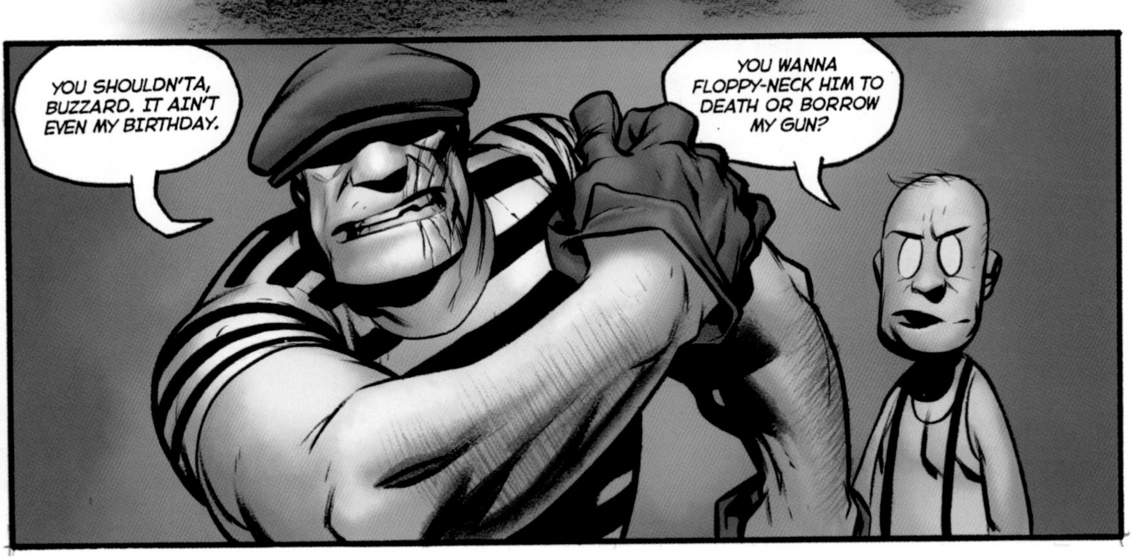
YOU SHOULDN'TA, BUZZARD. IT AIN'T EVEN MY BIRTHDAY.
YOU WANNA FLOPPY-NECK HIM TO DEATH OR BORROW MY GUN?

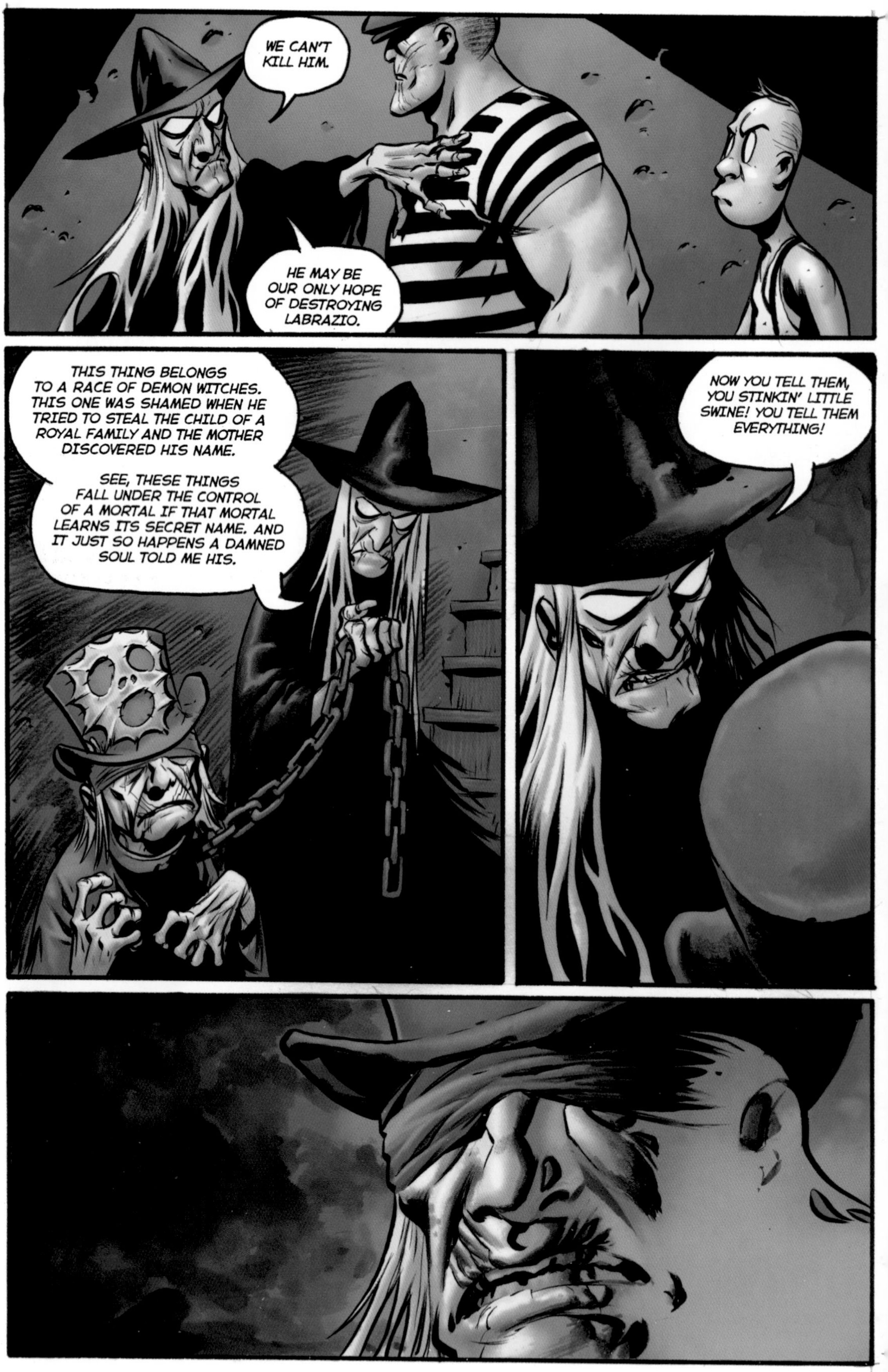
WE CAN'T KILL HIM.
HE MAY BE OUR ONLY HOPE OF DESTROYING LABRAZIO.
THIS THING BELONGS TO A RACE OF DEMON WITCHES. THIS ONE WAS SHAMED WHEN HE TRIED TO STEAL THE CHILD OF A ROYAL FAMILY AND THE MOTHER DISCOVERED HIS NAME.
SEE, THESE THINGS FALL UNDER THE CONTROL OF A MORTAL IF THAT MORTAL LEARNS ITS SECRET NAME. AND IT JUST SO HAPPENS A DAMNED SOUL TOLD ME HIS.
NOW YOU TELL THEM, YOU STINKIN' LITTLE SWINE! YOU TELL THEM EVERYTHING!

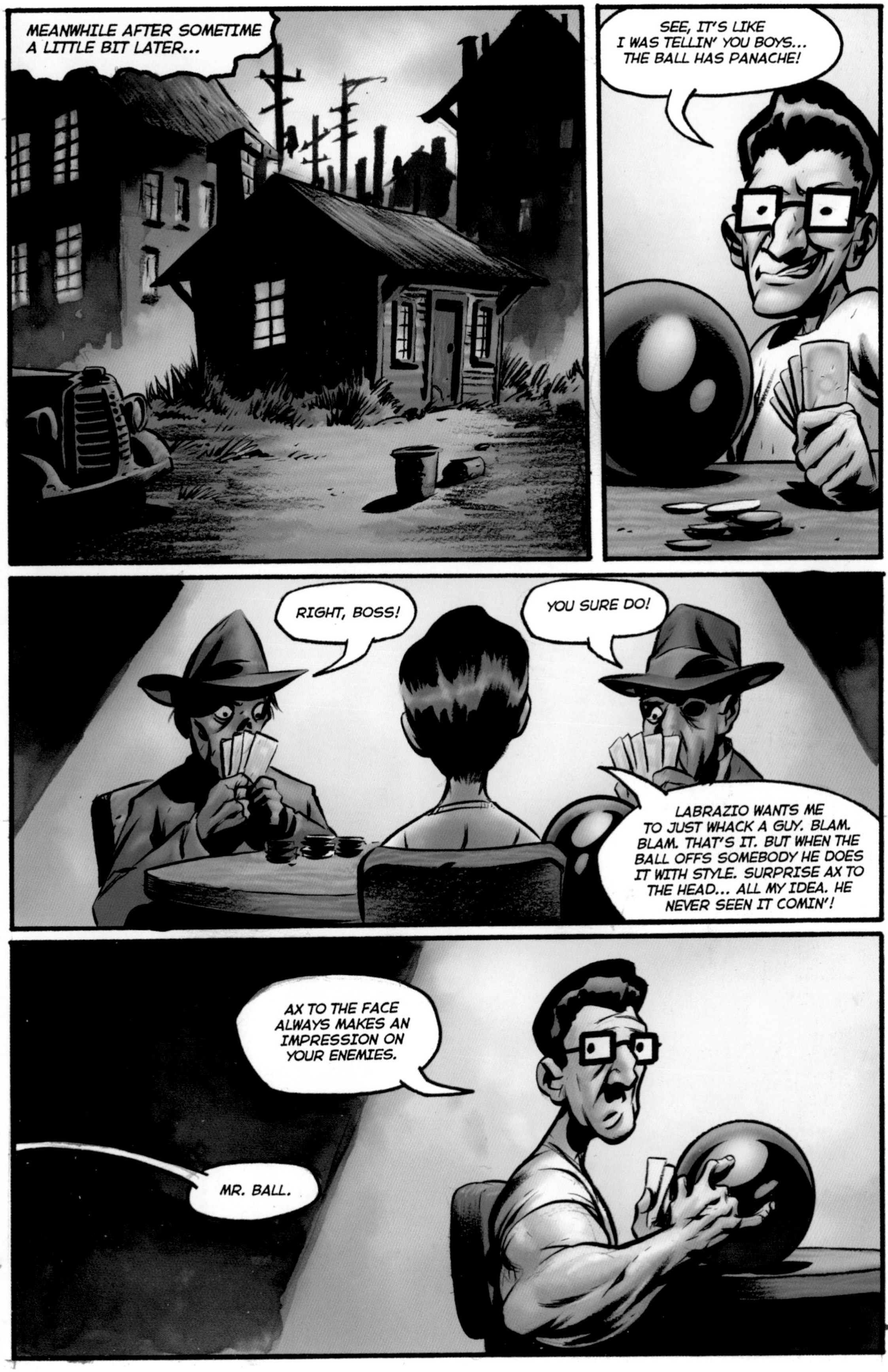
MEANWHILE AFTER SOMETIME A LITTLE BIT LATER...
SEE, IT'S LIKE I WAS TELLIN' YOU BOYS... THE BALL HAS PANACHE!
RIGHT, BOSS!
YOU SURE DO!
LABRAZIO WANTS ME TO JUST WHACK A GUY. BLAM. BLAM. THAT'S IT. BUT WHEN THE BALL OFFS SOMEBODY HE DOES IT WITH STYLE. SURPRISE AX TO THE HEAD... ALL MY IDEA. HE NEVER SEEN IT COMIN'!
AX TO THE FACE ALWAYS MAKES AN IMPRESSION ON YOUR ENEMIES.
MR. BALL.

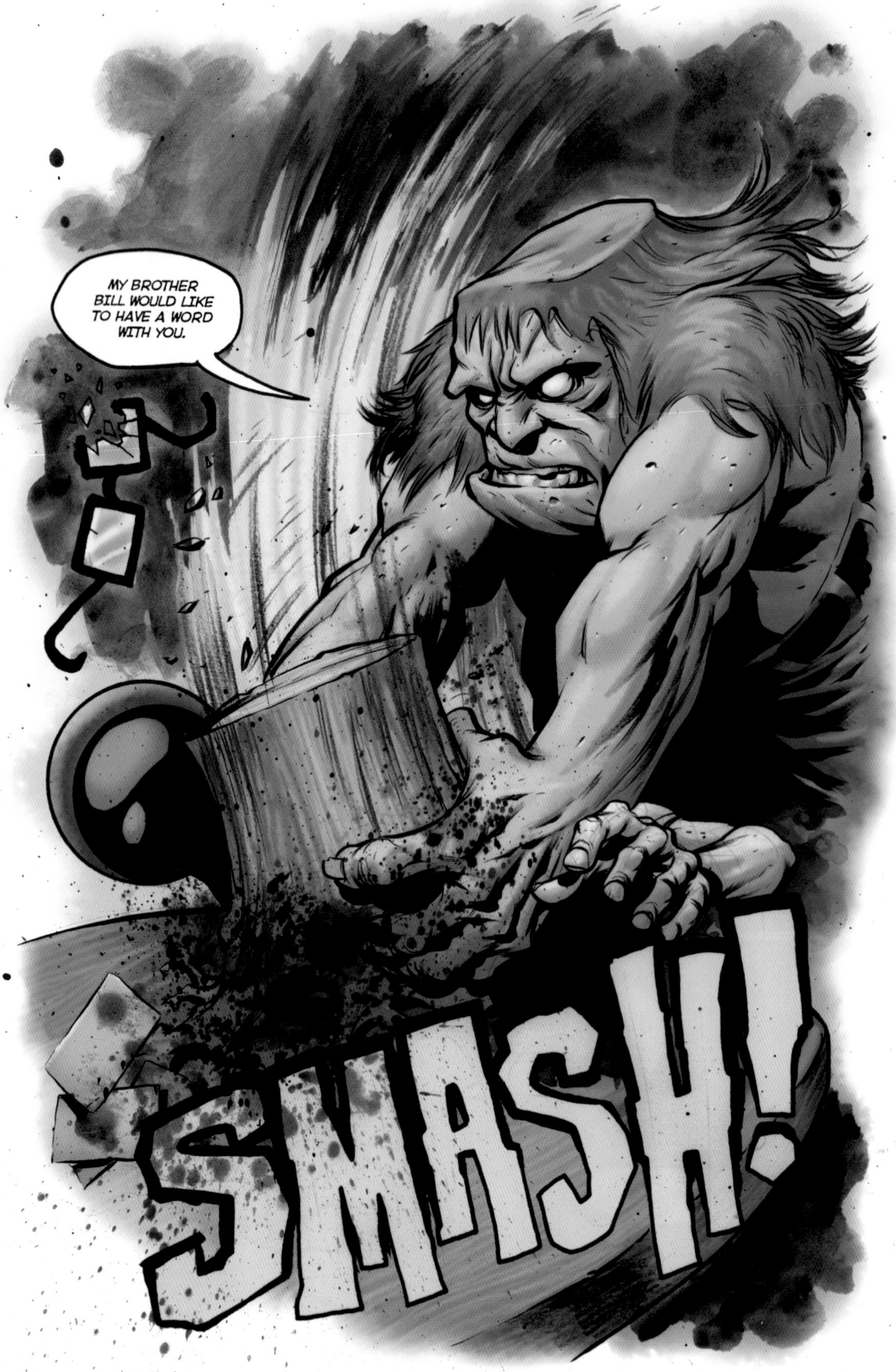
MY BROTHER BILL WOULD LIKE TO HAVE A WORD WITH YOU.
SMASH!

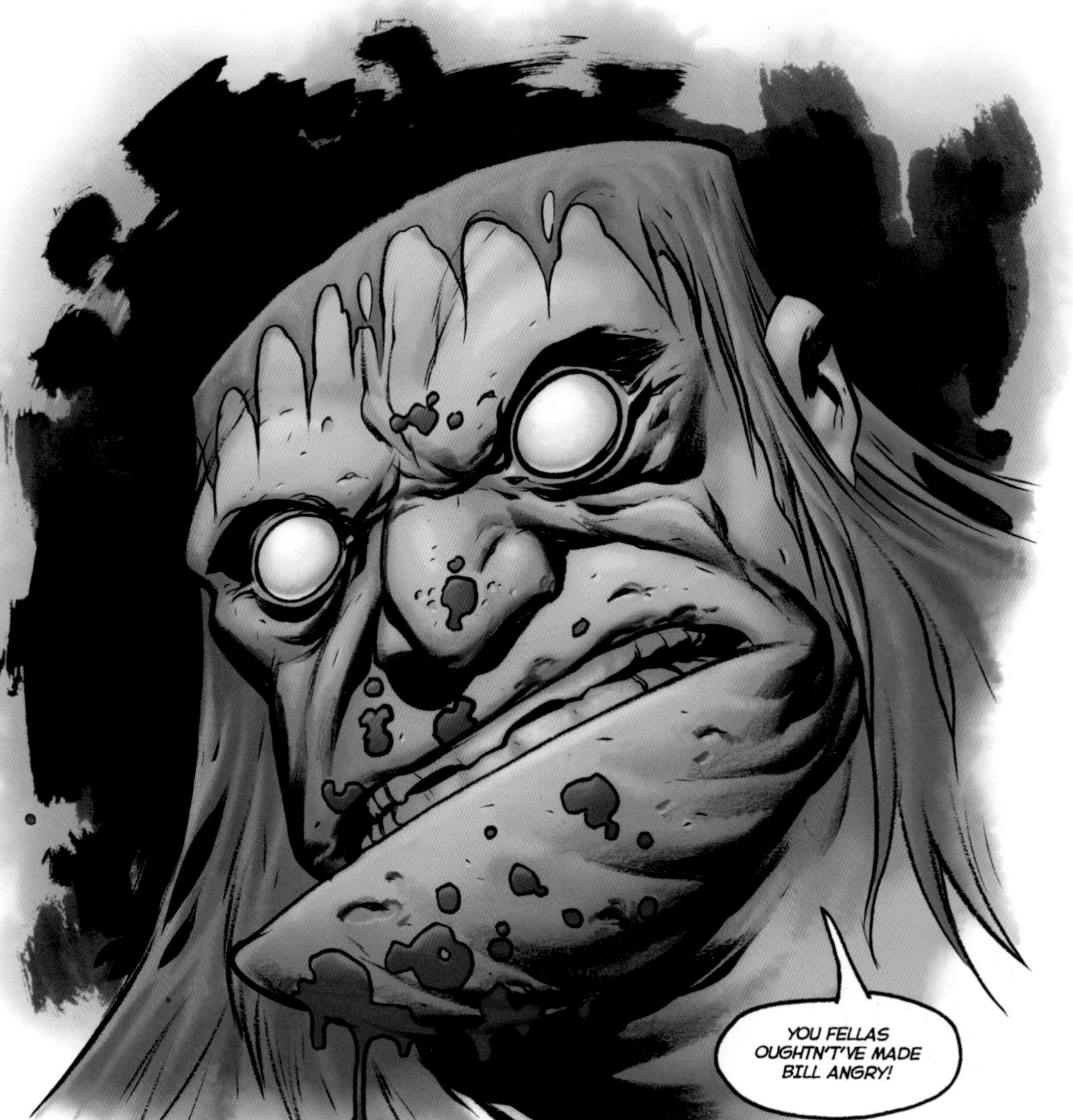
YOU FELLAS OUGHTN'T'VE MADE BILL ANGRY!

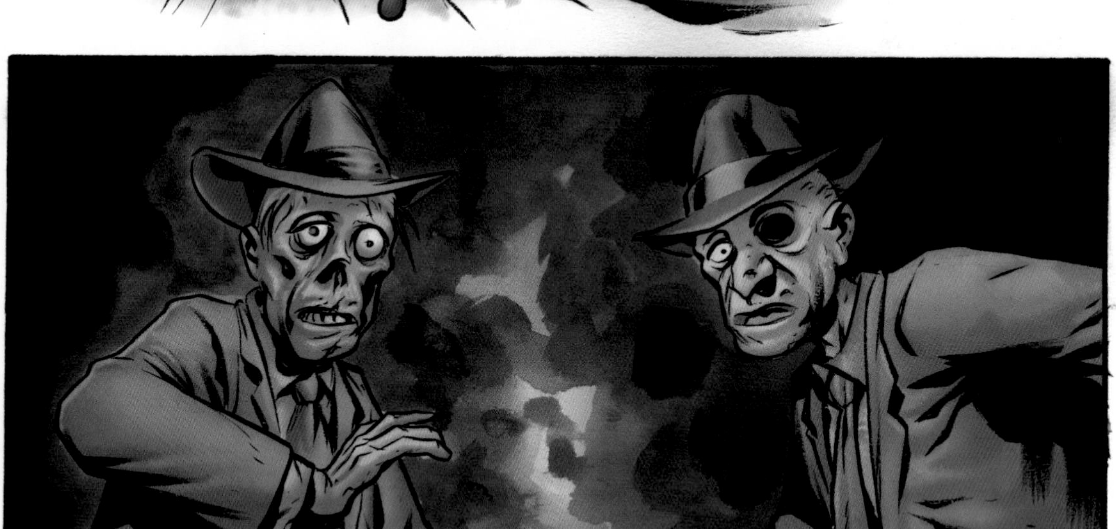

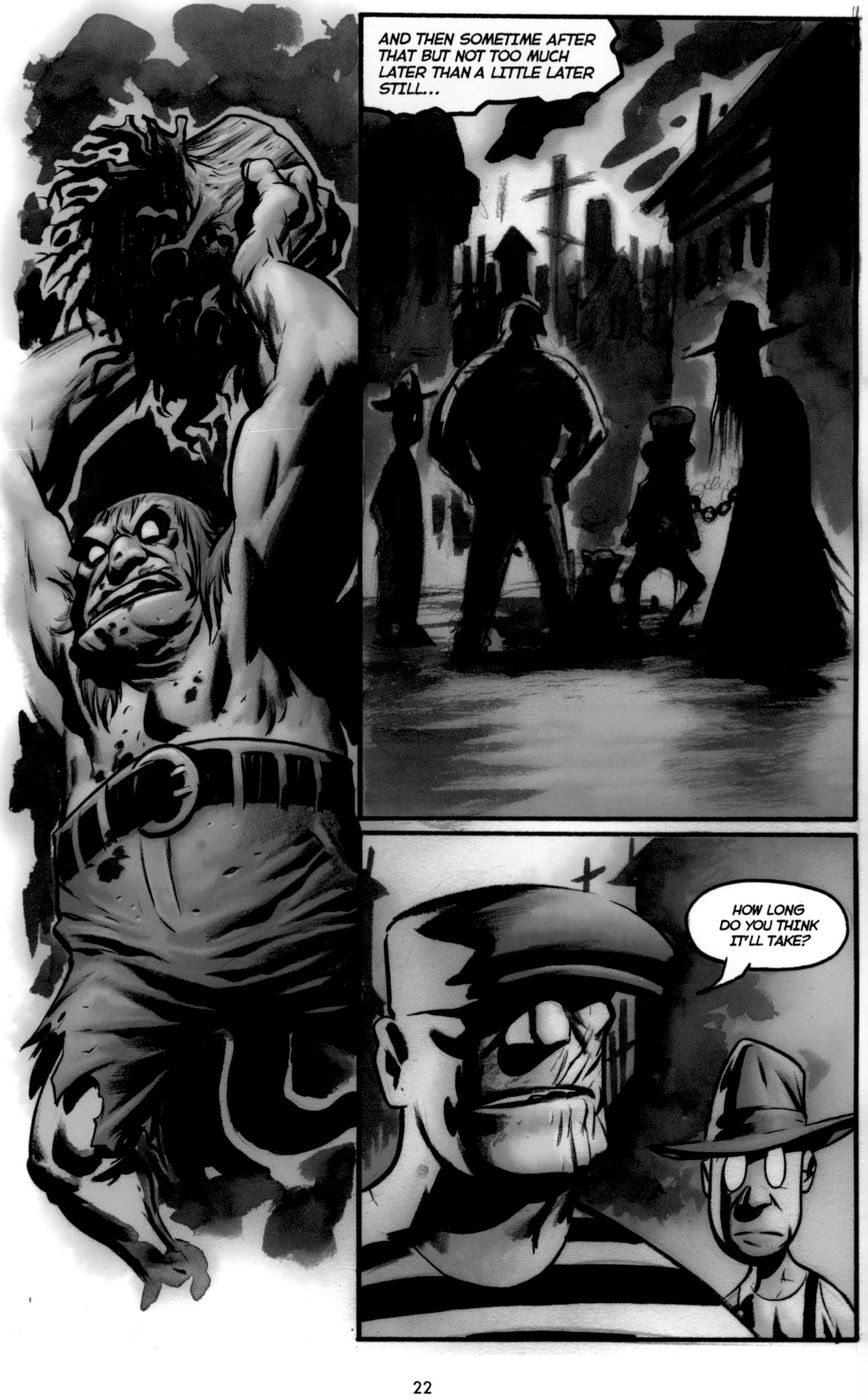
AND THEN SOMETIME AFTER THAT BUT NOT TOO MUCH LATER THAN A LITTLE LATER STILL...
HOW LONG DO YOU THINK IT'LL TAKE?

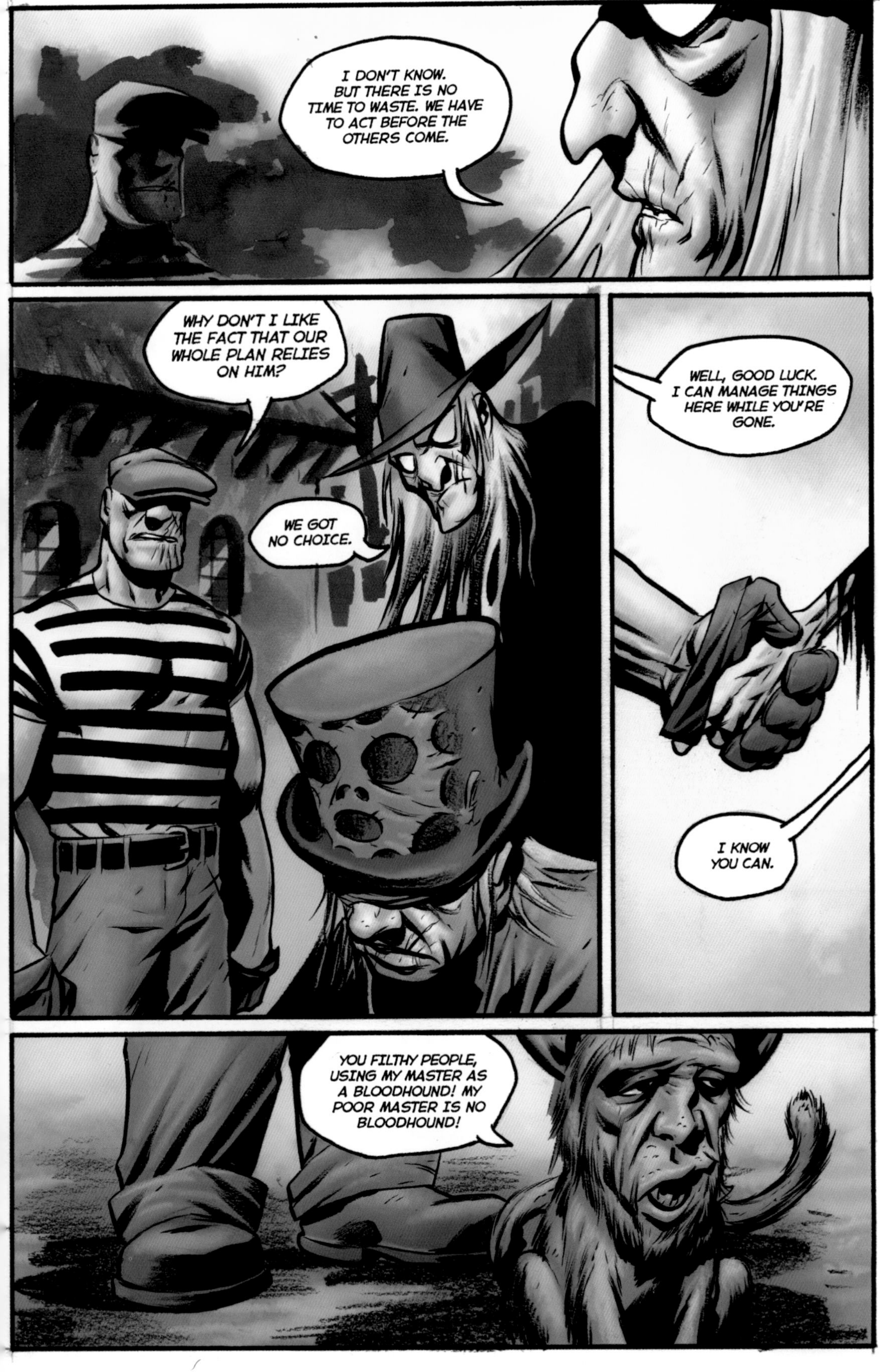
I DON'T KNOW. BUT THERE IS NO TIME TO WASTE. WE HAVE TO ACT BEFORE THE OTHERS COME.
WHY DON'T I LIKE THE FACT THAT OUR WHOLE PLAN RELIES ON HIM?
WE GOT NO CHOICE.
WELL, GOOD LUCK. I CAN MANAGE THINGS HERE WHILE YOU'RE GONE.
I KNOW YOU CAN.
YOU FILTHY PEOPLE, USING MY MASTER AS A BLOODHOUND! MY POOR MASTER IS NO BLOODHOUND!

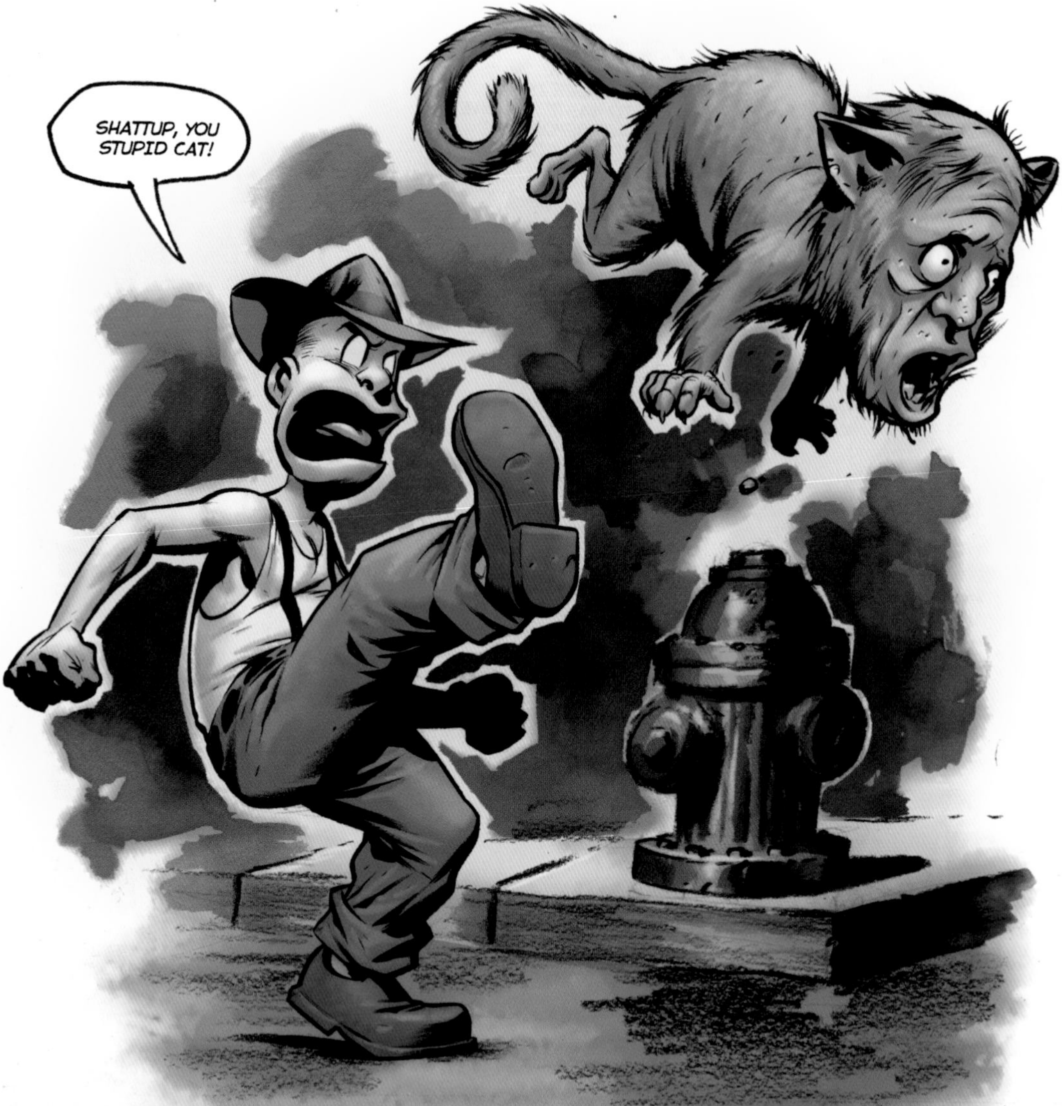
SHATTUP, YOU STUPID CAT!

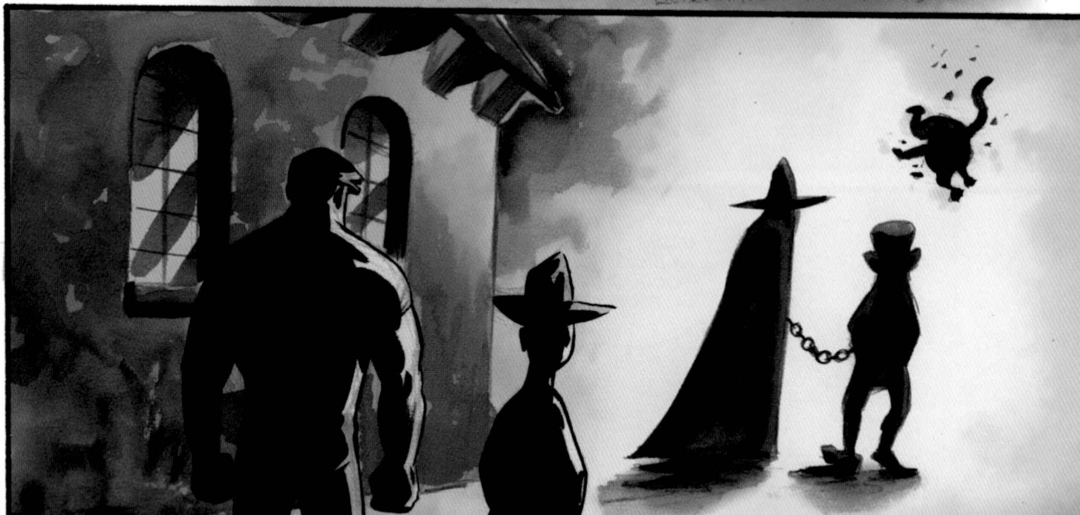

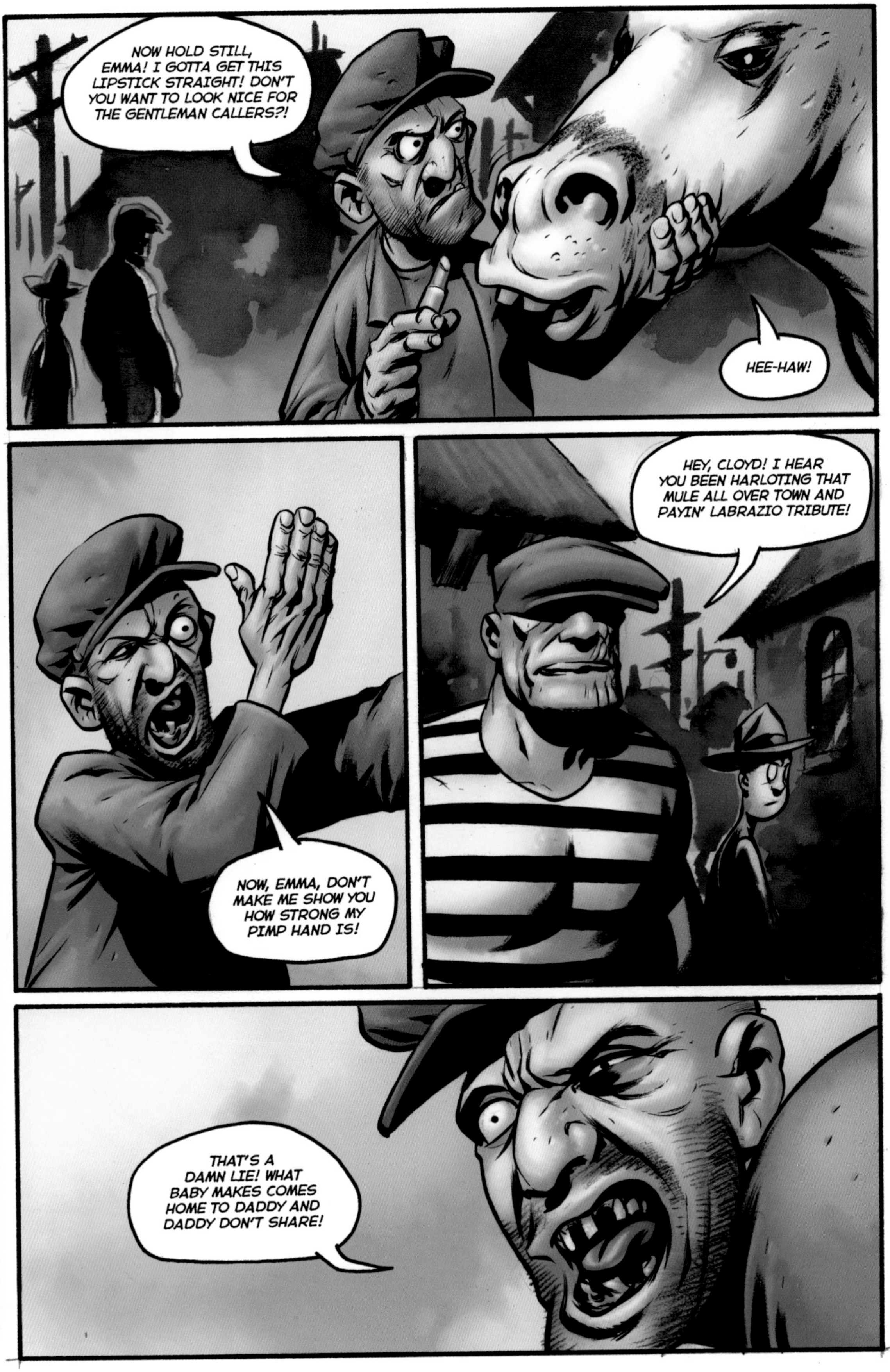
NOW HOLD STILL, EMMA! I GOTTA GET THIS LIPSTICK STRAIGHT! DON'T YOU WANT TO LOOK NICE FOR THE GENTLEMAN CALLERS?!
HEE-HAW!
NOW, EMMA, DON'T MAKE ME SHOW YOU HOW STRONG MY PIMP HAND IS!
HEY, CLOYD! I HEAR YOU BEEN HARLOTING THAT MULE ALL OVER TOWN AND PAYIN' LABRAZIO TRIBUTE!
THAT'S A DAMN LIE! WHAT BABY MAKES COMES HOME TO DADDY AND DADDY DON'T SHARE!

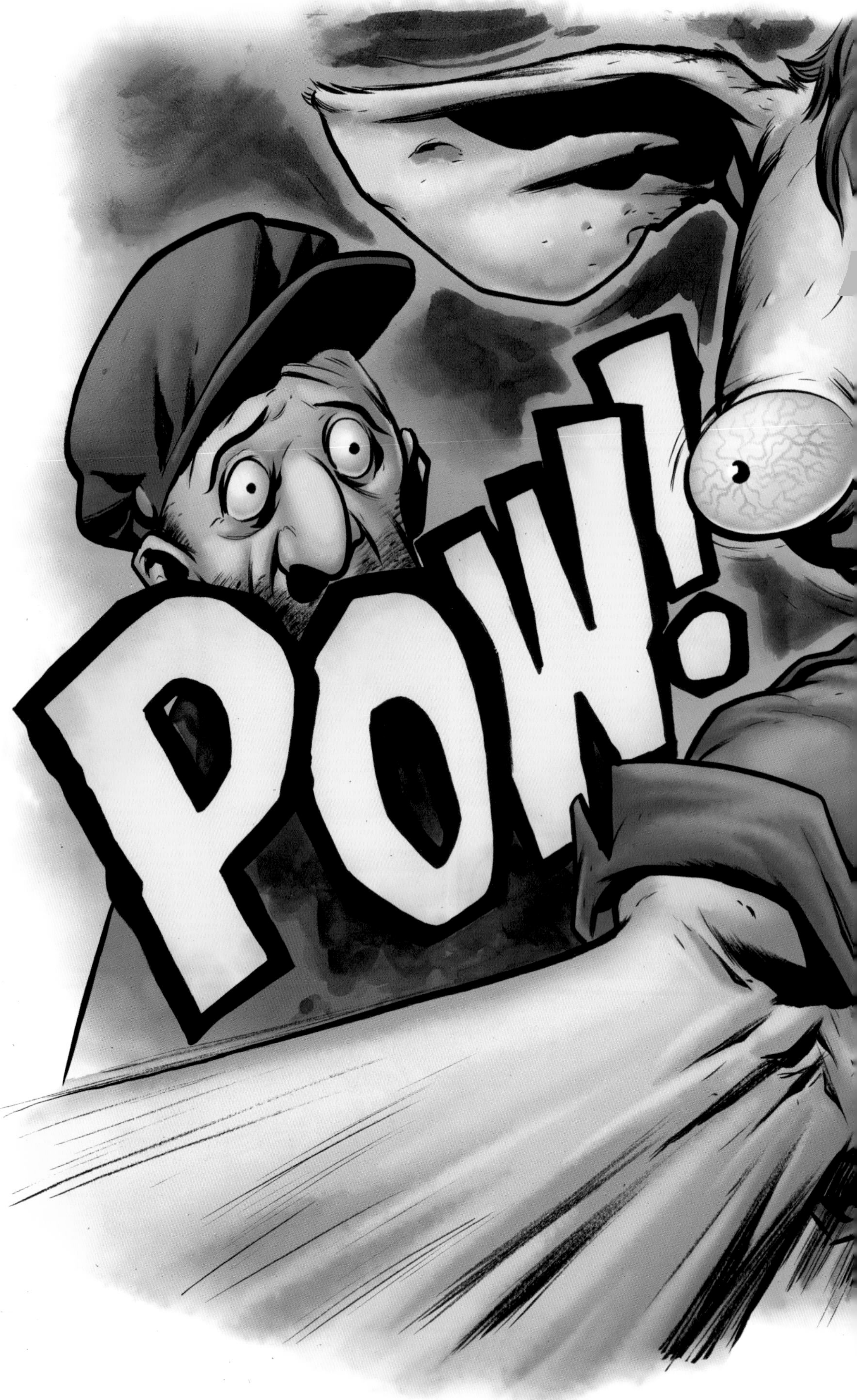
POW!

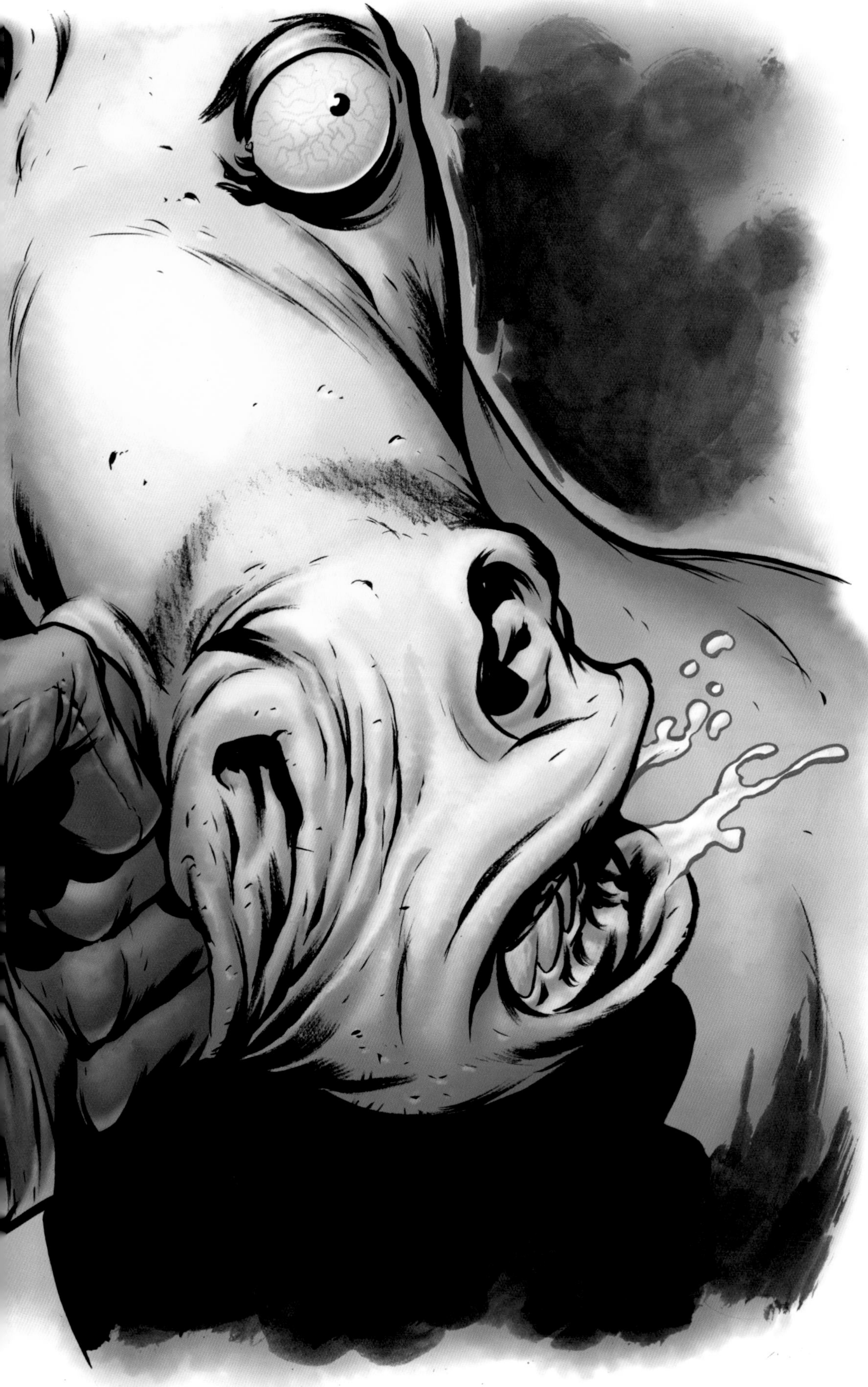

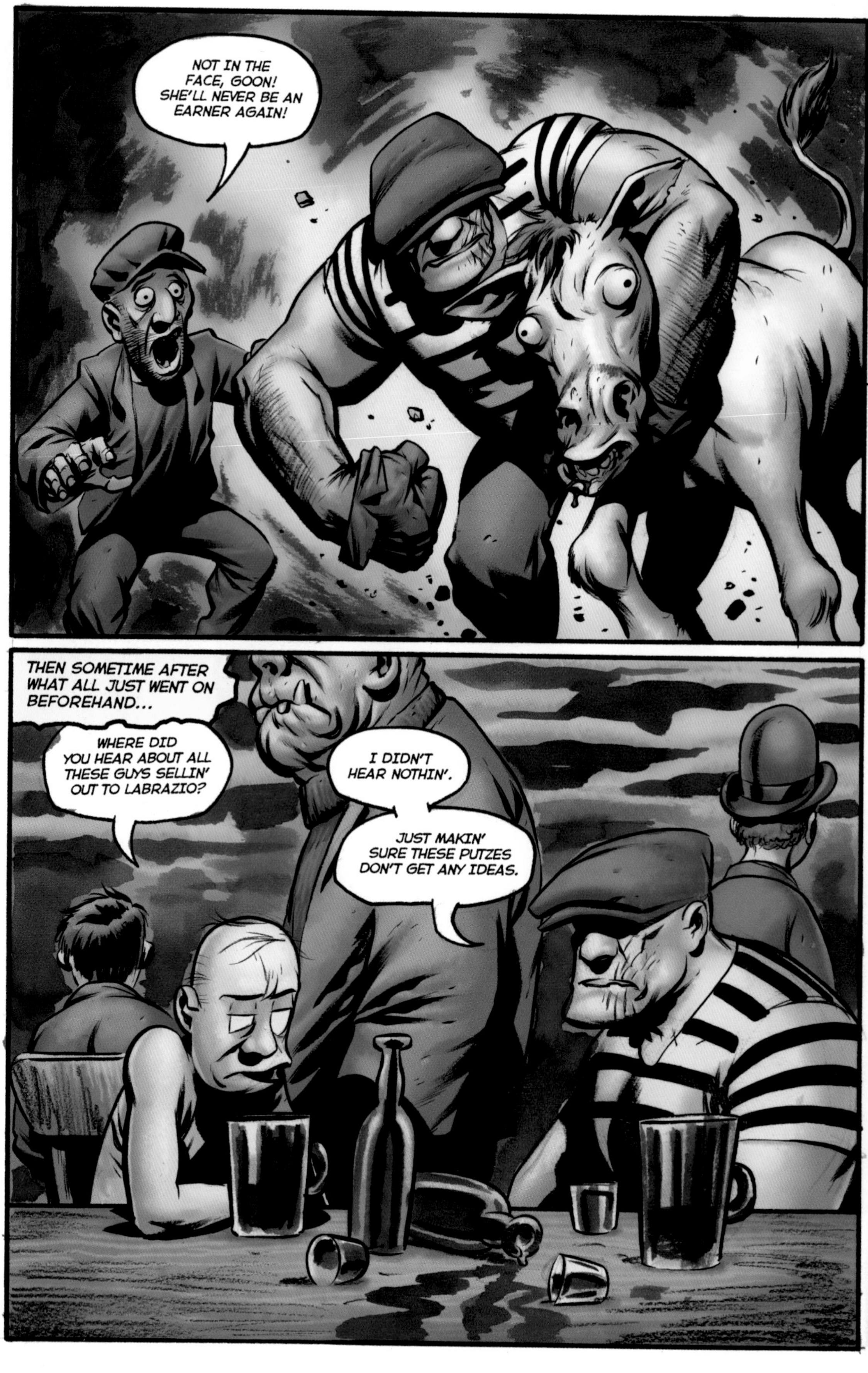
NOT IN THE FACE, GOON! SHE'LL NEVER BE AN EARNER AGAIN!
THEN SOMETIME AFTER WHAT ALL JUST WENT ON BEFOREHAND...
WHERE DID YOU HEAR ABOUT ALL THESE GUYS SELLIN' OUT TO LABRAZIO?
I DIDN'T HEAR NOTHIN'.
JUST MAKIN' SURE THESE PUTZES DON'T GET ANY IDEAS.

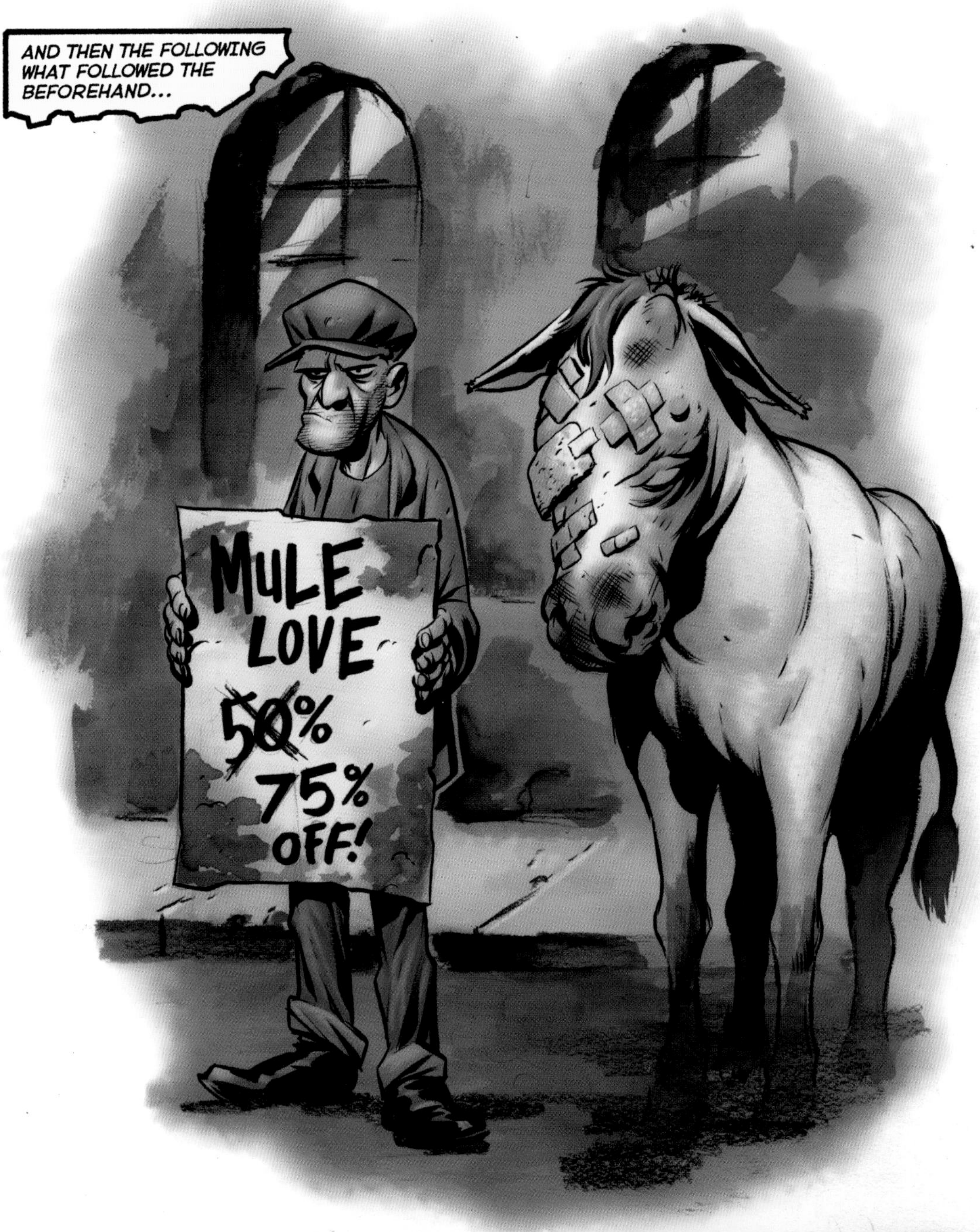
AND THEN THE FOLLOWING WHAT FOLLOWED THE BEFOREHAND...
MULE LOVE
~~50~~%
75% OFF!

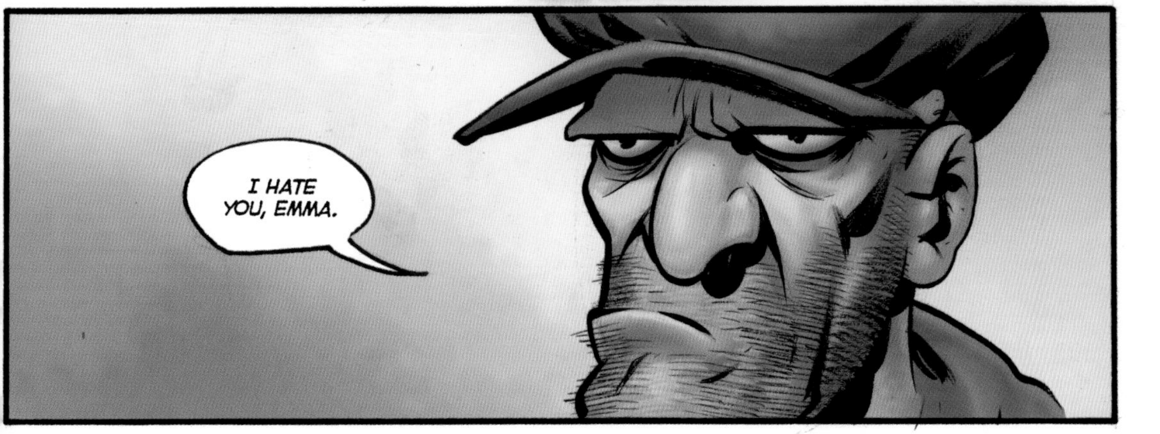
I HATE YOU, EMMA.

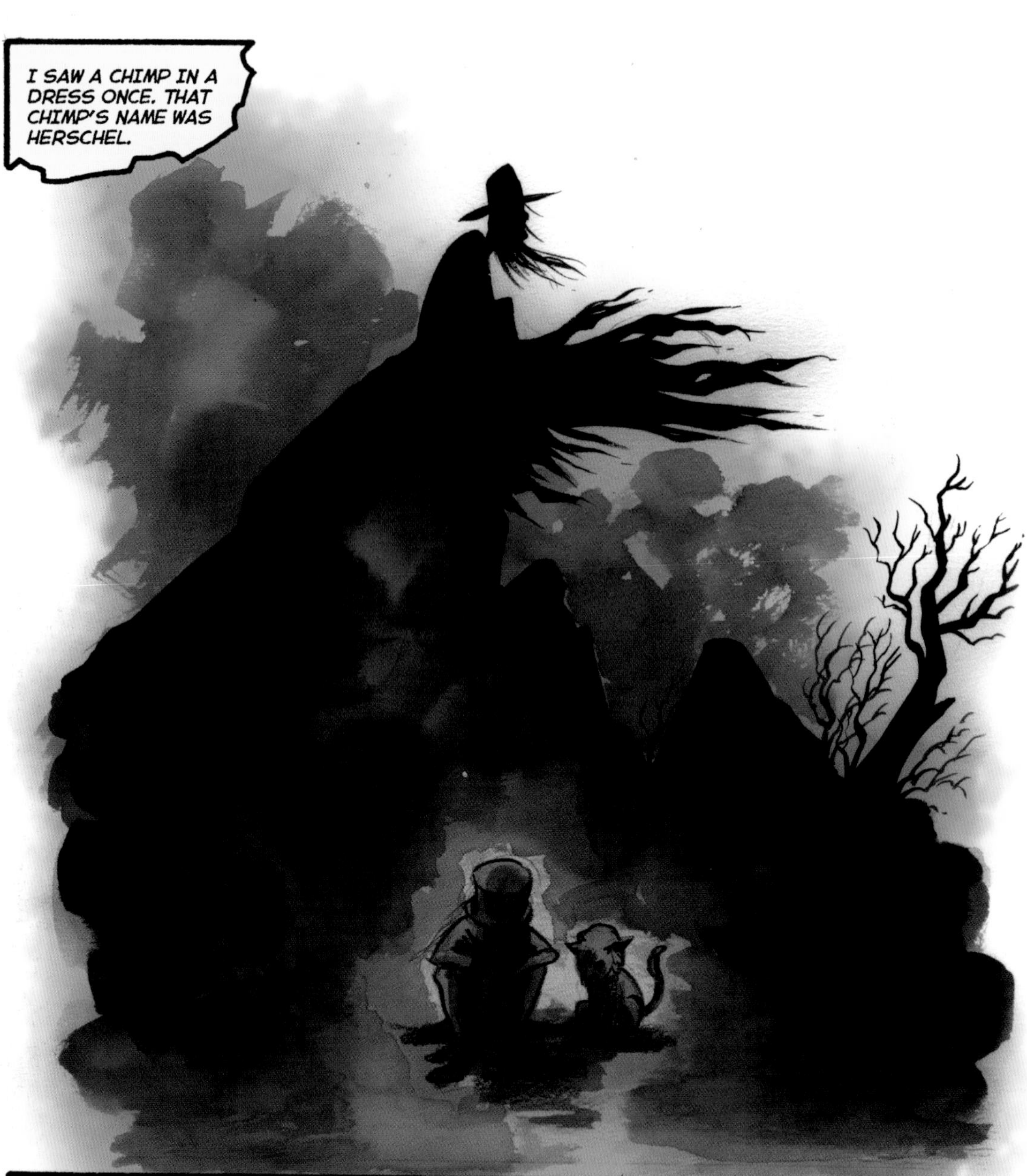
I SAW A CHIMP IN A DRESS ONCE. THAT CHIMP'S NAME WAS HERSCHEL.

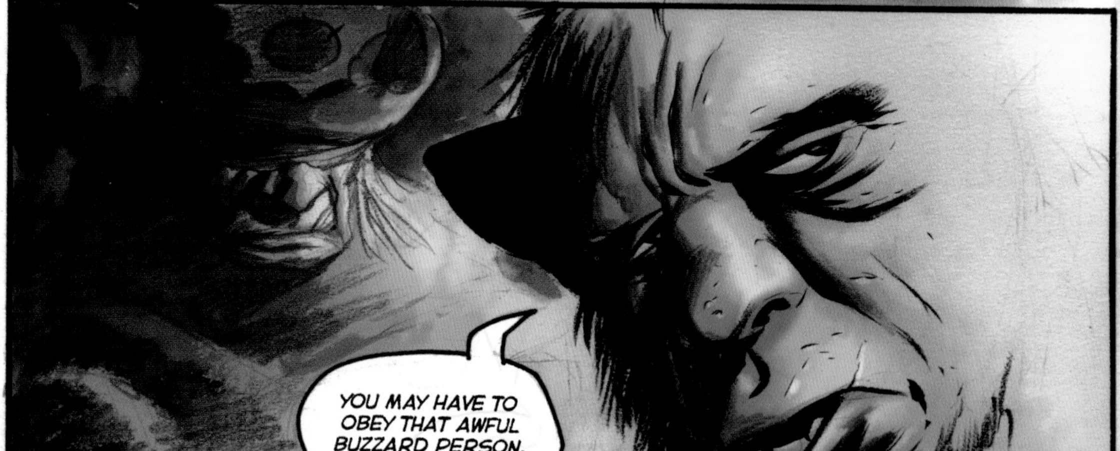
YOU MAY HAVE TO OBEY THAT AWFUL BUZZARD PERSON, MASTER, BUT CAT DOESN'T!

CHAPTER 2

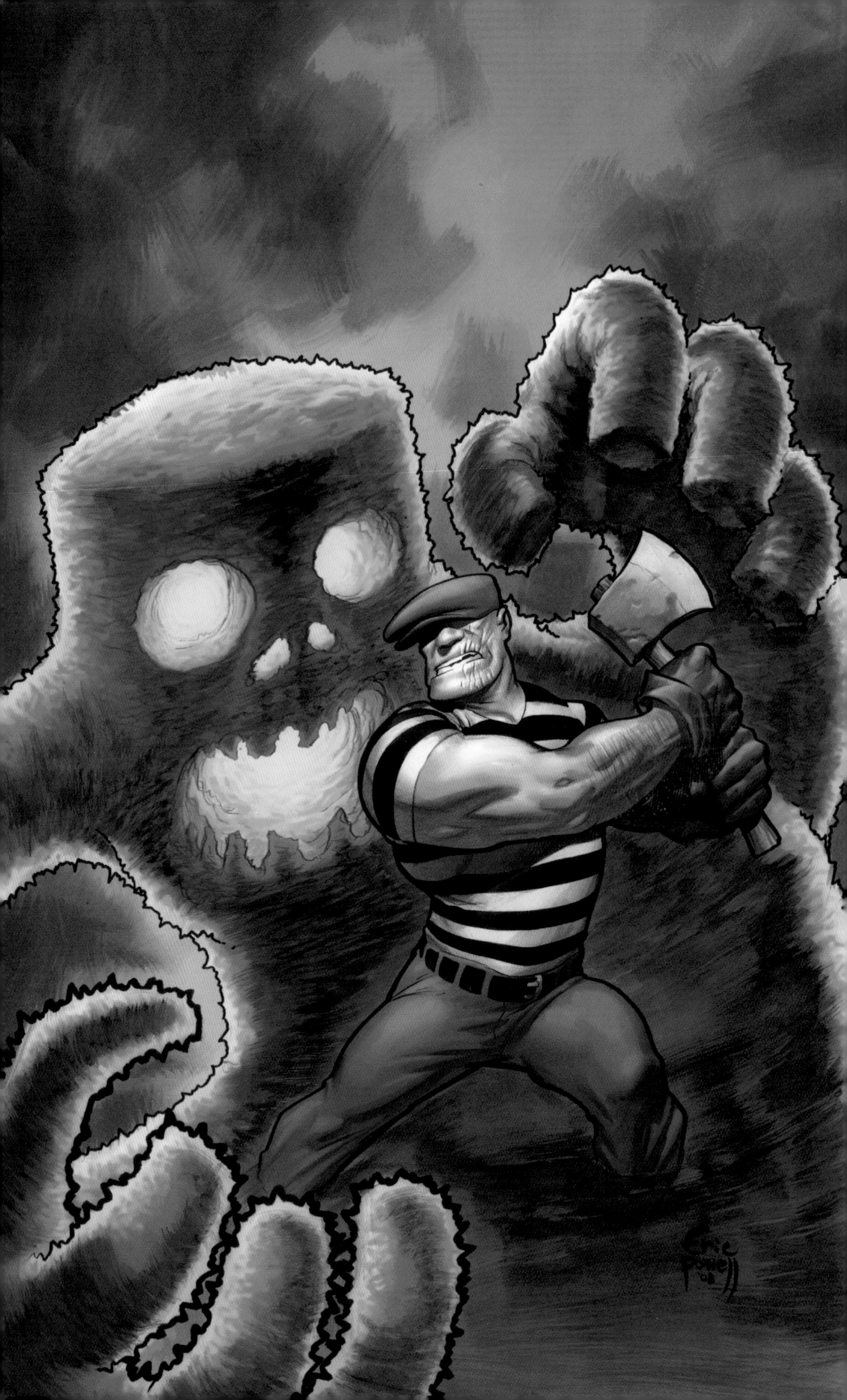

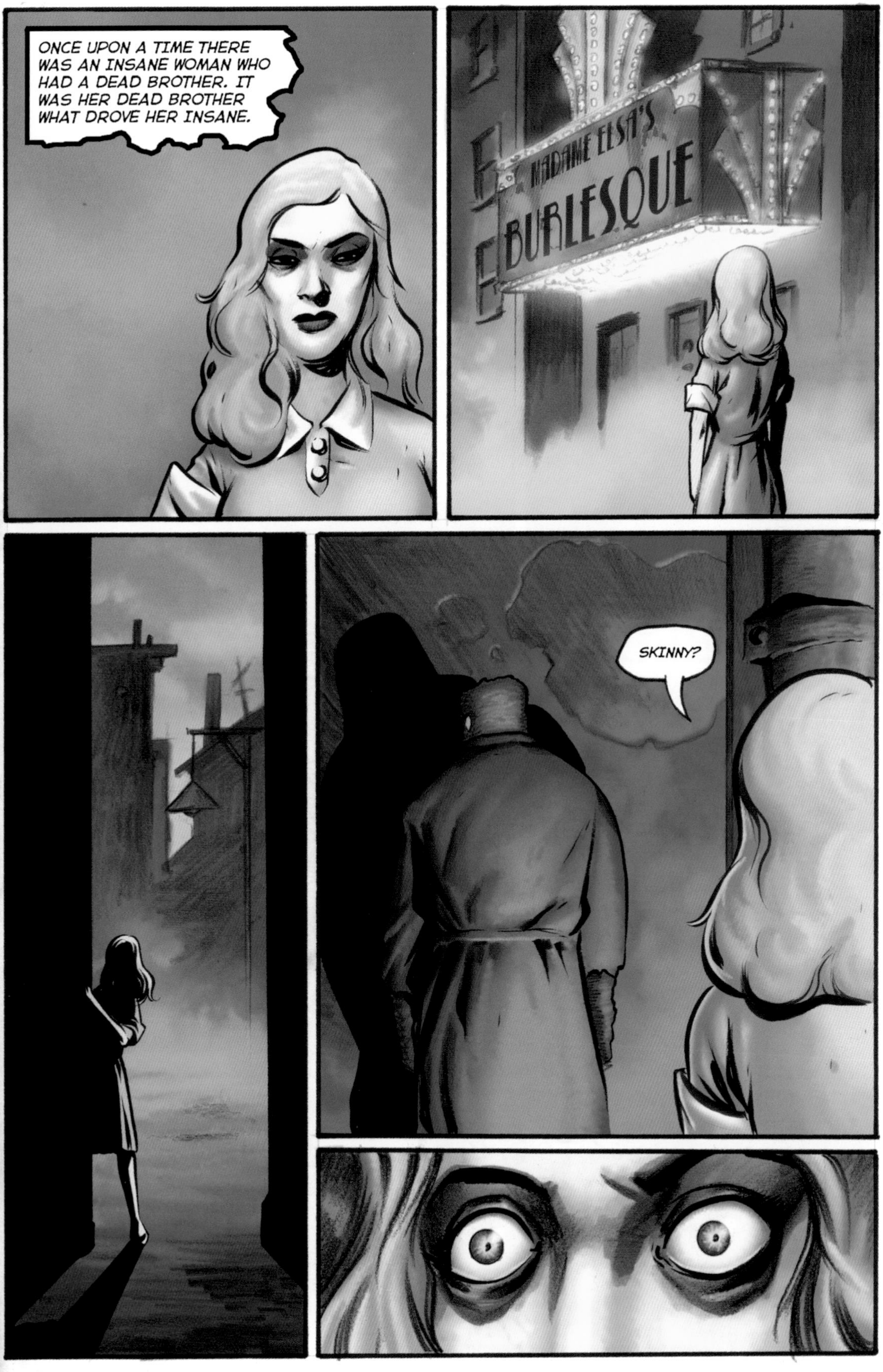
ONCE UPON A TIME THERE WAS AN INSANE WOMAN WHO HAD A DEAD BROTHER. IT WAS HER DEAD BROTHER WHAT DROVE HER INSANE.
MADAME ELSA'S
BURLESQUE
SKINNY?

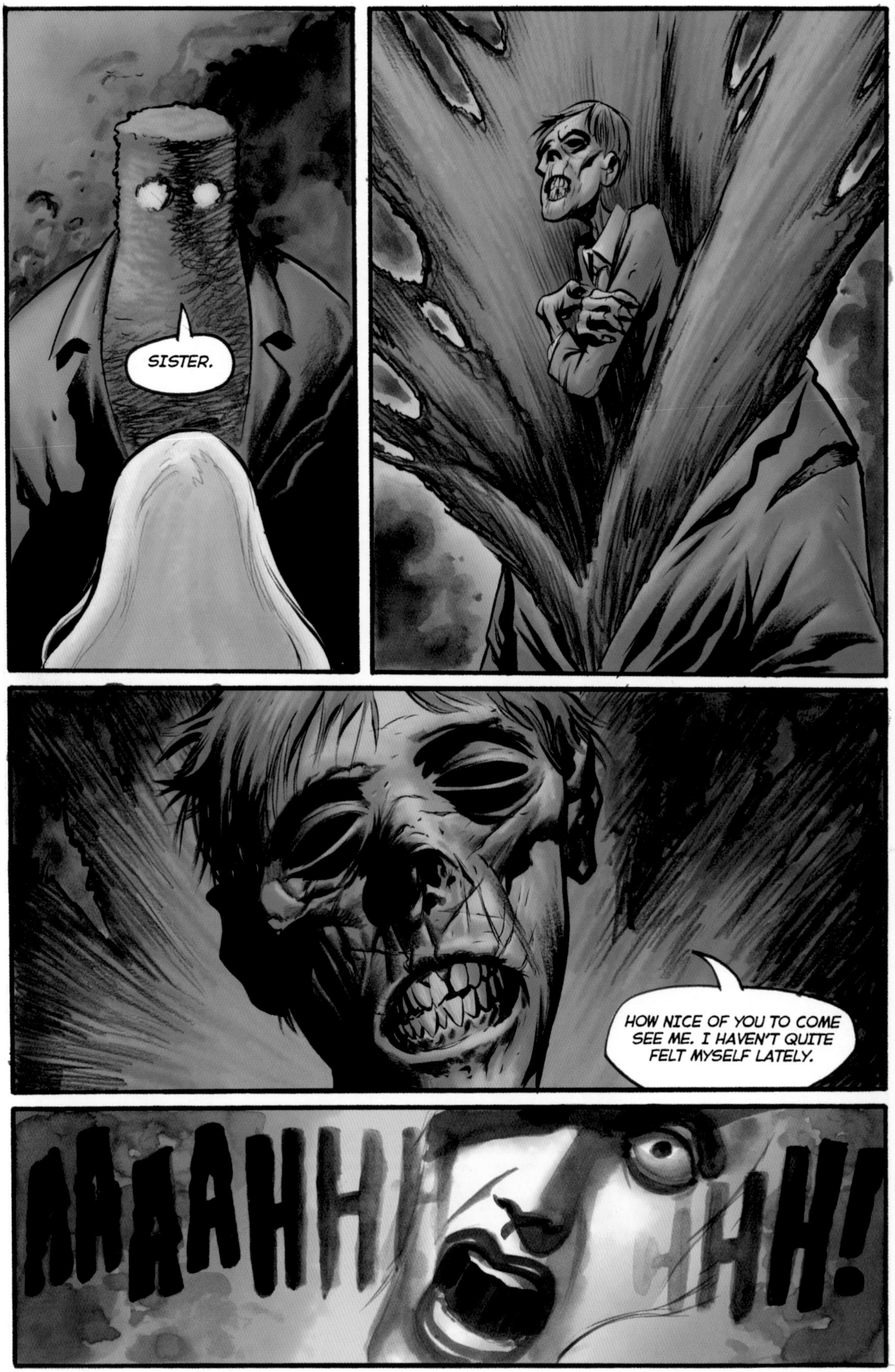
SISTER.
HOW NICE OF YOU TO COME SEE ME. I HAVEN'T QUITE FELT MYSELF LATELY.

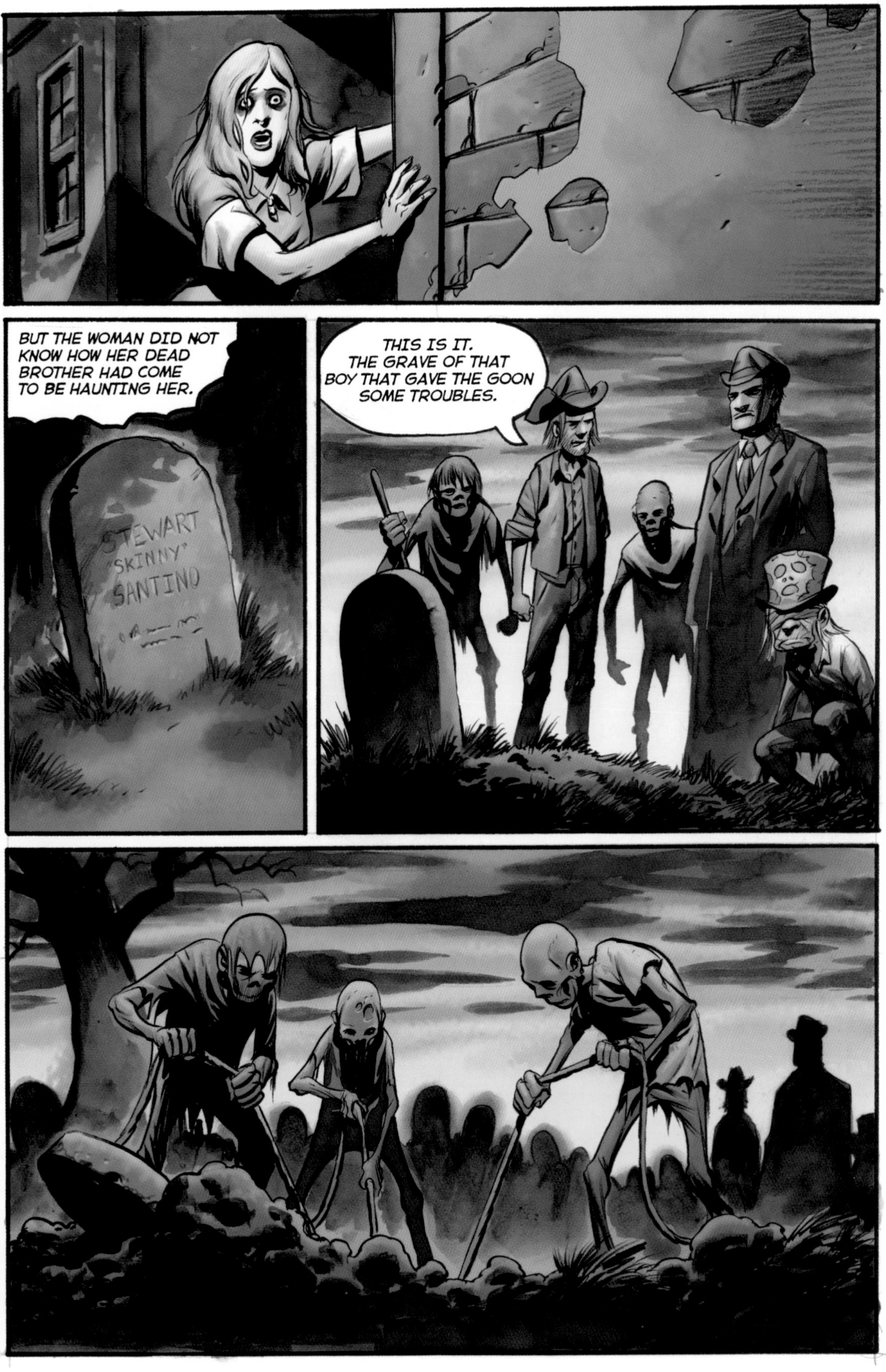
BUT THE WOMAN DID NOT KNOW HOW HER DEAD BROTHER HAD COME TO BE HAUNTING HER.
STEWART "SKINNY" SANTINO
THIS IS IT. THE GRAVE OF THAT BOY THAT GAVE THE GOON SOME TROUBLES.

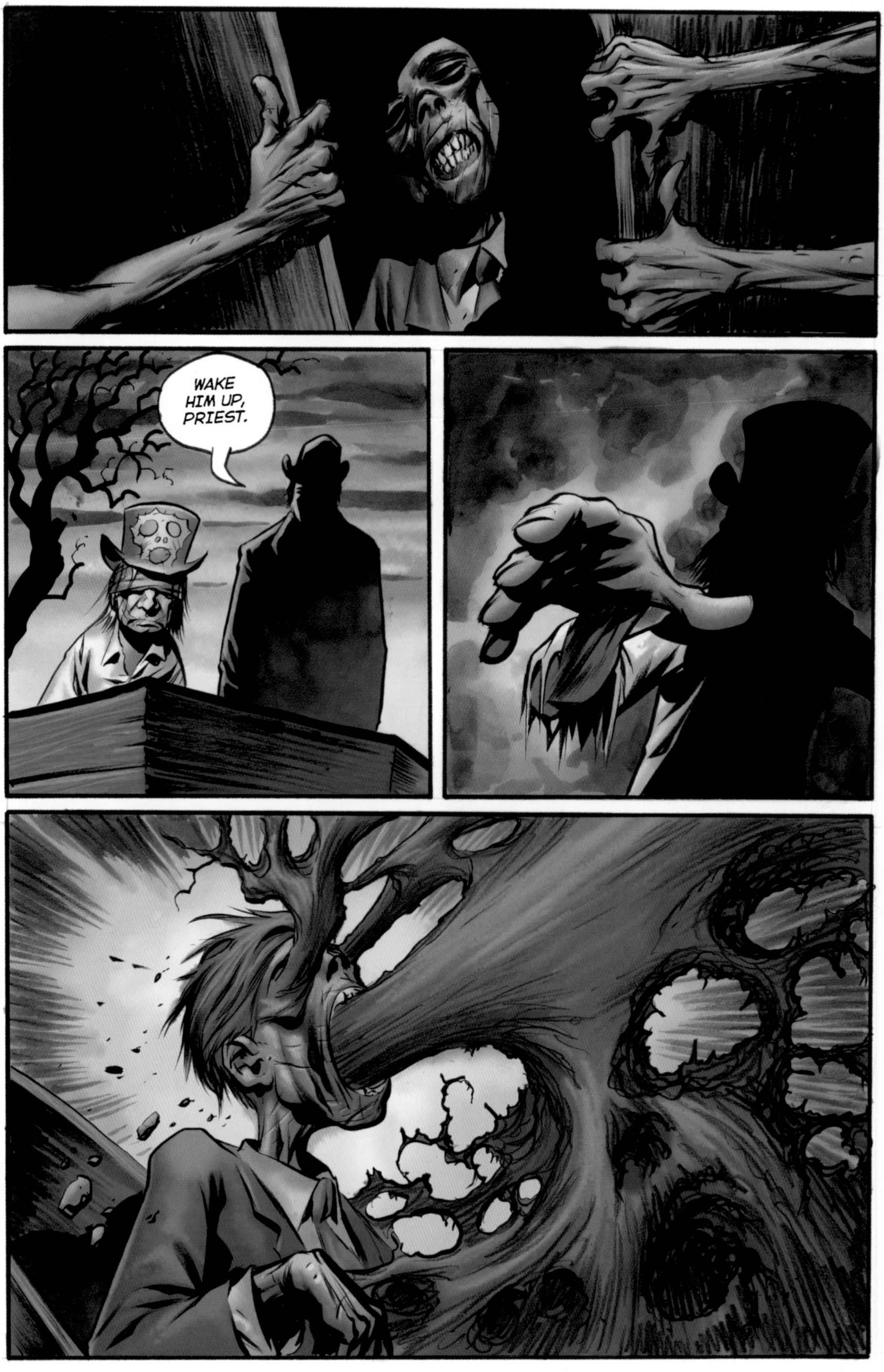
WAKE HIM UP, PRIEST.

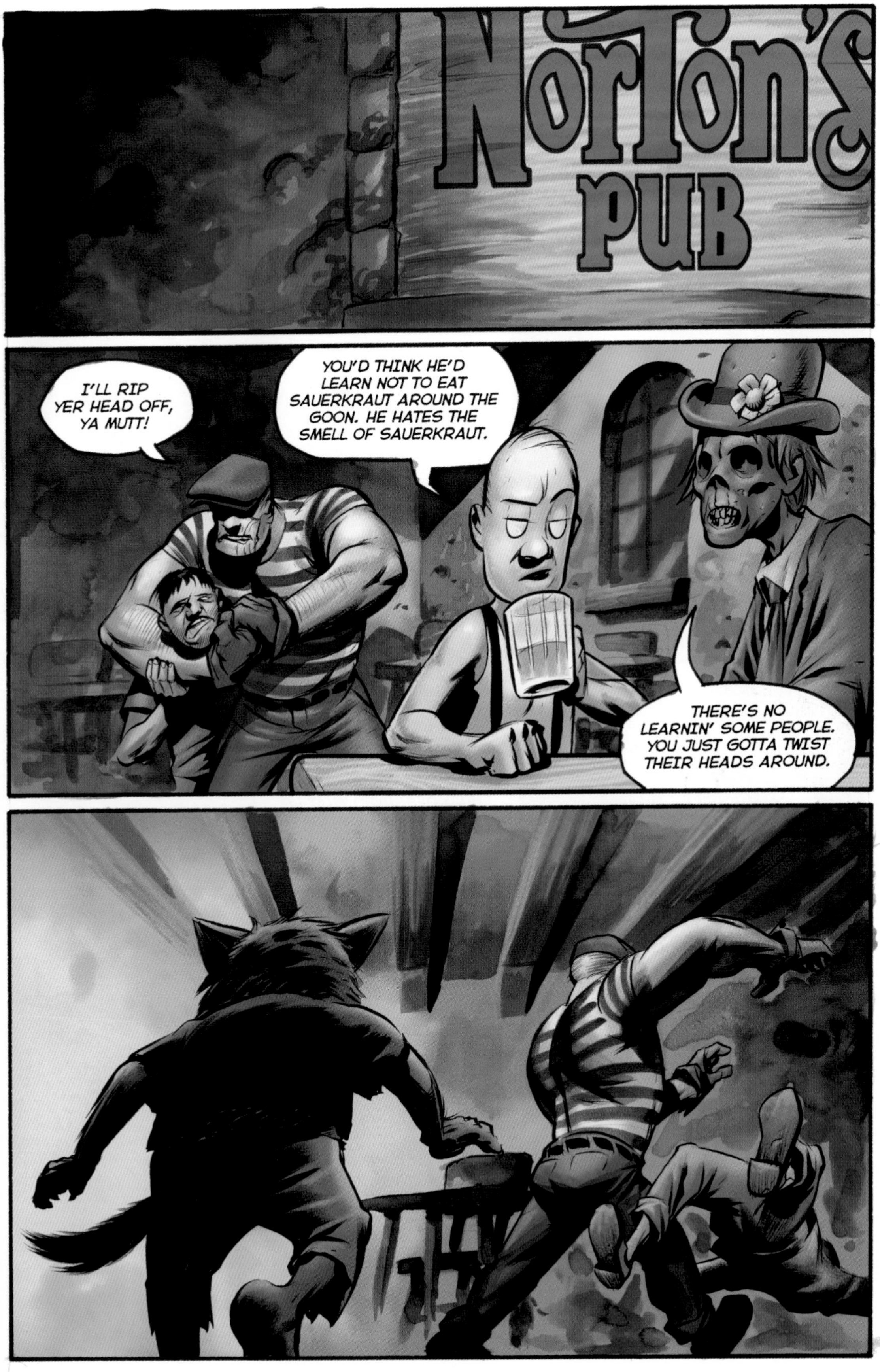
NORTON'S PUB
I'LL RIP YER HEAD OFF, YA MUTT!
YOU'D THINK HE'D LEARN NOT TO EAT SAUERKRAUT AROUND THE GOON. HE HATES THE SMELL OF SAUERKRAUT.
THERE'S NO LEARNIN' SOME PEOPLE. YOU JUST GOTTA TWIST THEIR HEADS AROUND.

WHAT THE--!

YOU KILLED MY PA!

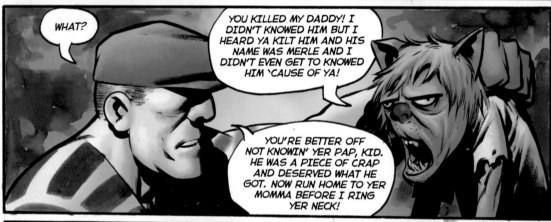

WHAT?

YOU KILLED MY DADDY! I DIDN'T KNOWED HIM BUT I HEARD YA KILT HIM AND HIS NAME WAS MERLE AND I DIDN'T EVEN GET TO KNOWED HIM 'CAUSE OF YA!

YOU'RE BETTER OFF NOT KNOWIN' YER PAP, KID. HE WAS A PIECE OF CRAP AND DESERVED WHAT HE GOT. NOW RUN HOME TO YER MOMMA BEFORE I RING YER NECK!

I AIN'T GOT NO MOMMA! SHE DIED OF THE WHOOPIN' COUGH!

ORPHAN, HUH? I GOT JUST THE PLACE FOR YOU!

THE McGREGGHO FOR ILLEGIT: WAYWARD, AN HOMICIDAL

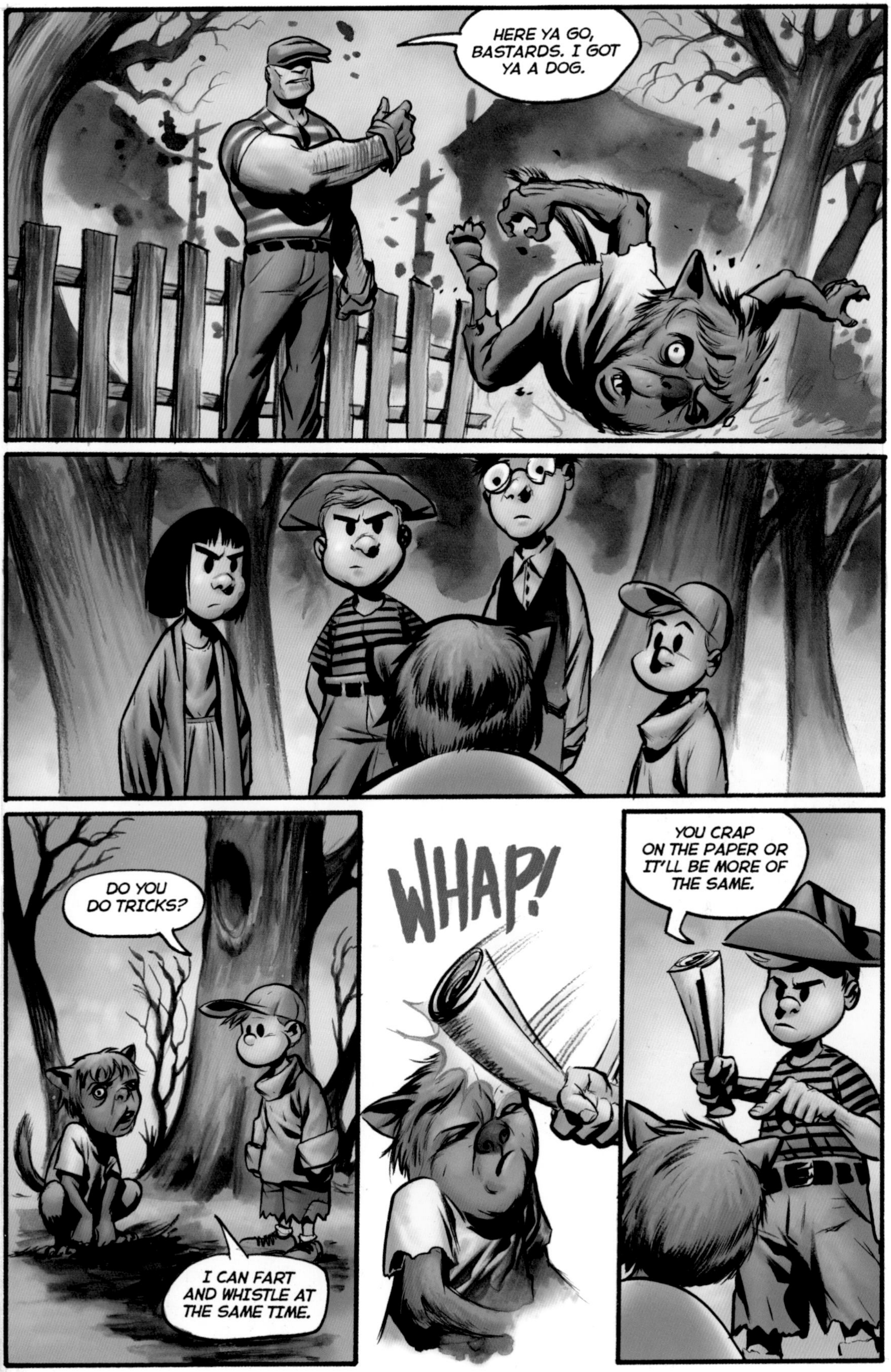

HERE YA GO, BASTARDS. I GOT YA A DOG.
DO YOU DO TRICKS?
I CAN FART AND WHISTLE AT THE SAME TIME.
WHAP!
YOU CRAP ON THE PAPER OR IT'LL BE MORE OF THE SAME.

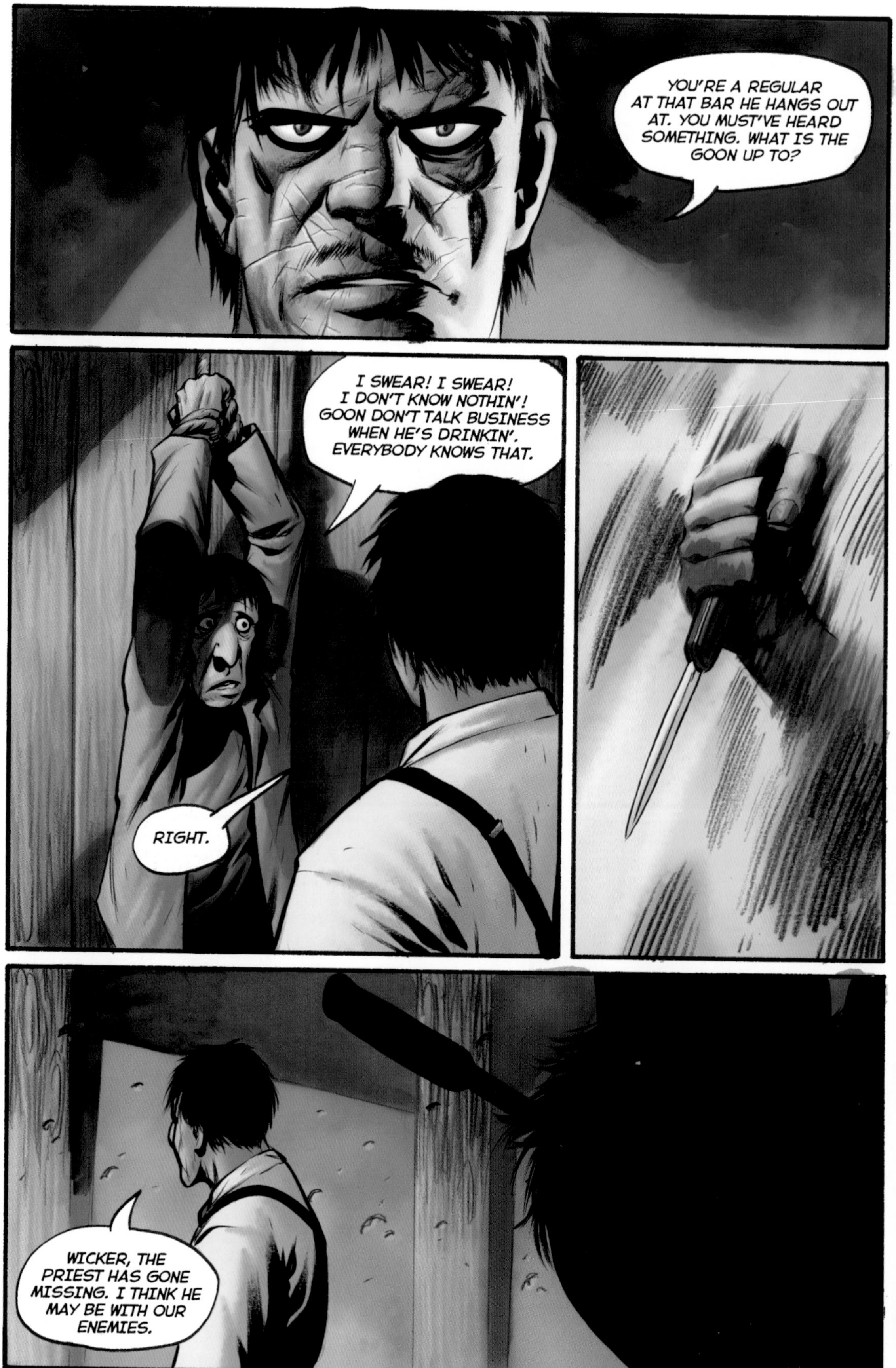
YOU'RE A REGULAR AT THAT BAR HE HANGS OUT AT. YOU MUST'VE HEARD SOMETHING. WHAT IS THE GOON UP TO?
I SWEAR! I SWEAR! I DON'T KNOW NOTHIN'! GOON DON'T TALK BUSINESS WHEN HE'S DRINKIN'. EVERYBODY KNOWS THAT.
RIGHT.
WICKER, THE PRIEST HAS GONE MISSING. I THINK HE MAY BE WITH OUR ENEMIES.

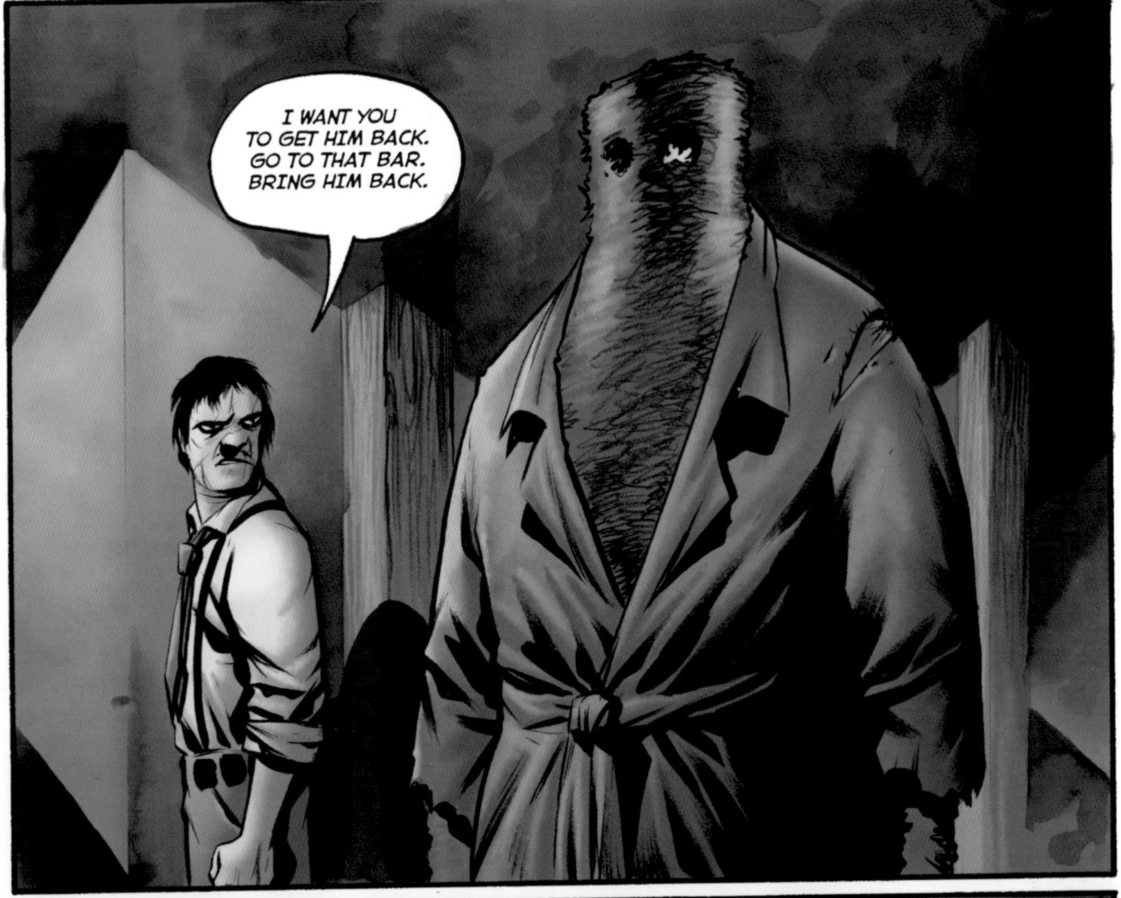
I WANT YOU TO GET HIM BACK. GO TO THAT BAR. BRING HIM BACK.

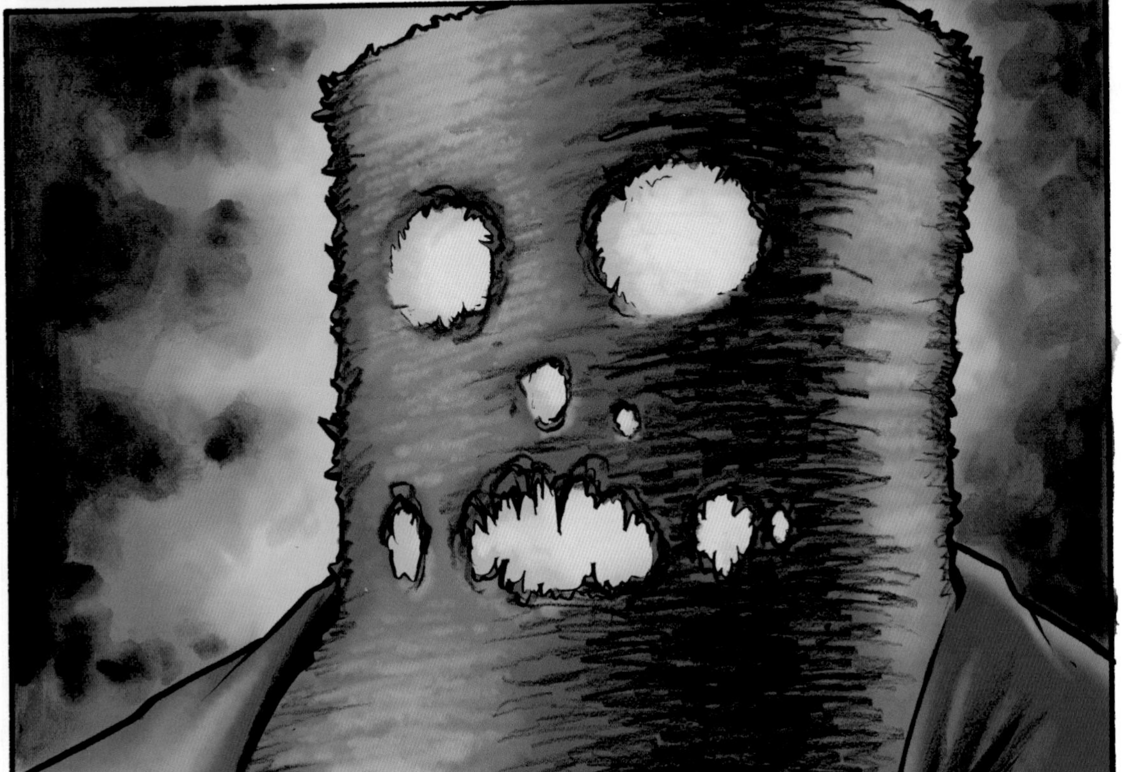

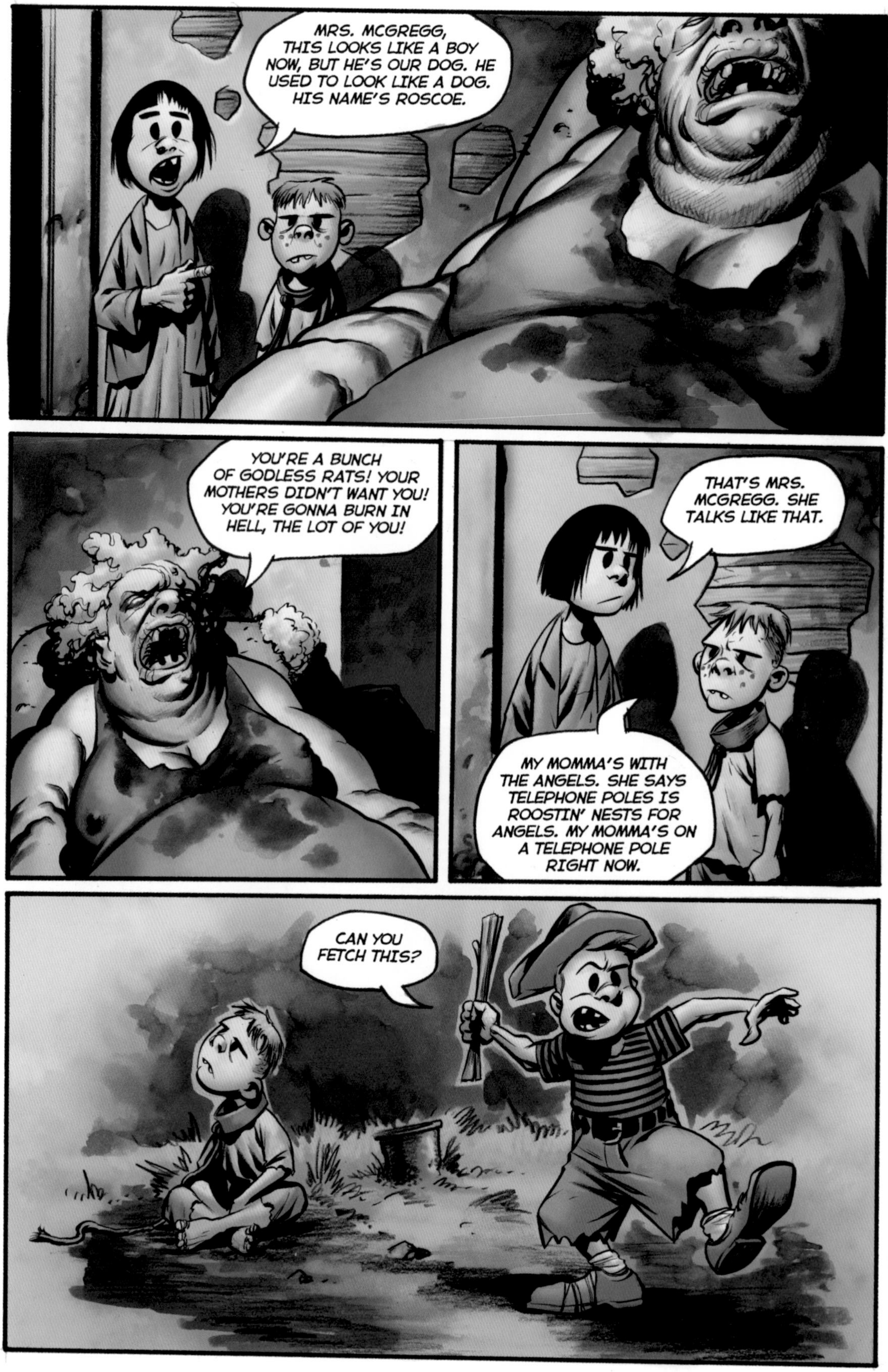
MRS. MCGREGG, THIS LOOKS LIKE A BOY NOW, BUT HE'S OUR DOG. HE USED TO LOOK LIKE A DOG. HIS NAME'S ROSCOE.
YOU'RE A BUNCH OF GODLESS RATS! YOUR MOTHERS DIDN'T WANT YOU! YOU'RE GONNA BURN IN HELL, THE LOT OF YOU!
THAT'S MRS. MCGREGG. SHE TALKS LIKE THAT.
MY MOMMA'S WITH THE ANGELS. SHE SAYS TELEPHONE POLES IS ROOSTIN' NESTS FOR ANGELS. MY MOMMA'S ON A TELEPHONE POLE RIGHT NOW.
CAN YOU FETCH THIS?

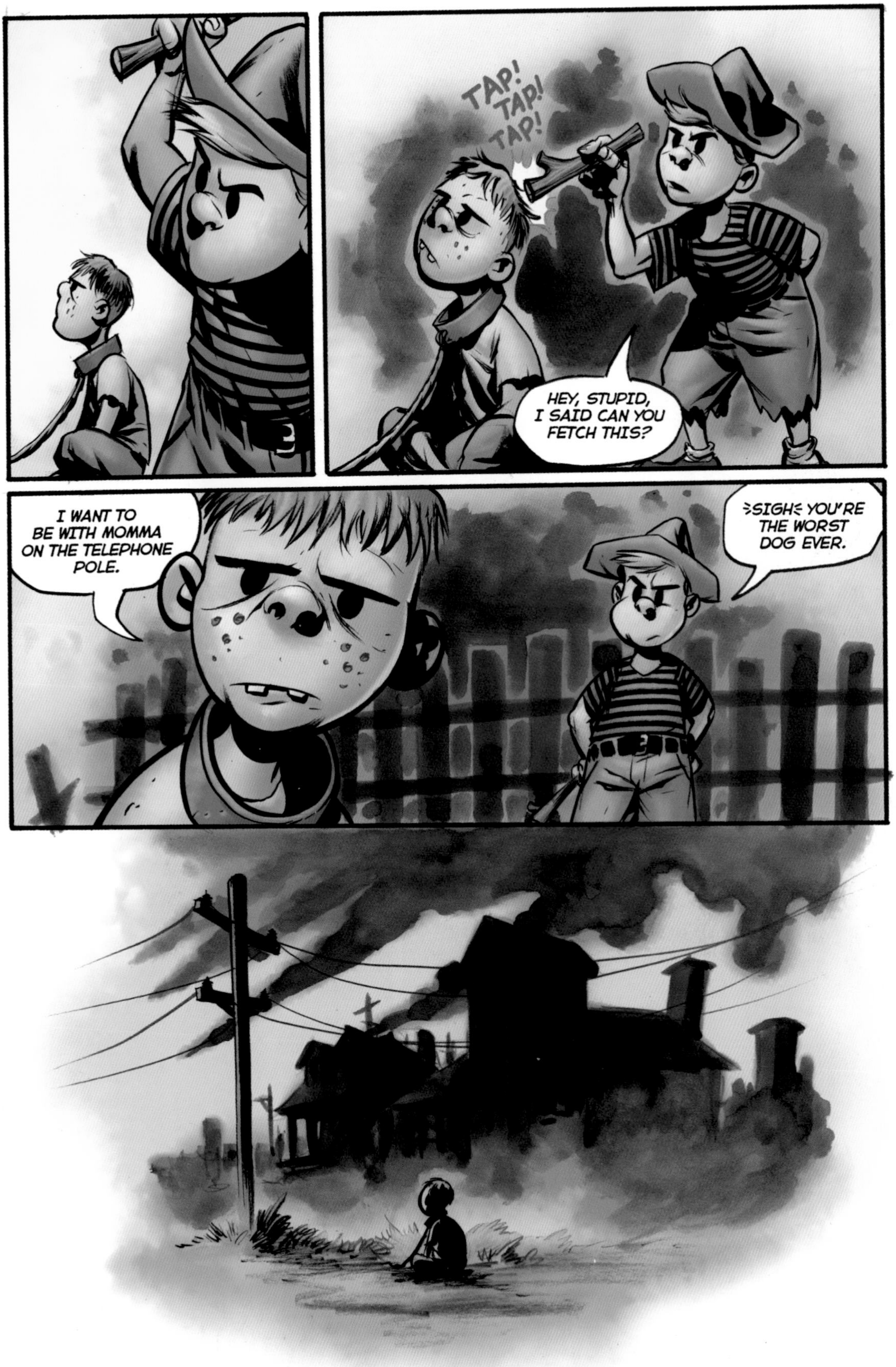
TAP! TAP! TAP!
HEY, STUPID, I SAID CAN YOU FETCH THIS?
I WANT TO BE WITH MOMMA ON THE TELEPHONE POLE.
≷SIGH≶ YOU'RE THE WORST DOG EVER.

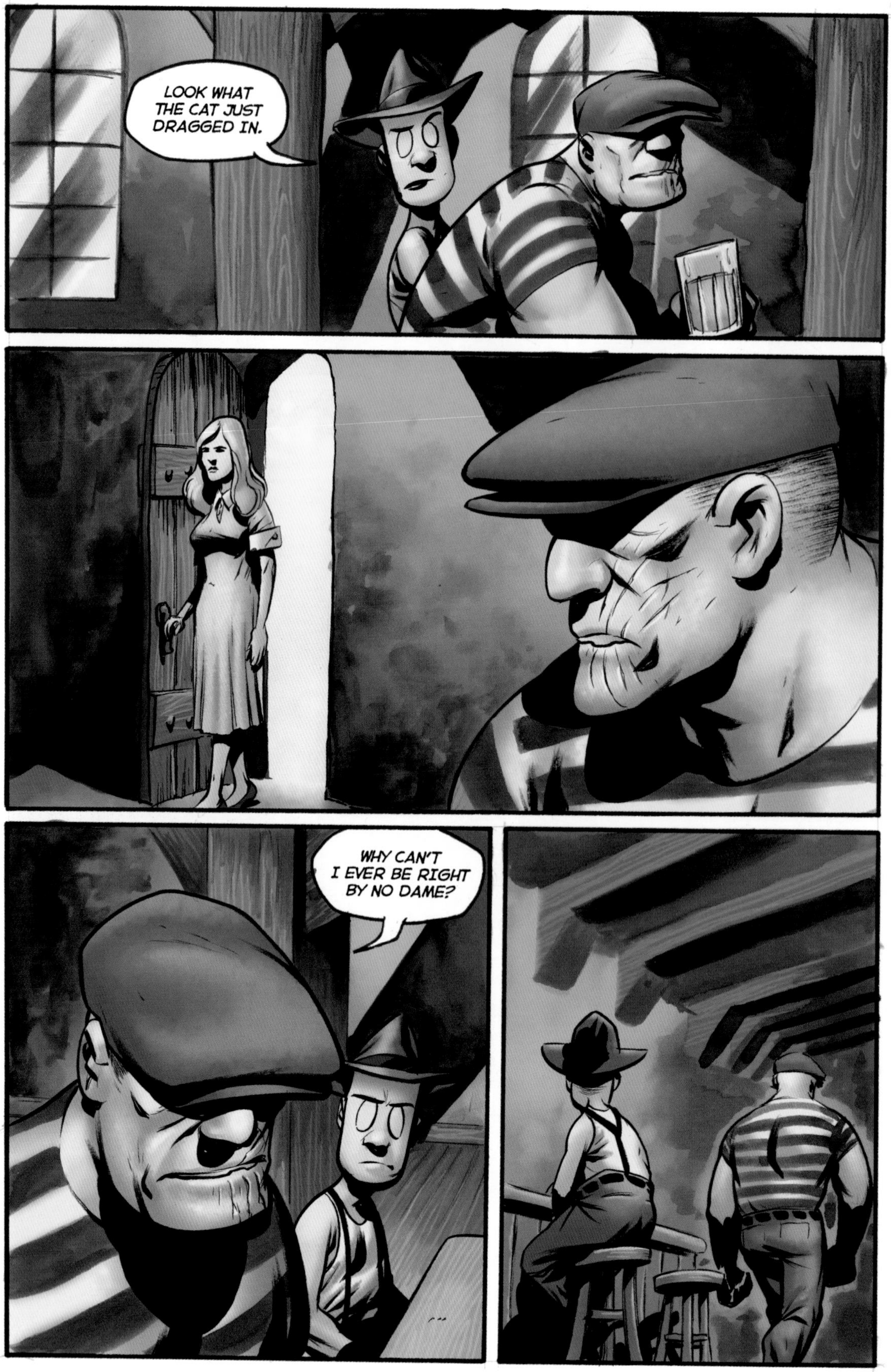
LOOK WHAT THE CAT JUST DRAGGED IN.
WHY CAN'T I EVER BE RIGHT BY NO DAME?

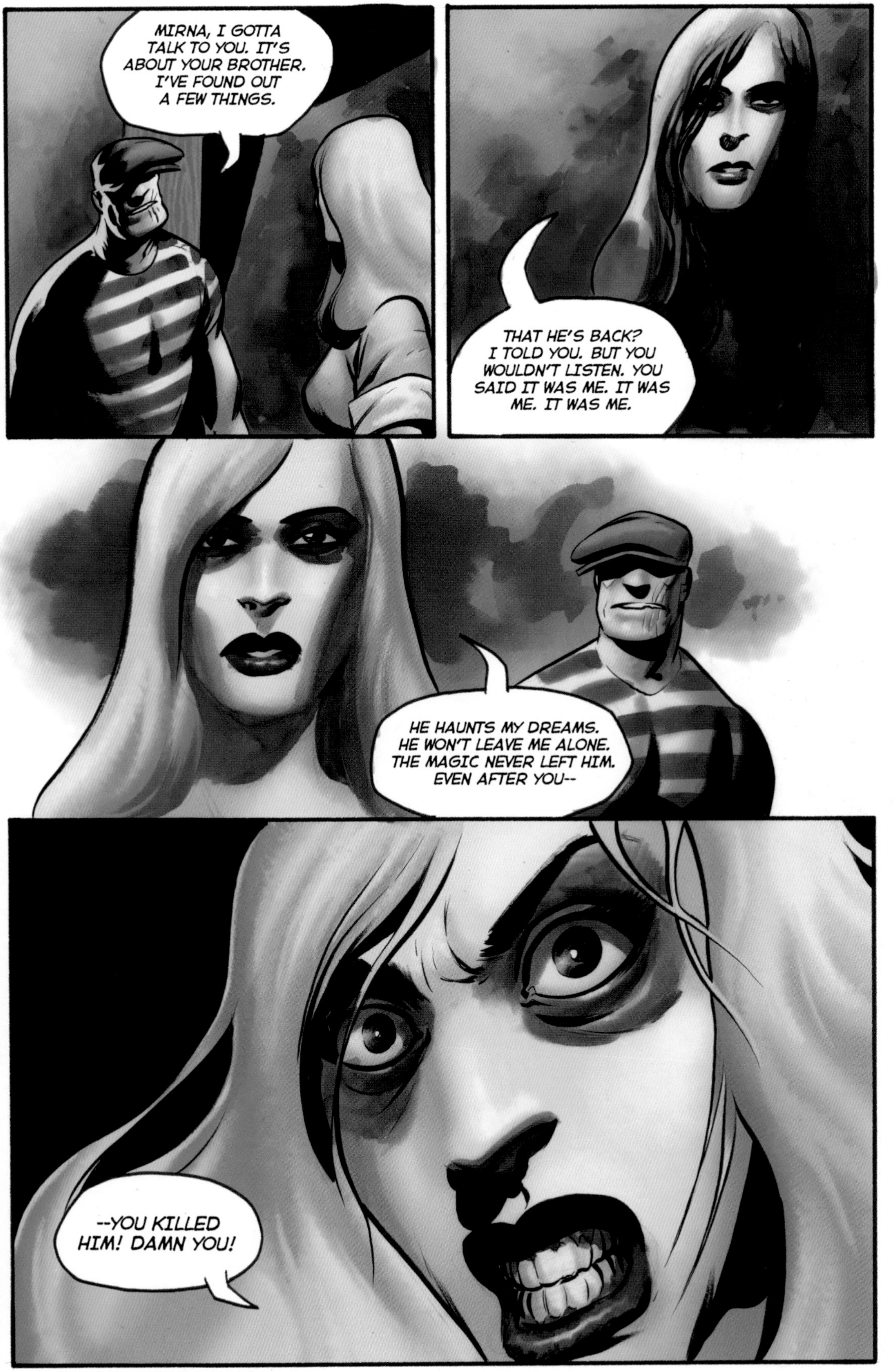
MIRNA, I GOTTA TALK TO YOU. IT'S ABOUT YOUR BROTHER. I'VE FOUND OUT A FEW THINGS.
THAT HE'S BACK? I TOLD YOU. BUT YOU WOULDN'T LISTEN. YOU SAID IT WAS ME. IT WAS ME. IT WAS ME.
HE HAUNTS MY DREAMS. HE WON'T LEAVE ME ALONE. THE MAGIC NEVER LEFT HIM. EVEN AFTER YOU--
--YOU KILLED HIM! DAMN YOU!

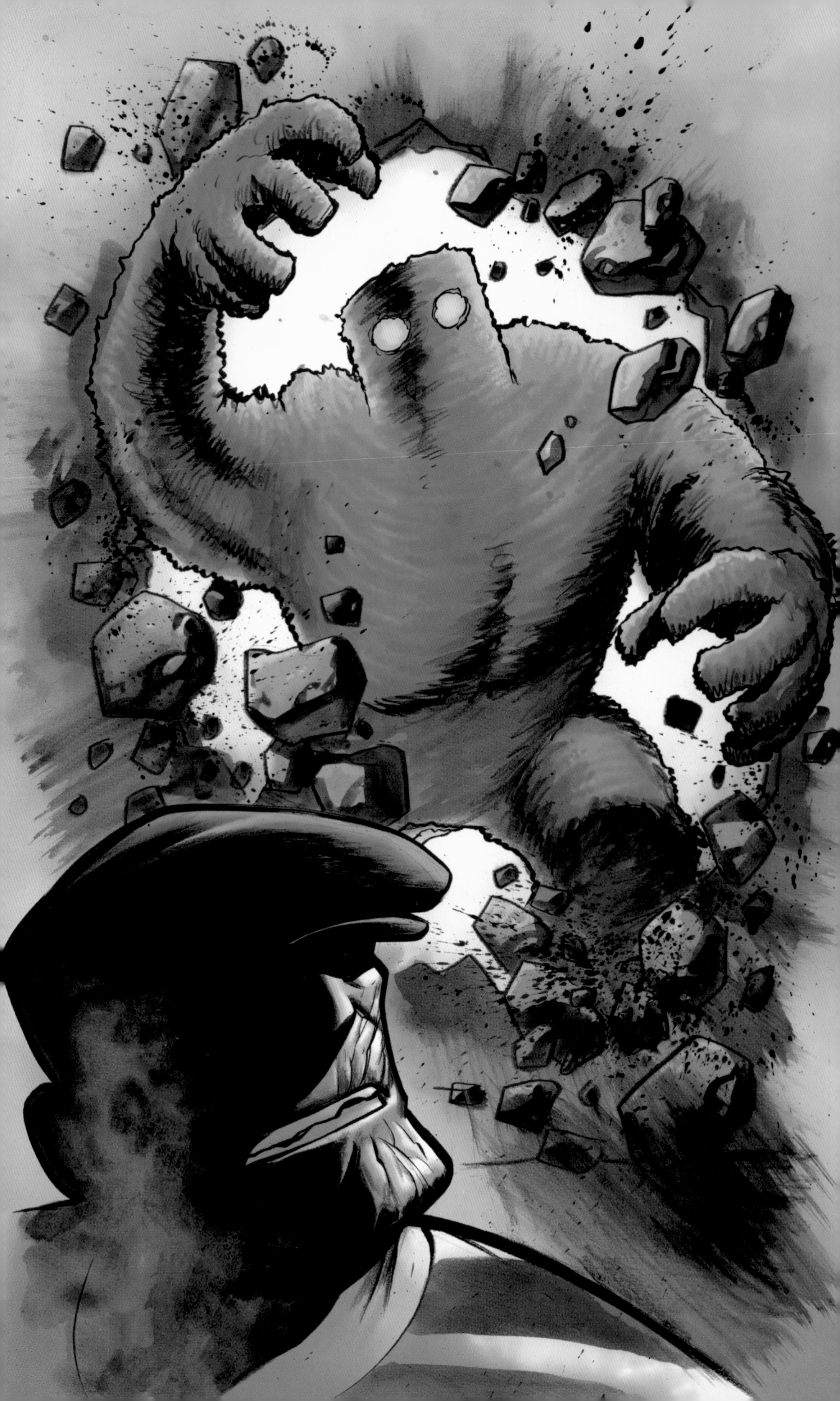

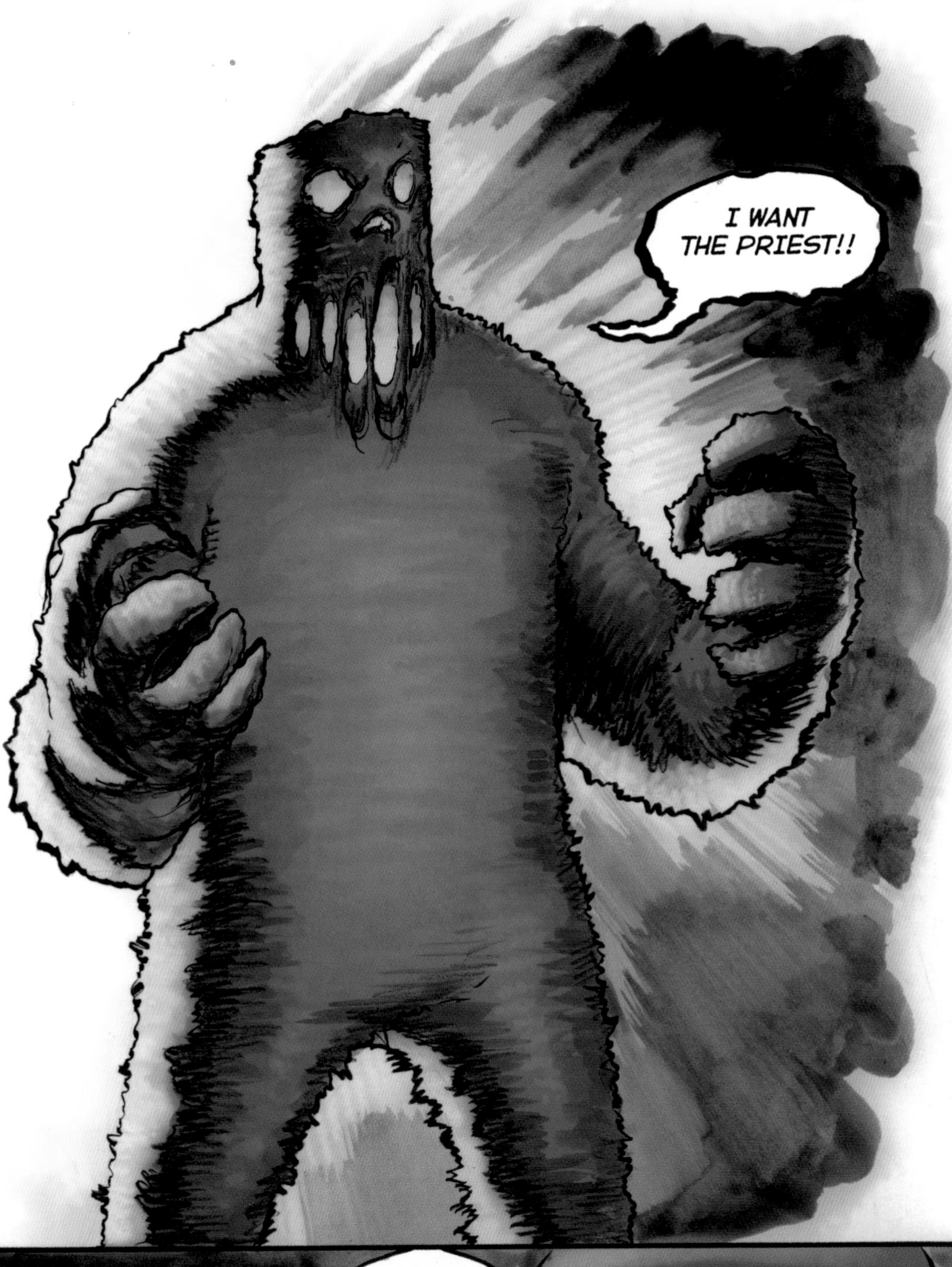
I WANT THE PRIEST!!

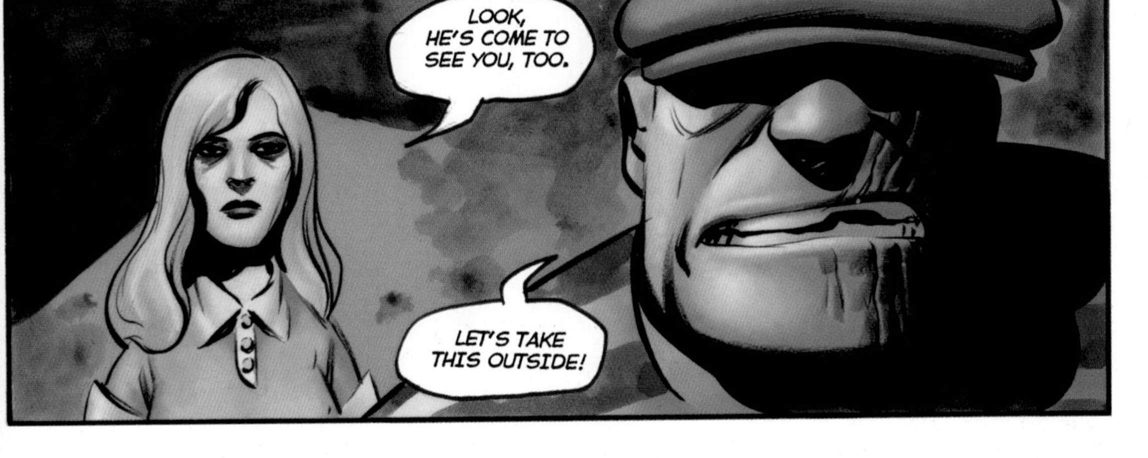
LOOK, HE'S COME TO SEE YOU, TOO.
LET'S TAKE THIS OUTSIDE!

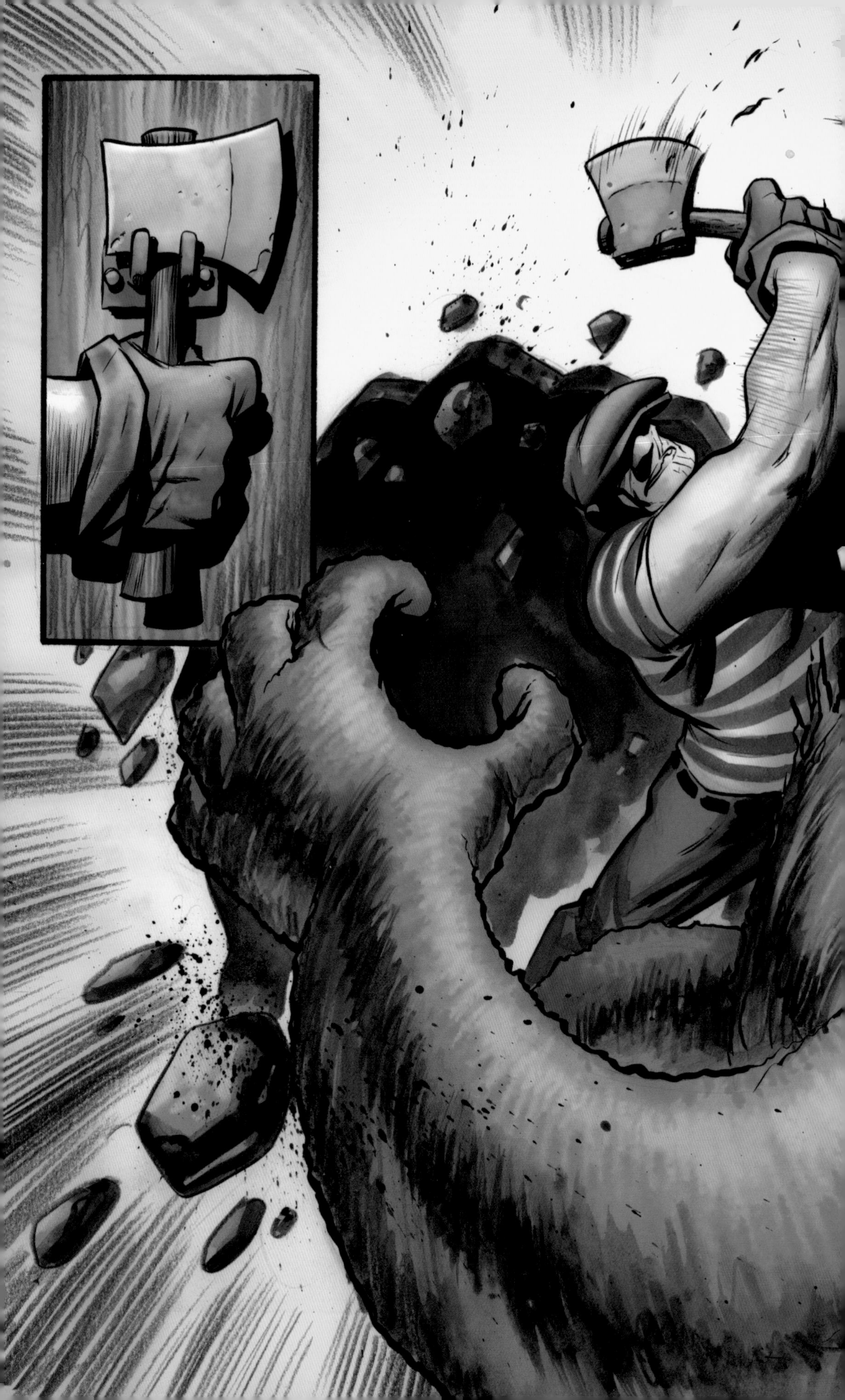

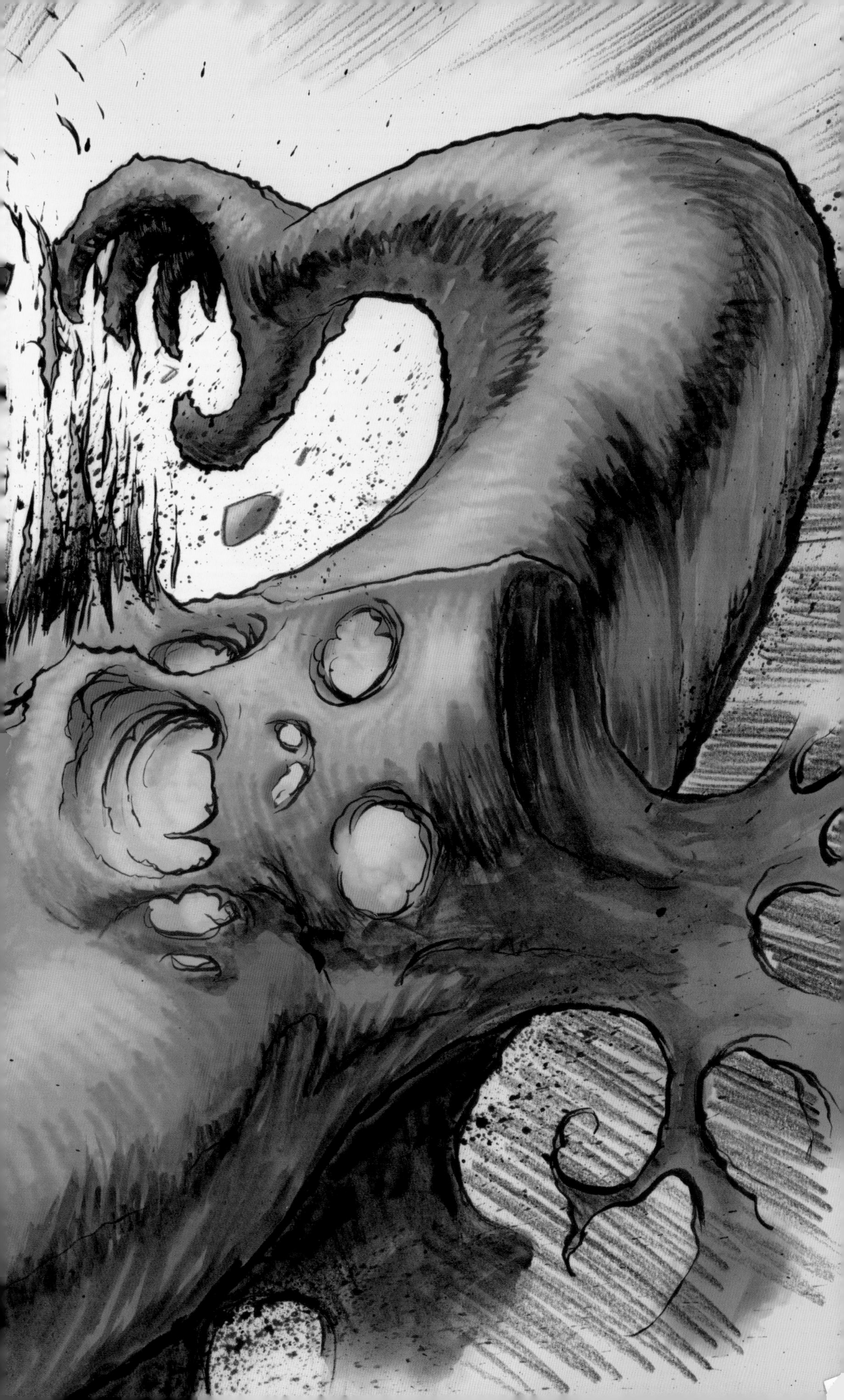

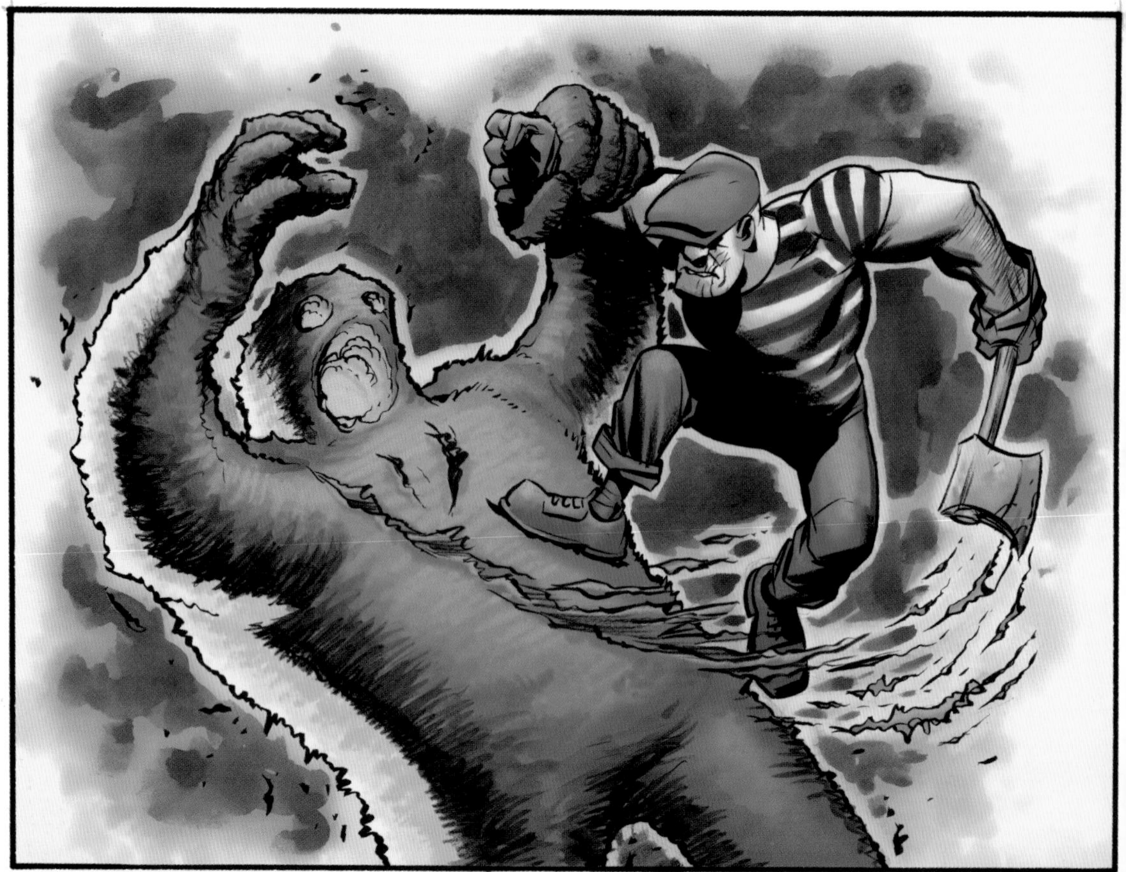

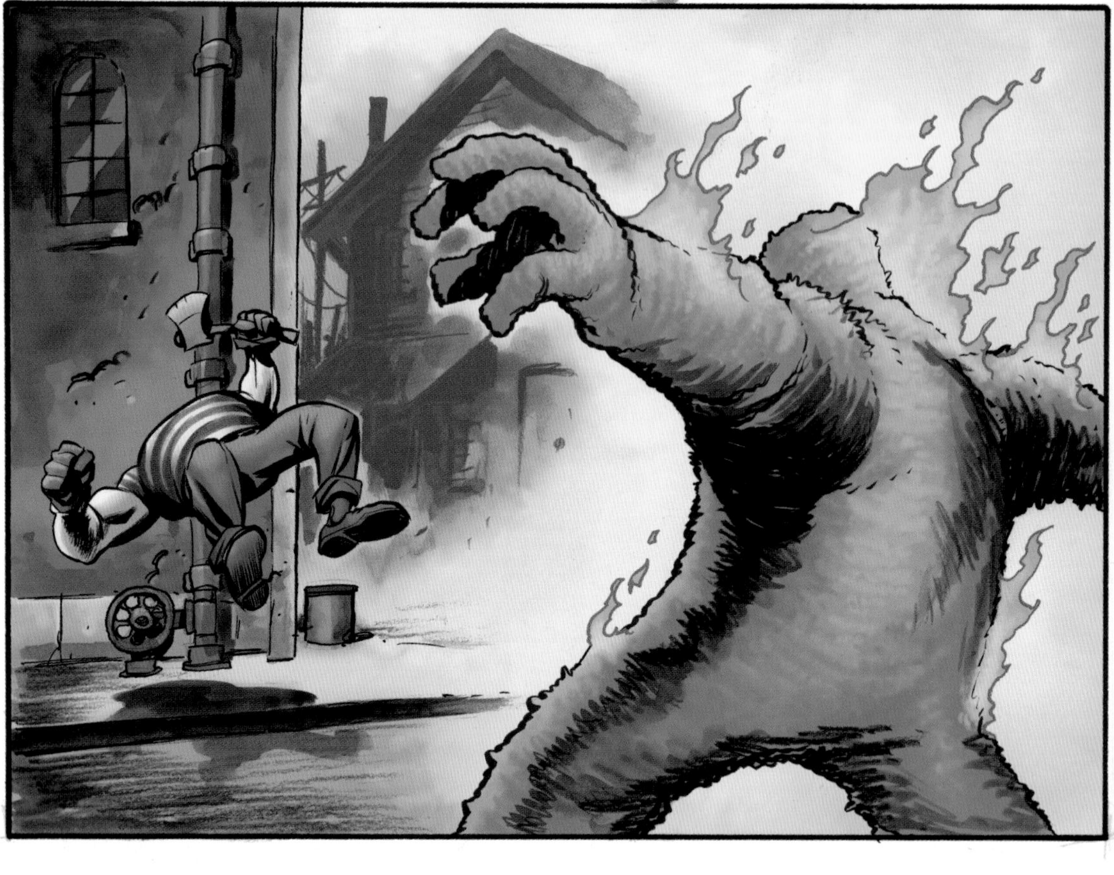

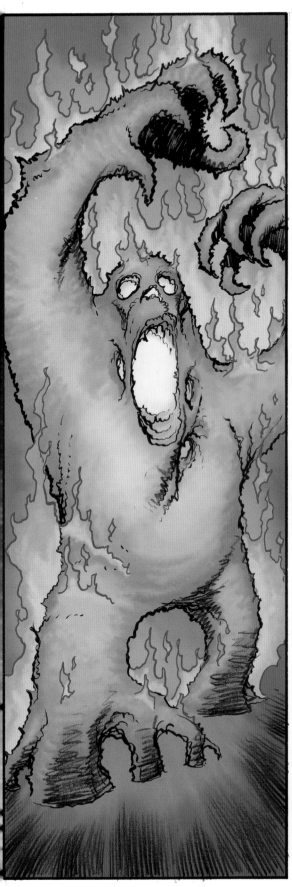

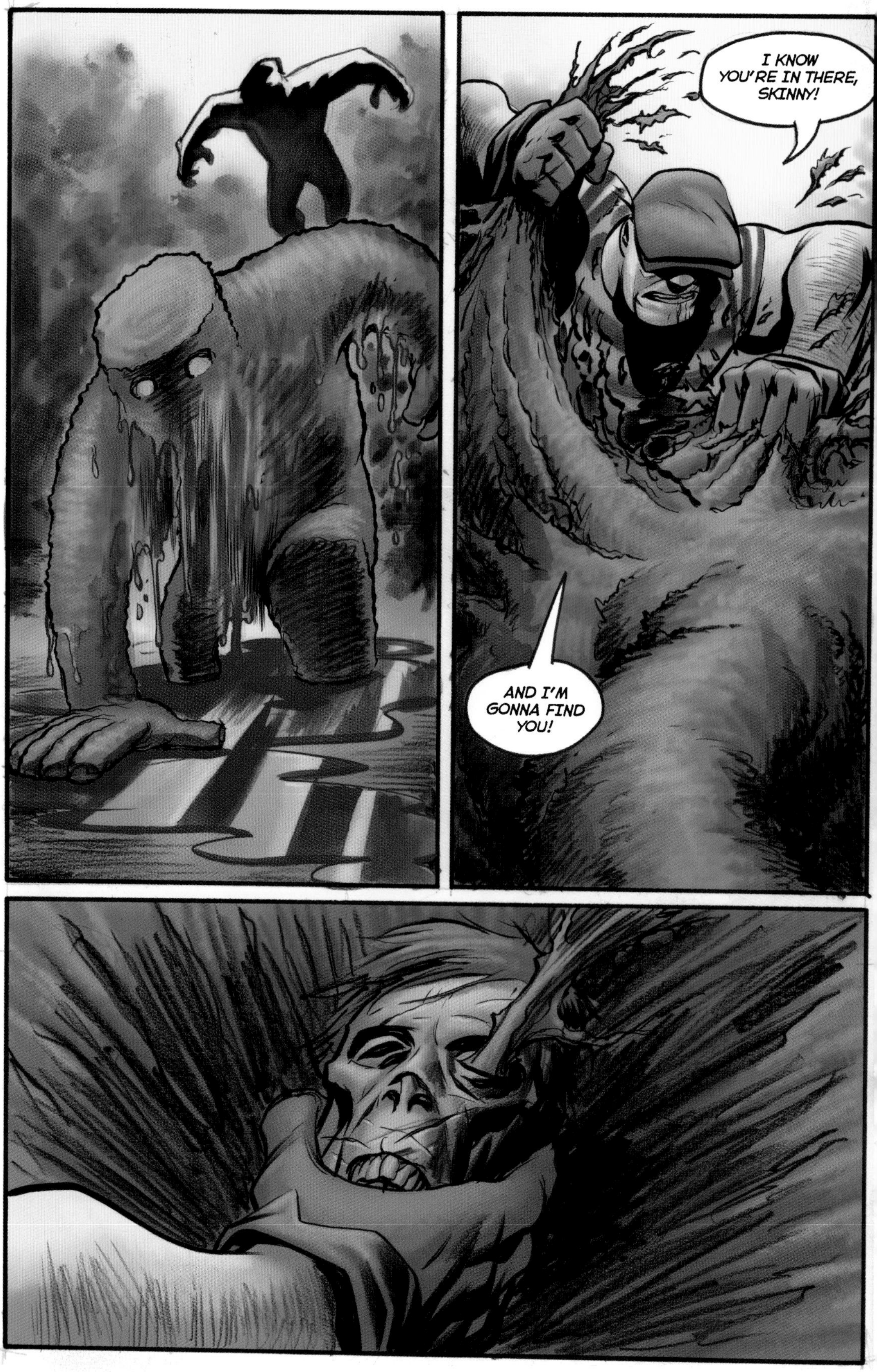
I KNOW YOU'RE IN THERE, SKINNY!
AND I'M GONNA FIND YOU!

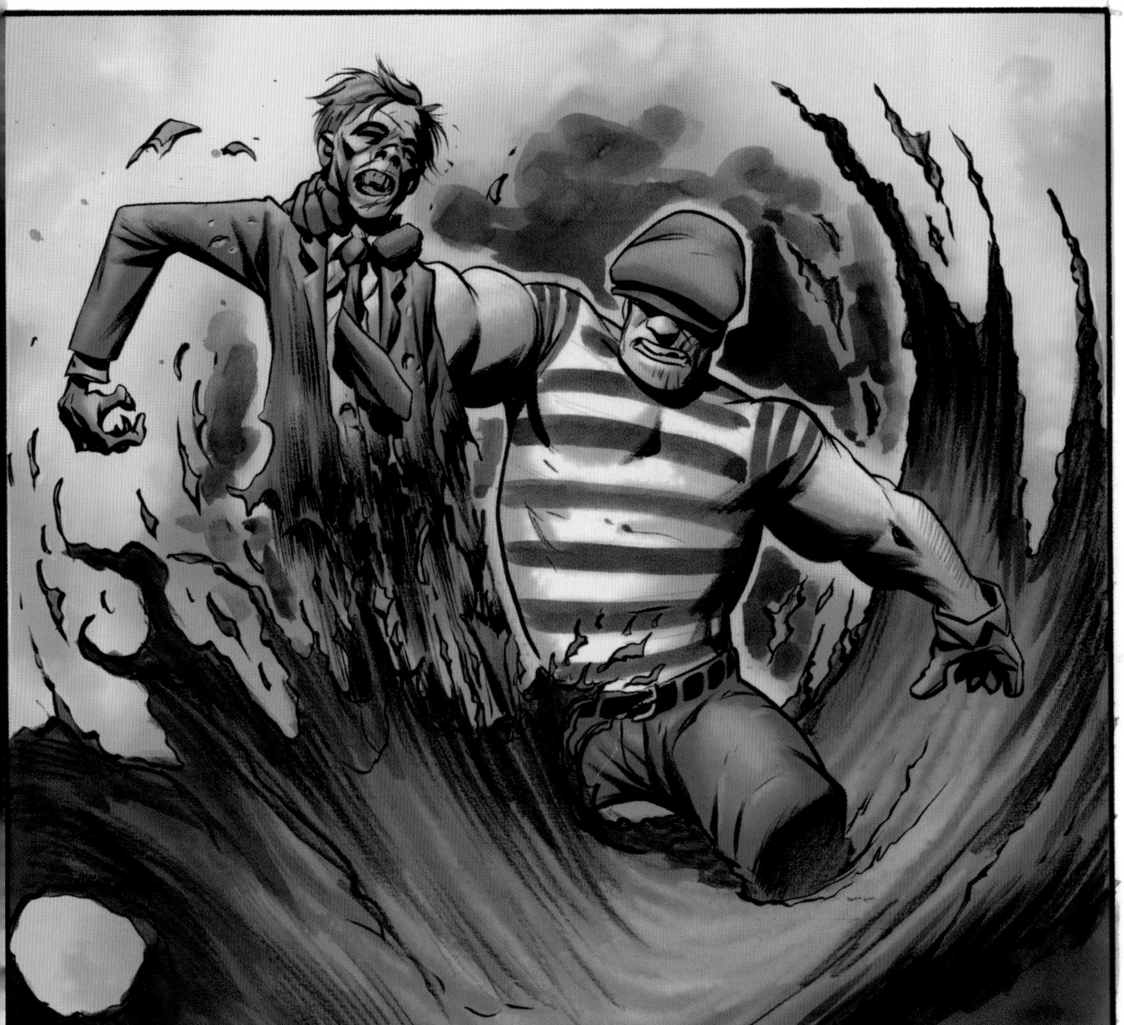

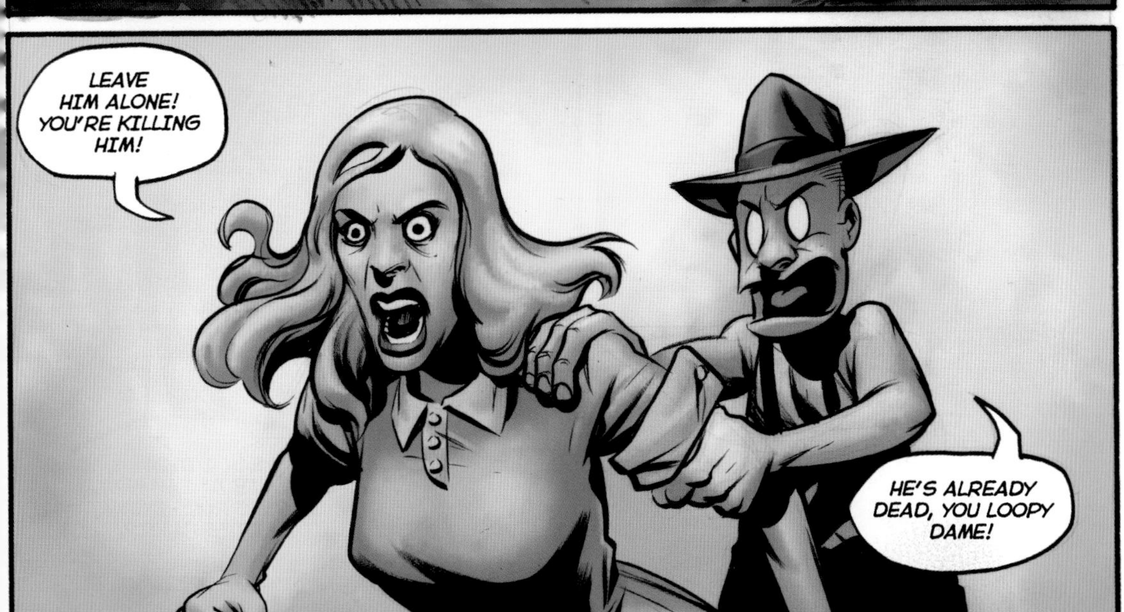
LEAVE HIM ALONE! YOU'RE KILLING HIM!
HE'S ALREADY DEAD, YOU LOOPY DAME!

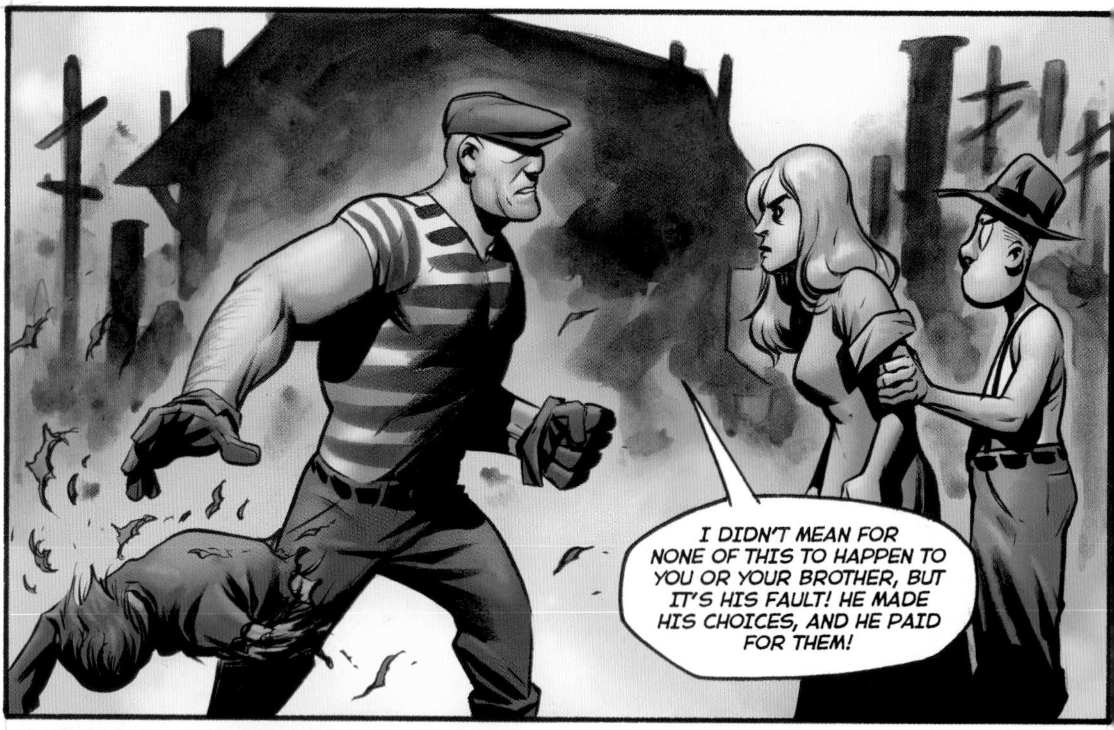
I DIDN'T MEAN FOR NONE OF THIS TO HAPPEN TO YOU OR YOUR BROTHER, BUT IT'S HIS FAULT! HE MADE HIS CHOICES, AND HE PAID FOR THEM!

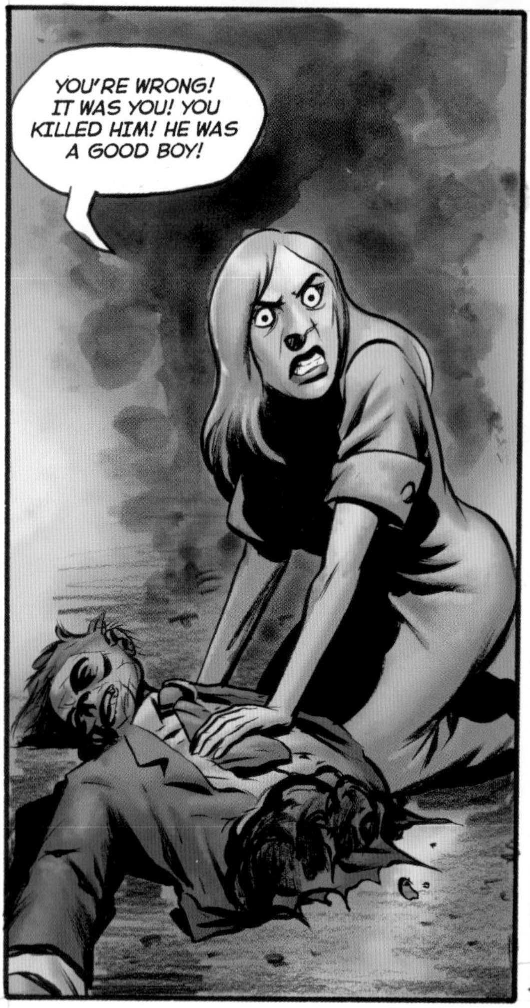
YOU'RE WRONG! IT WAS YOU! YOU KILLED HIM! HE WAS A GOOD BOY!

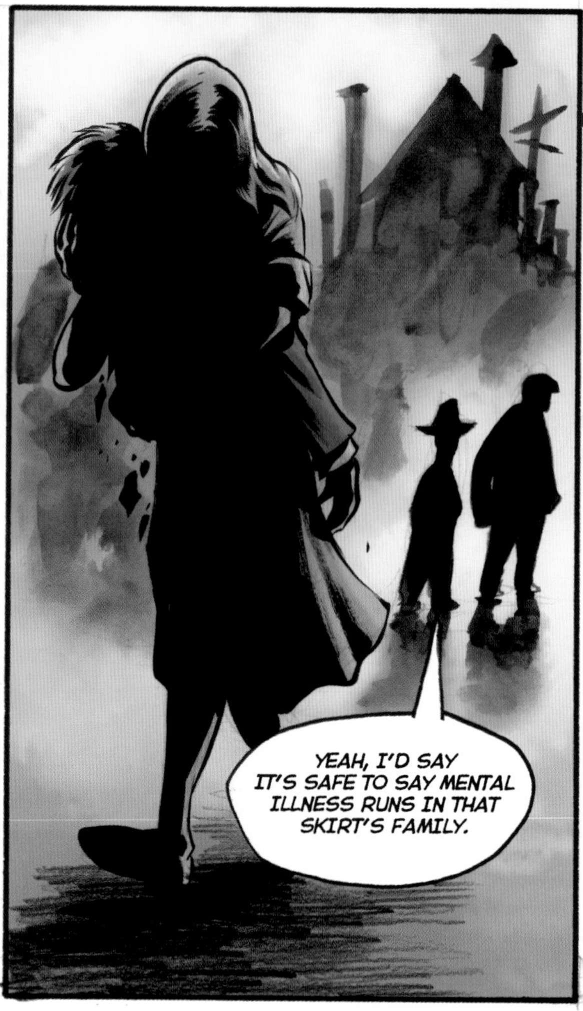
YEAH, I'D SAY IT'S SAFE TO SAY MENTAL ILLNESS RUNS IN THAT SKIRT'S FAMILY.

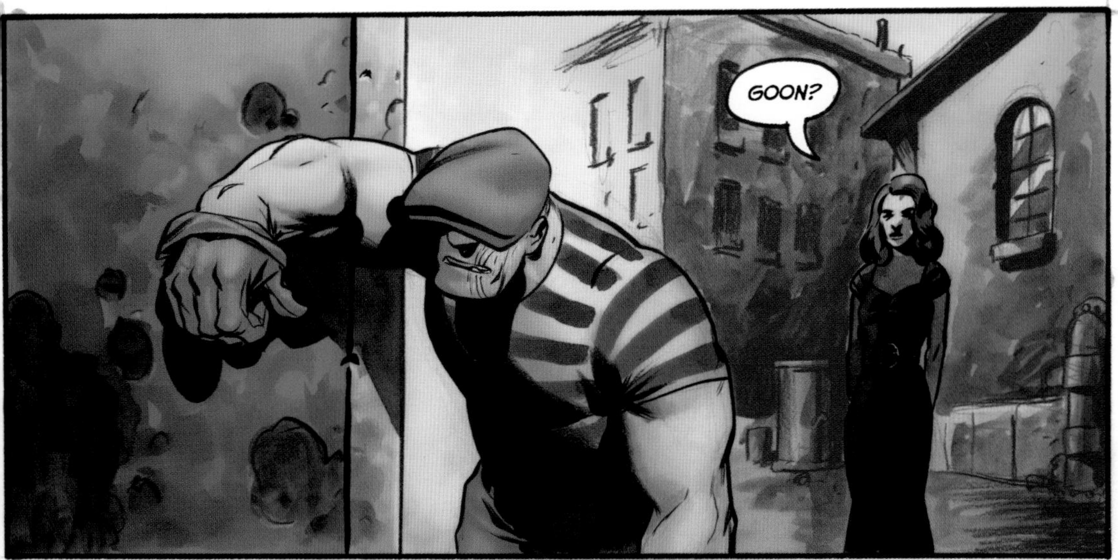
GOON?

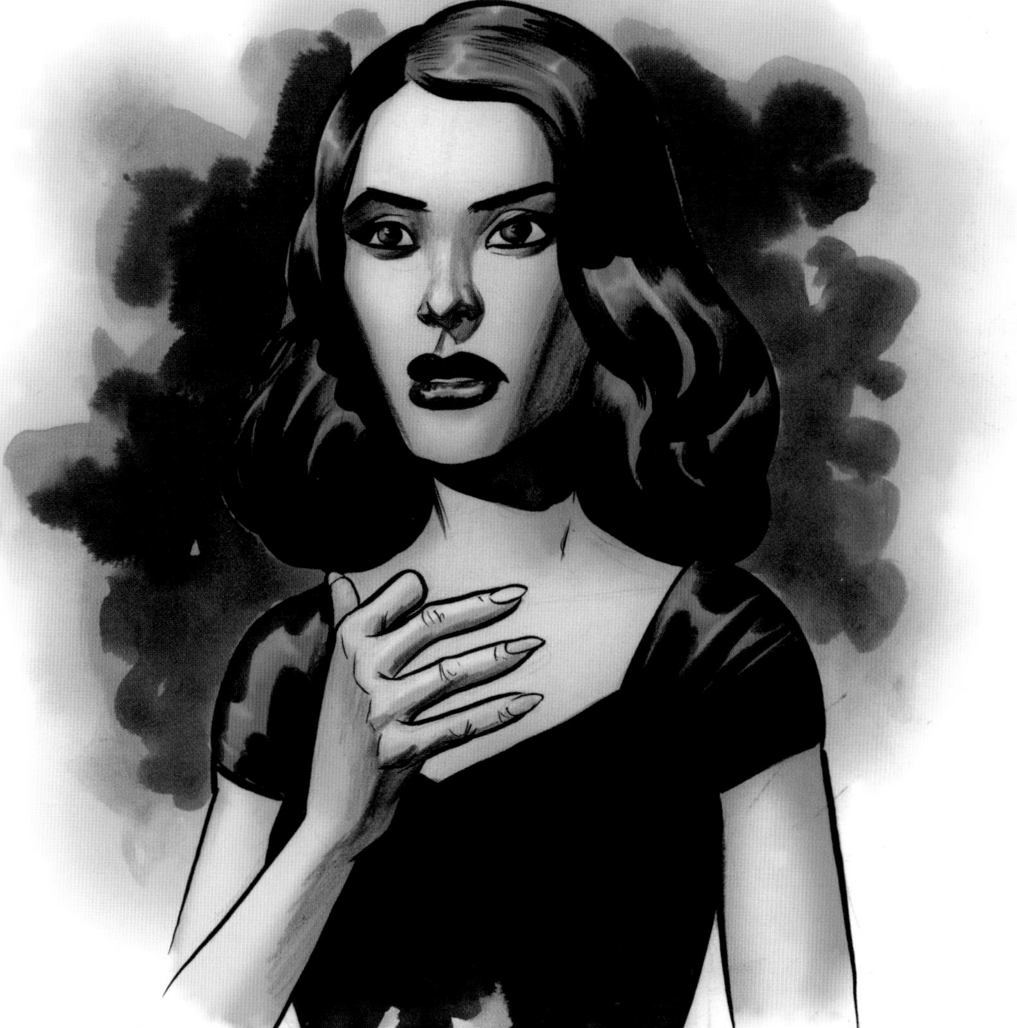

CHAPTER 3

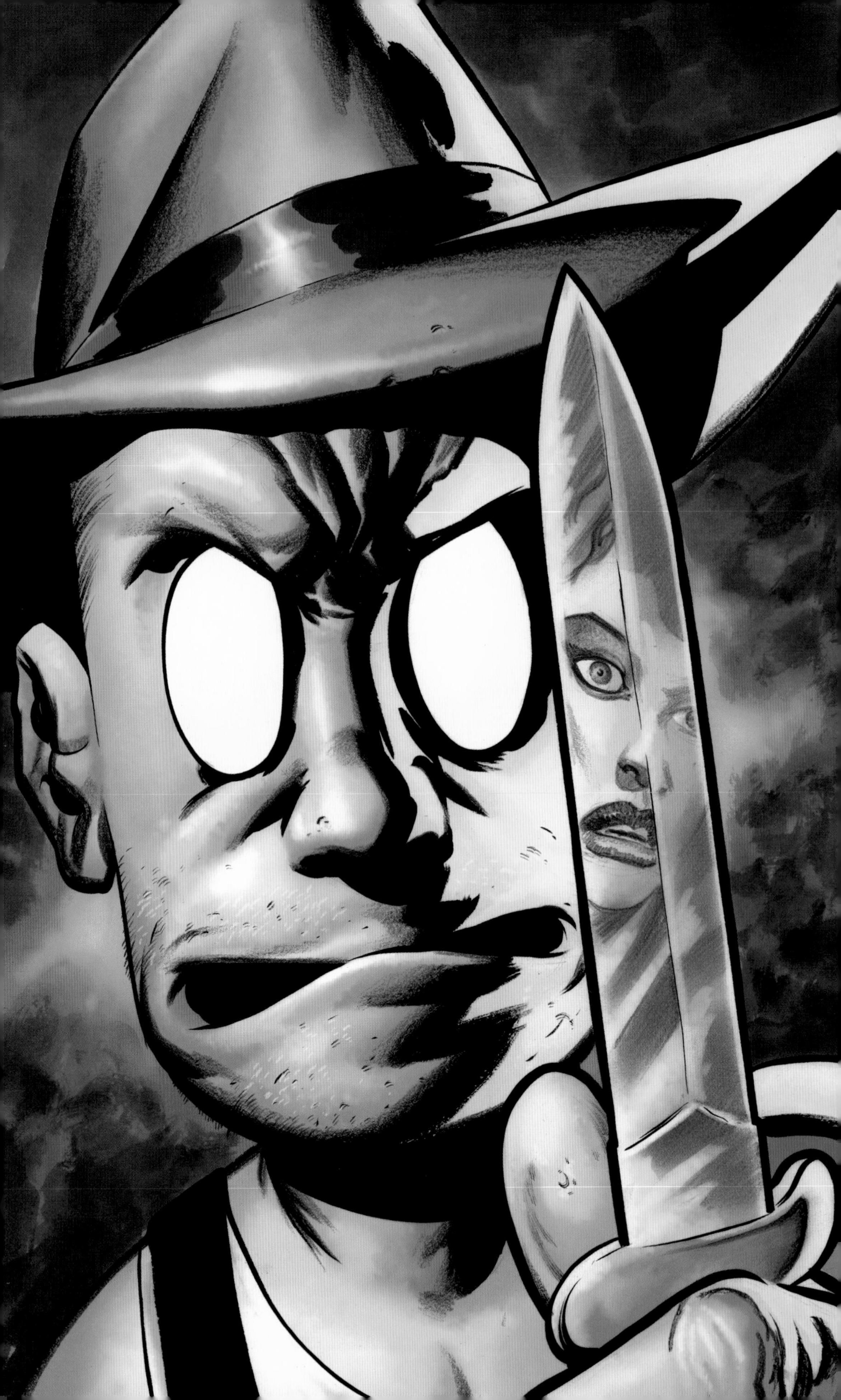

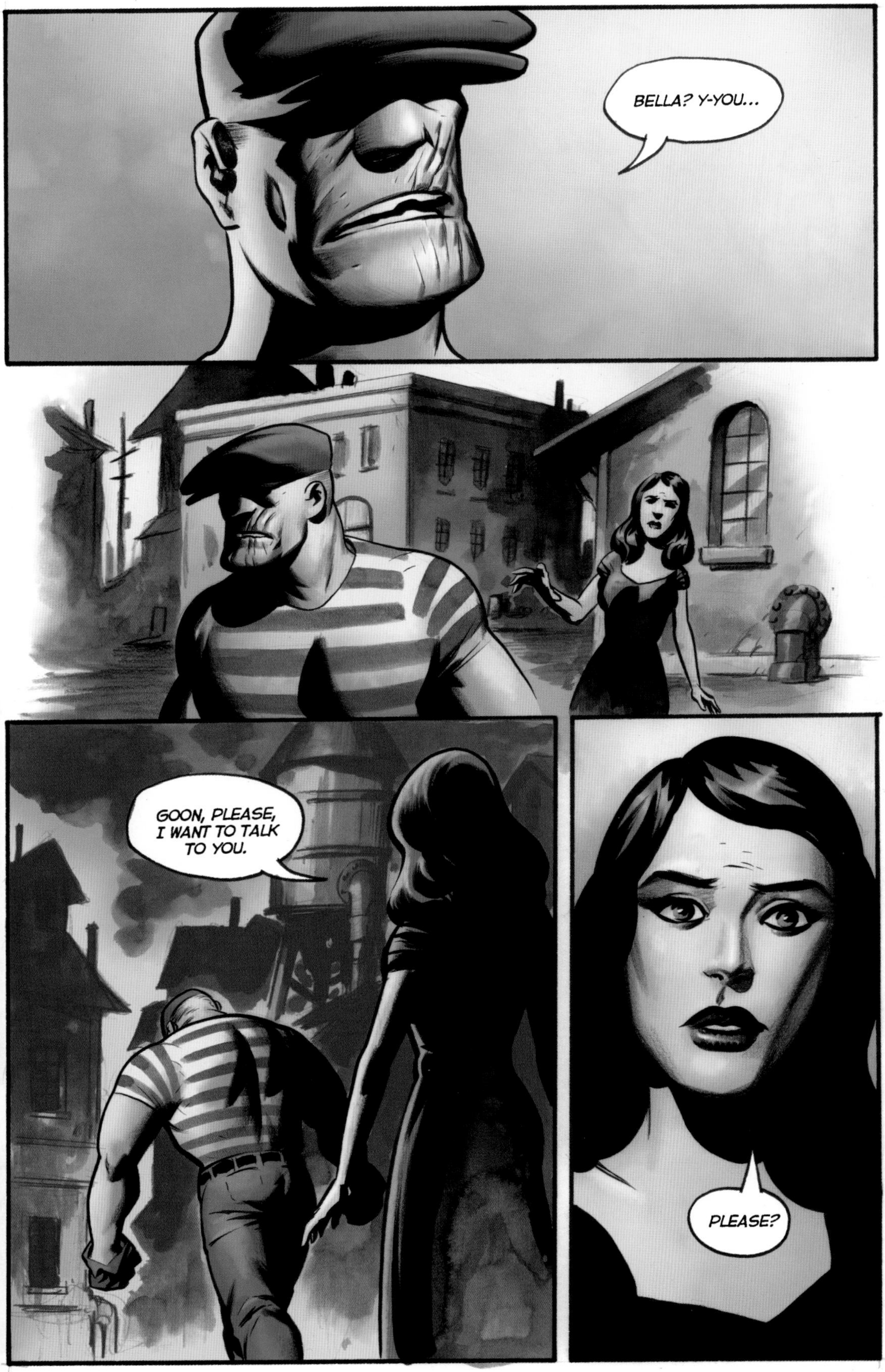
BELLA? Y-YOU...
GOON, PLEASE, I WANT TO TALK TO YOU.
PLEASE?

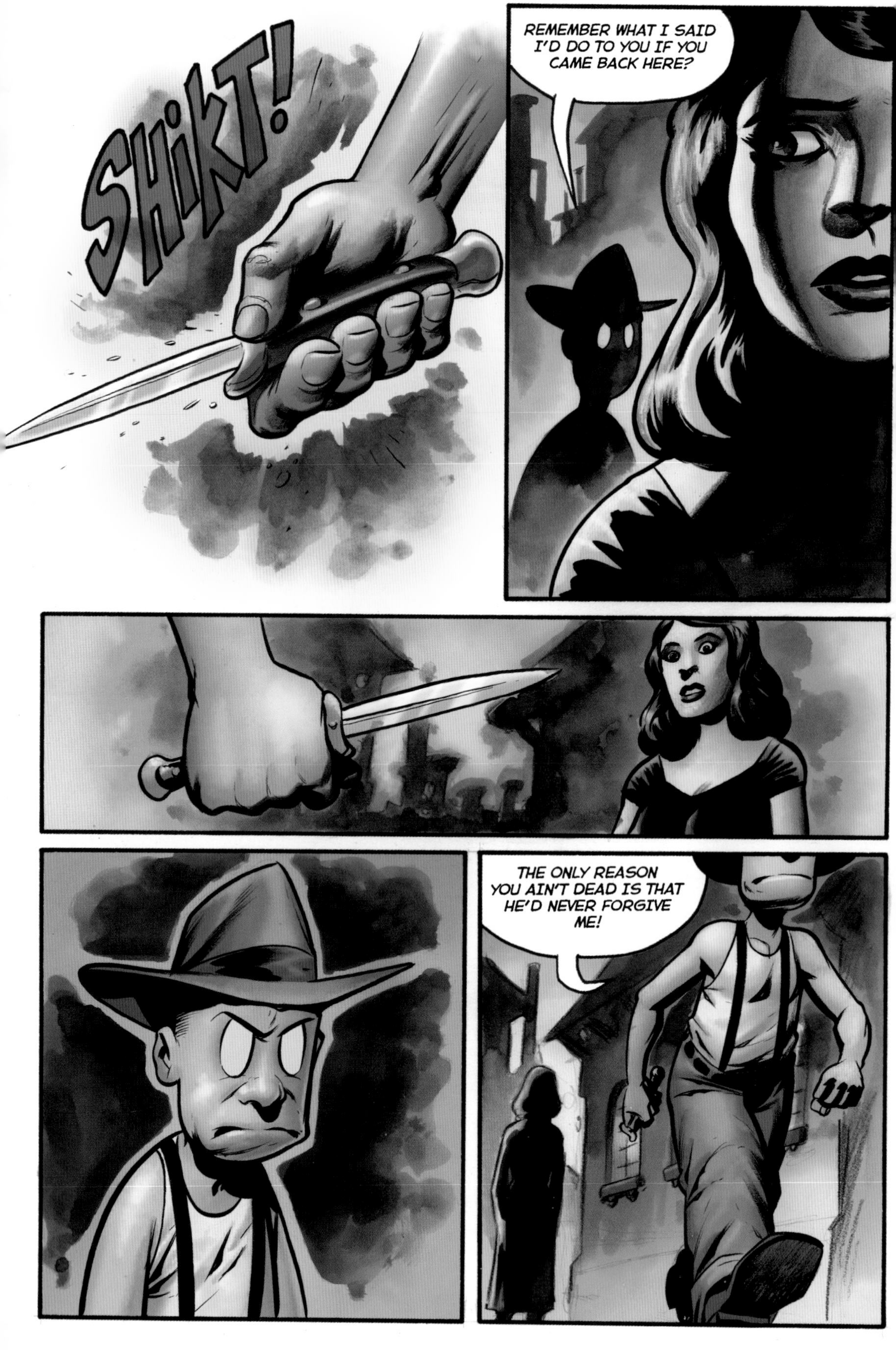
SHIKT!
REMEMBER WHAT I SAID I'D DO TO YOU IF YOU CAME BACK HERE?
THE ONLY REASON YOU AIN'T DEAD IS THAT HE'D NEVER FORGIVE ME!

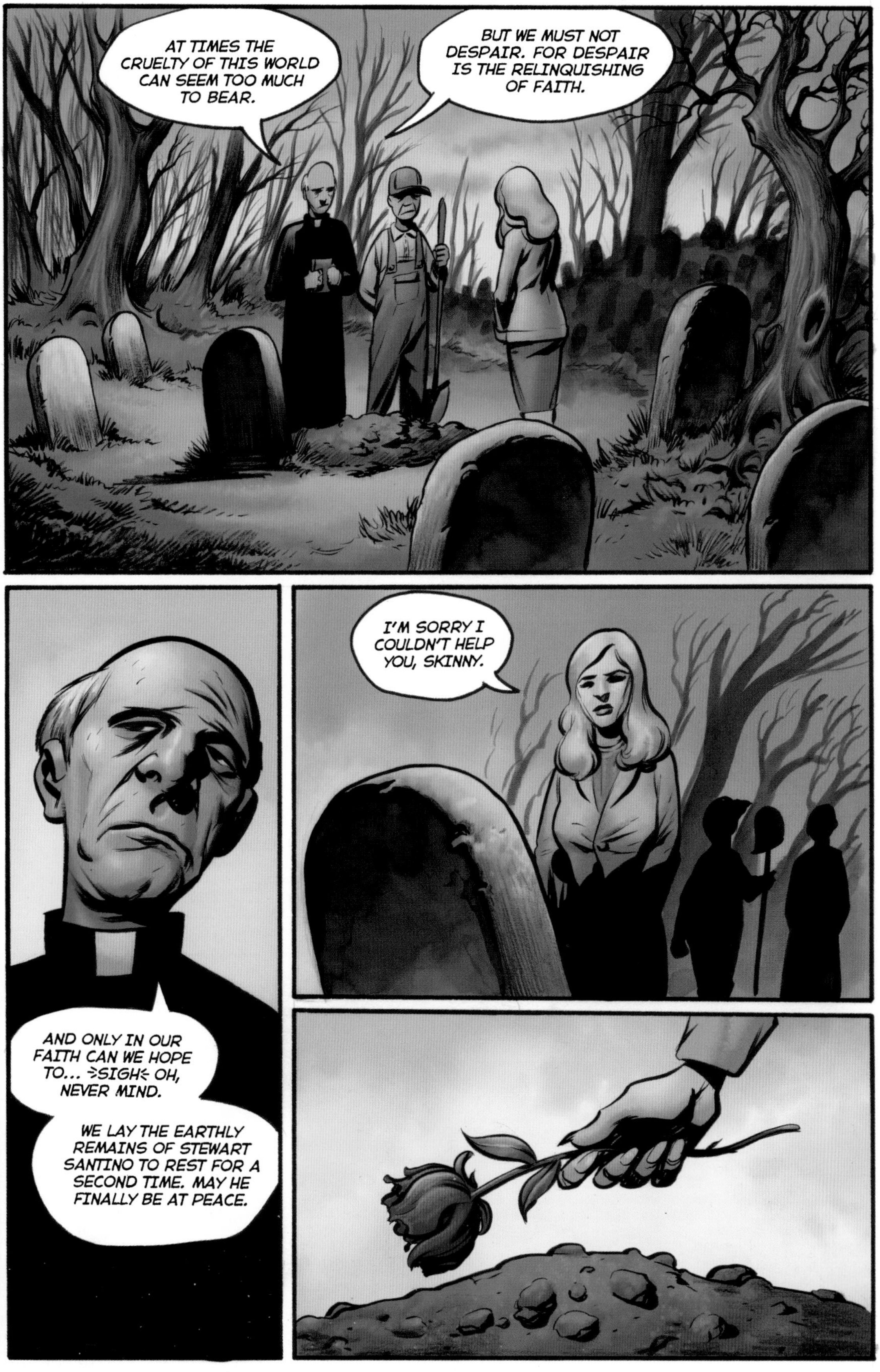
AT TIMES THE CRUELTY OF THIS WORLD CAN SEEM TOO MUCH TO BEAR.
BUT WE MUST NOT DESPAIR. FOR DESPAIR IS THE RELINQUISHING OF FAITH.
I'M SORRY I COULDN'T HELP YOU, SKINNY.
AND ONLY IN OUR FAITH CAN WE HOPE TO... >SIGH< OH, NEVER MIND.
WE LAY THE EARTHLY REMAINS OF STEWART SANTINO TO REST FOR A SECOND TIME. MAY HE FINALLY BE AT PEACE.

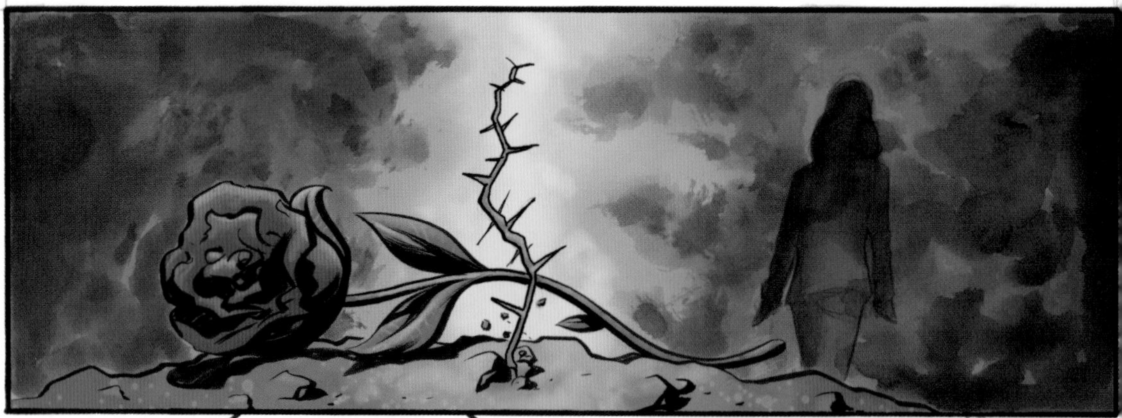

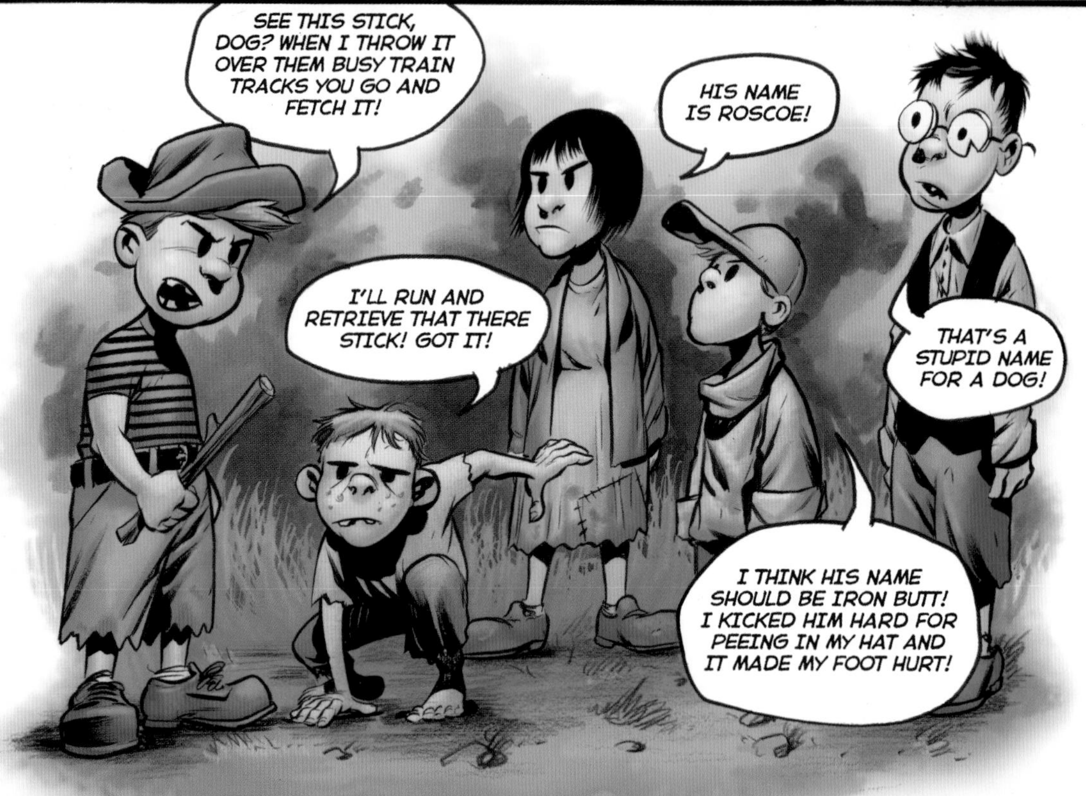

SEE THIS STICK, DOG? WHEN I THROW IT OVER THEM BUSY TRAIN TRACKS YOU GO AND FETCH IT!
HIS NAME IS ROSCOE!
I'LL RUN AND RETRIEVE THAT THERE STICK! GOT IT!
THAT'S A STUPID NAME FOR A DOG!
I THINK HIS NAME SHOULD BE IRON BUTT! I KICKED HIM HARD FOR PEEING IN MY HAT AND IT MADE MY FOOT HURT!

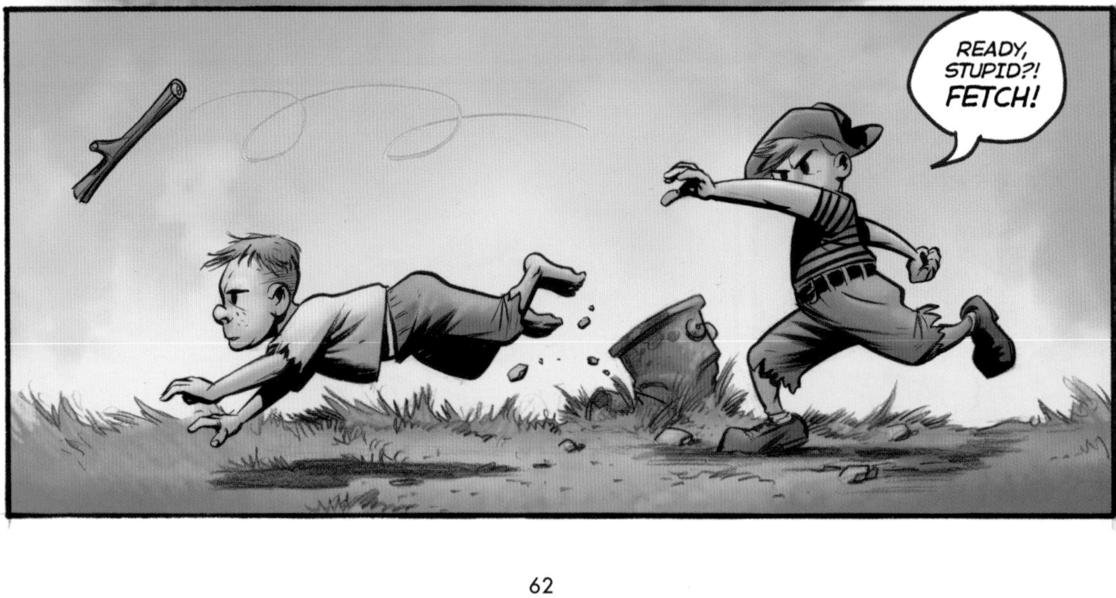

READY, STUPID?! FETCH!

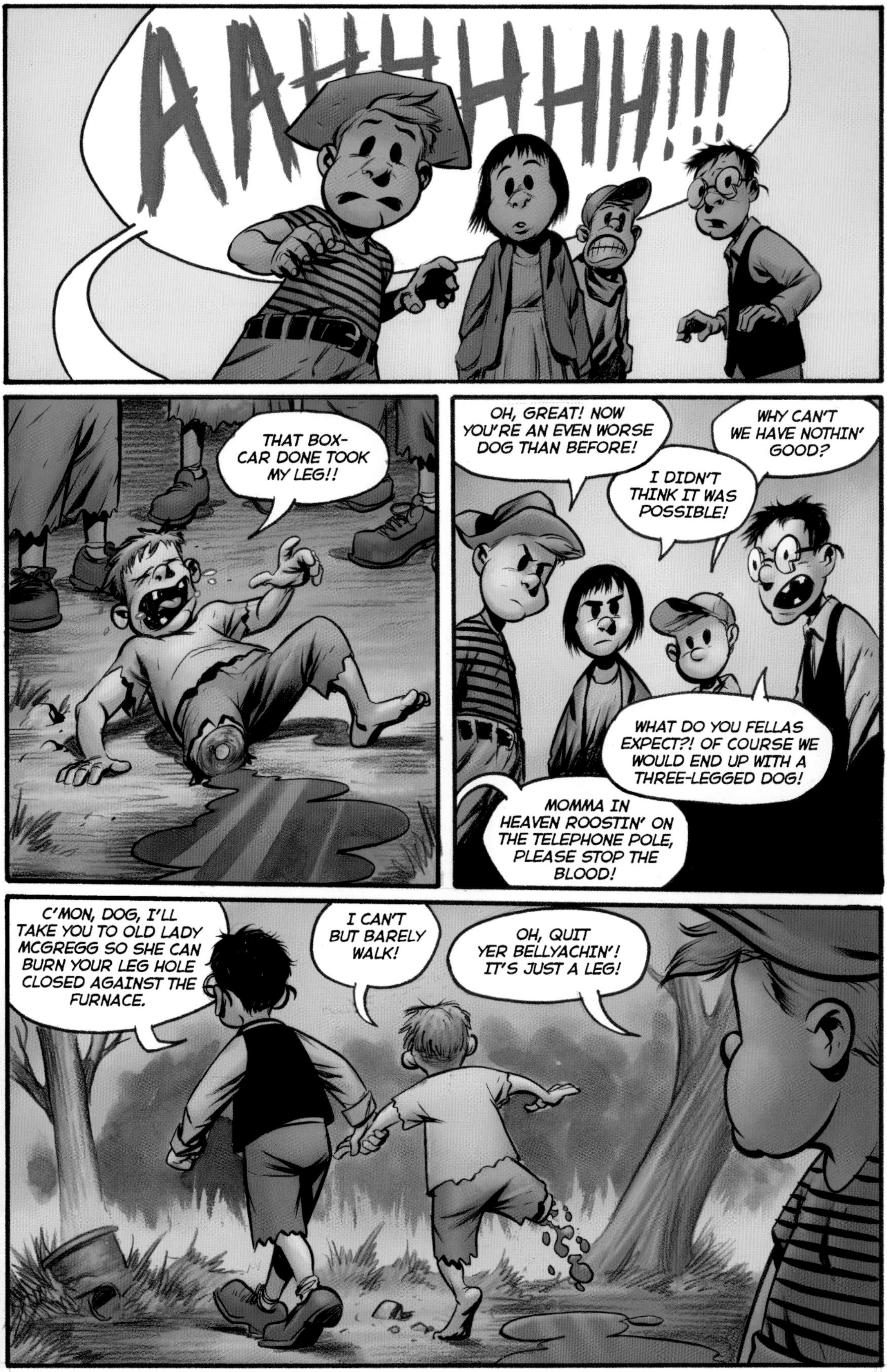
AAHHHHH!!!
THAT BOX-CAR DONE TOOK MY LEG!!
OH, GREAT! NOW YOU'RE AN EVEN WORSE DOG THAN BEFORE!
I DIDN'T THINK IT WAS POSSIBLE!
WHY CAN'T WE HAVE NOTHIN' GOOD?
WHAT DO YOU FELLAS EXPECT?! OF COURSE WE WOULD END UP WITH A THREE-LEGGED DOG!
MOMMA IN HEAVEN ROOSTIN' ON THE TELEPHONE POLE, PLEASE STOP THE BLOOD!
C'MON, DOG, I'LL TAKE YOU TO OLD LADY MCGREGG SO SHE CAN BURN YOUR LEG HOLE CLOSED AGAINST THE FURNACE.
I CAN'T BUT BARELY WALK!
OH, QUIT YER BELLYACHIN'! IT'S JUST A LEG!

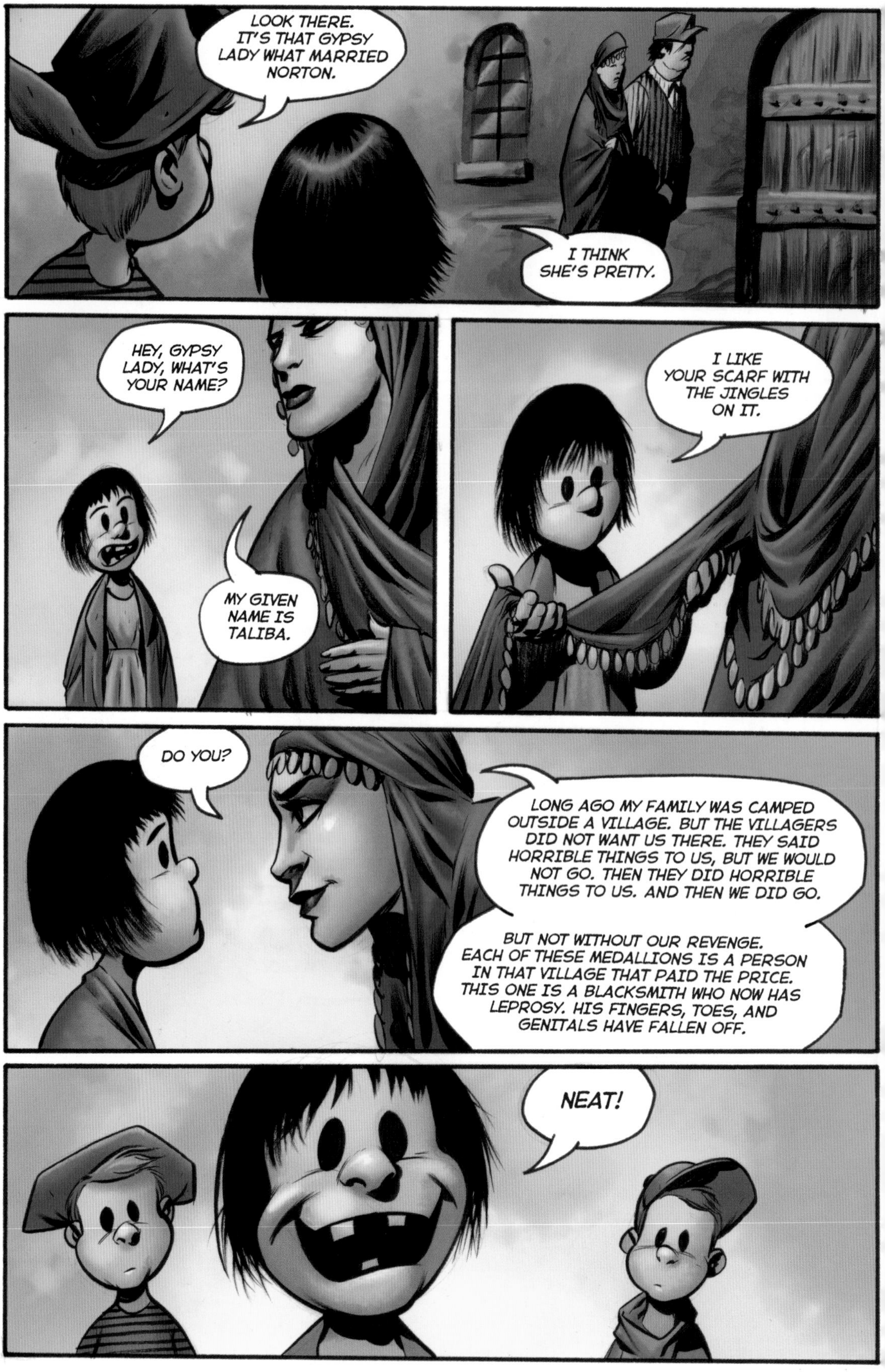
LOOK THERE. IT'S THAT GYPSY LADY WHAT MARRIED NORTON.
I THINK SHE'S PRETTY.
HEY, GYPSY LADY, WHAT'S YOUR NAME?
MY GIVEN NAME IS TALIBA.
I LIKE YOUR SCARF WITH THE JINGLES ON IT.
DO YOU?
LONG AGO MY FAMILY WAS CAMPED OUTSIDE A VILLAGE. BUT THE VILLAGERS DID NOT WANT US THERE. THEY SAID HORRIBLE THINGS TO US, BUT WE WOULD NOT GO. THEN THEY DID HORRIBLE THINGS TO US. AND THEN WE DID GO.
BUT NOT WITHOUT OUR REVENGE. EACH OF THESE MEDALLIONS IS A PERSON IN THAT VILLAGE THAT PAID THE PRICE. THIS ONE IS A BLACKSMITH WHO NOW HAS LEPROSY. HIS FINGERS, TOES, AND GENITALS HAVE FALLEN OFF.
NEAT!

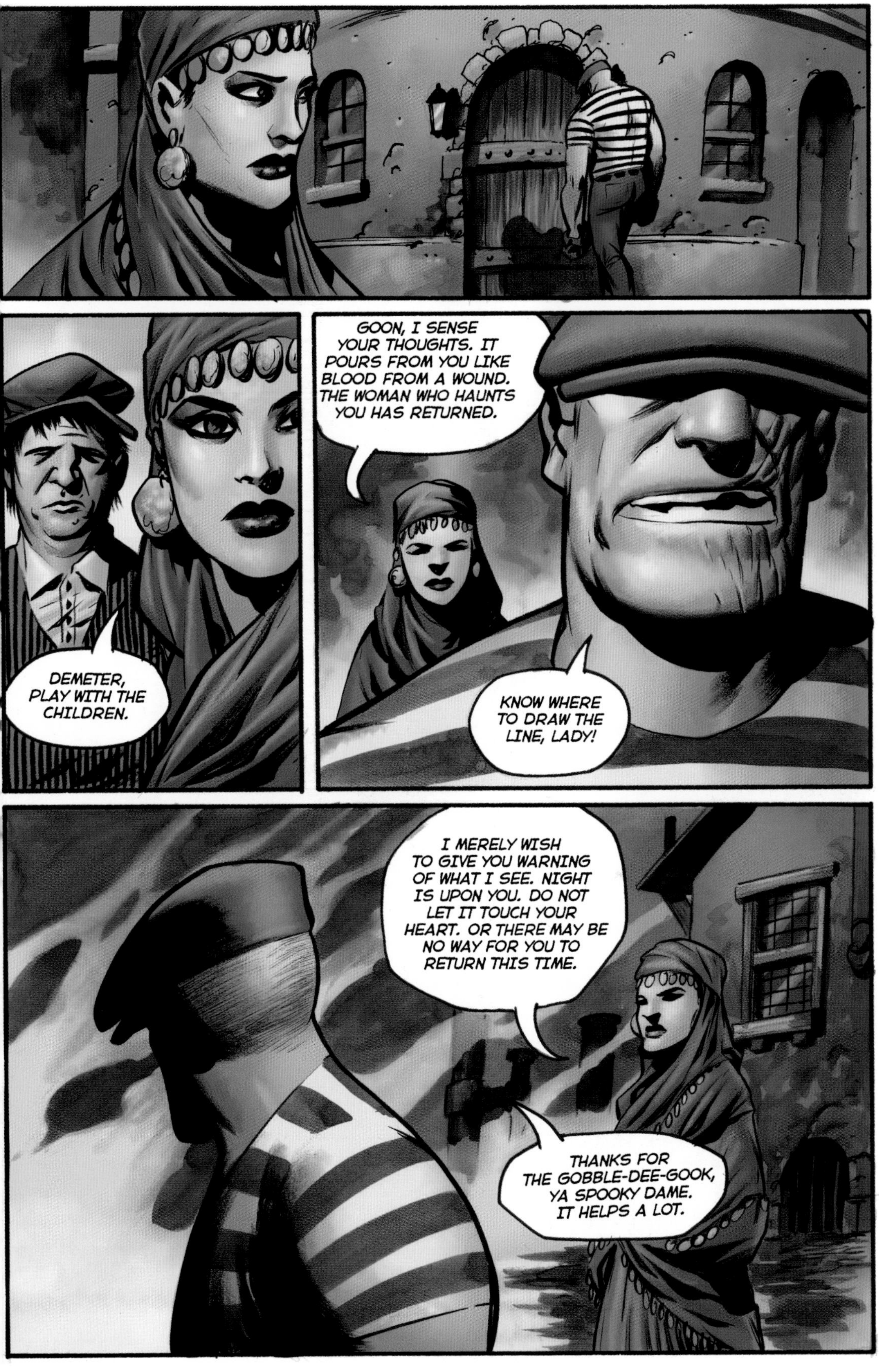
GOON, I SENSE YOUR THOUGHTS. IT POURS FROM YOU LIKE BLOOD FROM A WOUND. THE WOMAN WHO HAUNTS YOU HAS RETURNED.
DEMETER, PLAY WITH THE CHILDREN.
KNOW WHERE TO DRAW THE LINE, LADY!
I MERELY WISH TO GIVE YOU WARNING OF WHAT I SEE. NIGHT IS UPON YOU. DO NOT LET IT TOUCH YOUR HEART. OR THERE MAY BE NO WAY FOR YOU TO RETURN THIS TIME.
THANKS FOR THE GOBBLE-DEE-GOOK, YA SPOOKY DAME. IT HELPS A LOT.

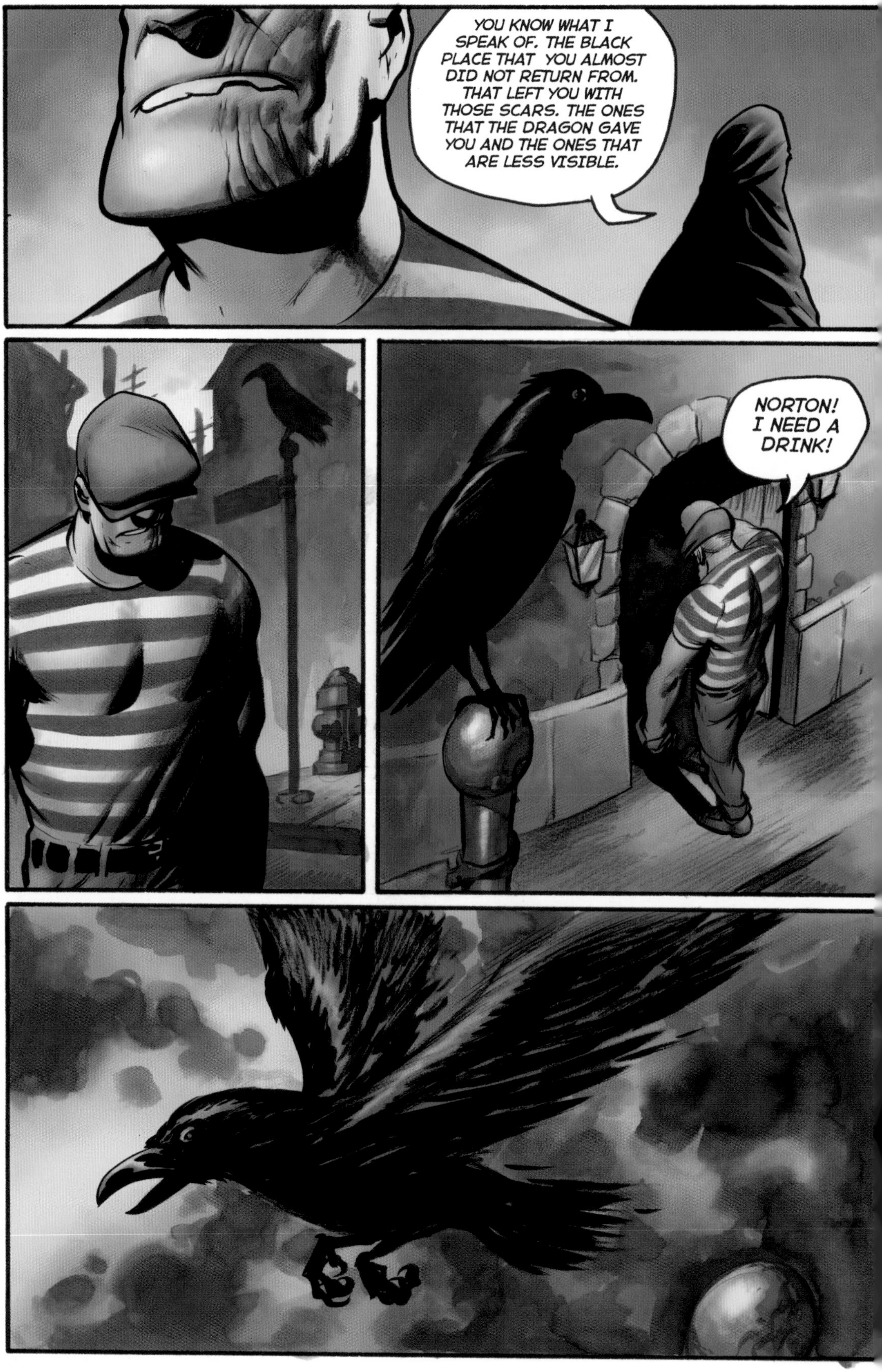

YOU KNOW WHAT I SPEAK OF. THE BLACK PLACE THAT YOU ALMOST DID NOT RETURN FROM. THAT LEFT YOU WITH THOSE SCARS. THE ONES THAT THE DRAGON GAVE YOU AND THE ONES THAT ARE LESS VISIBLE.
NORTON! I NEED A DRINK!

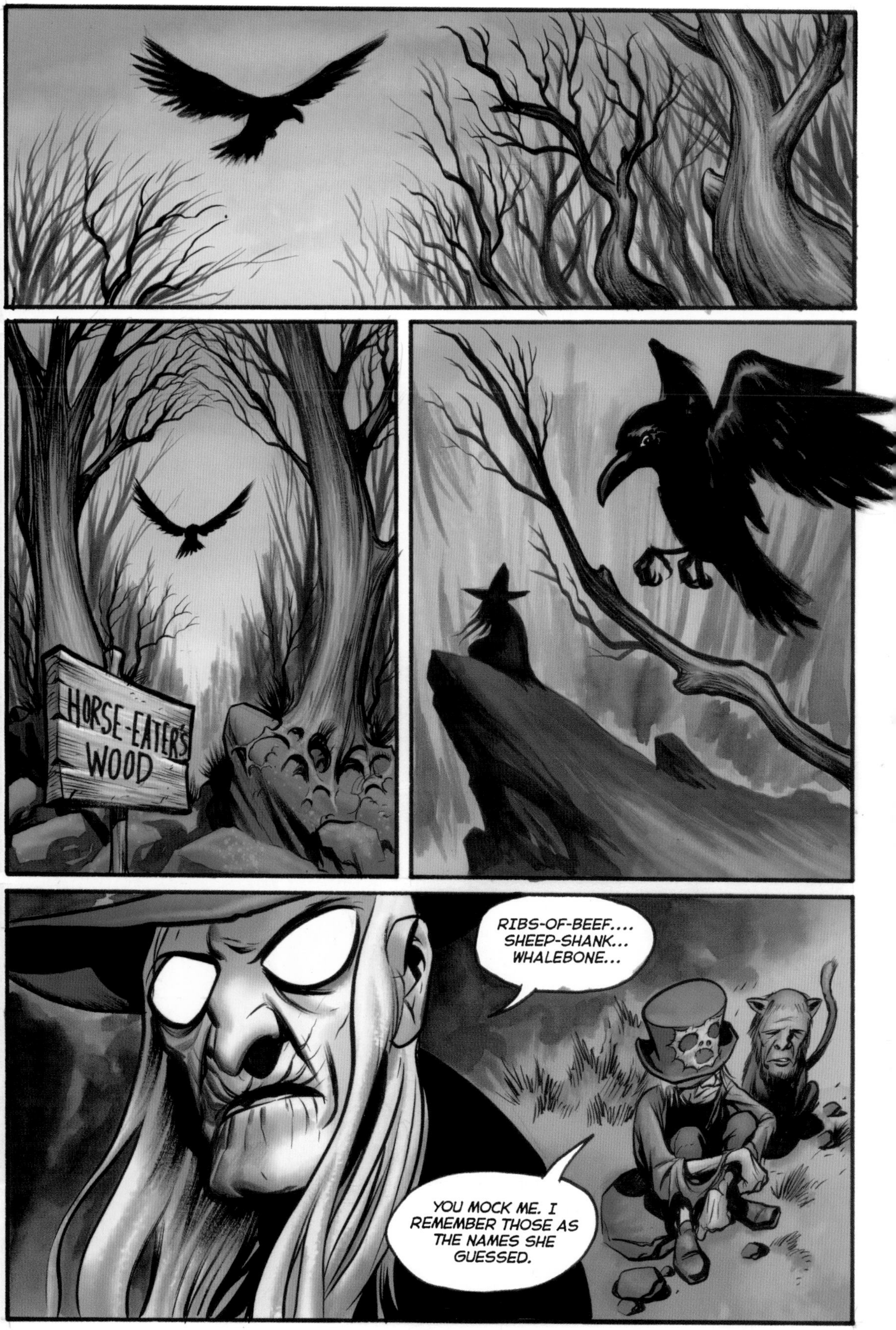
HORSE-EATER'S WOOD
RIBS-OF-BEEF.... SHEEP-SHANK... WHALEBONE...
YOU MOCK ME. I REMEMBER THOSE AS THE NAMES SHE GUESSED.

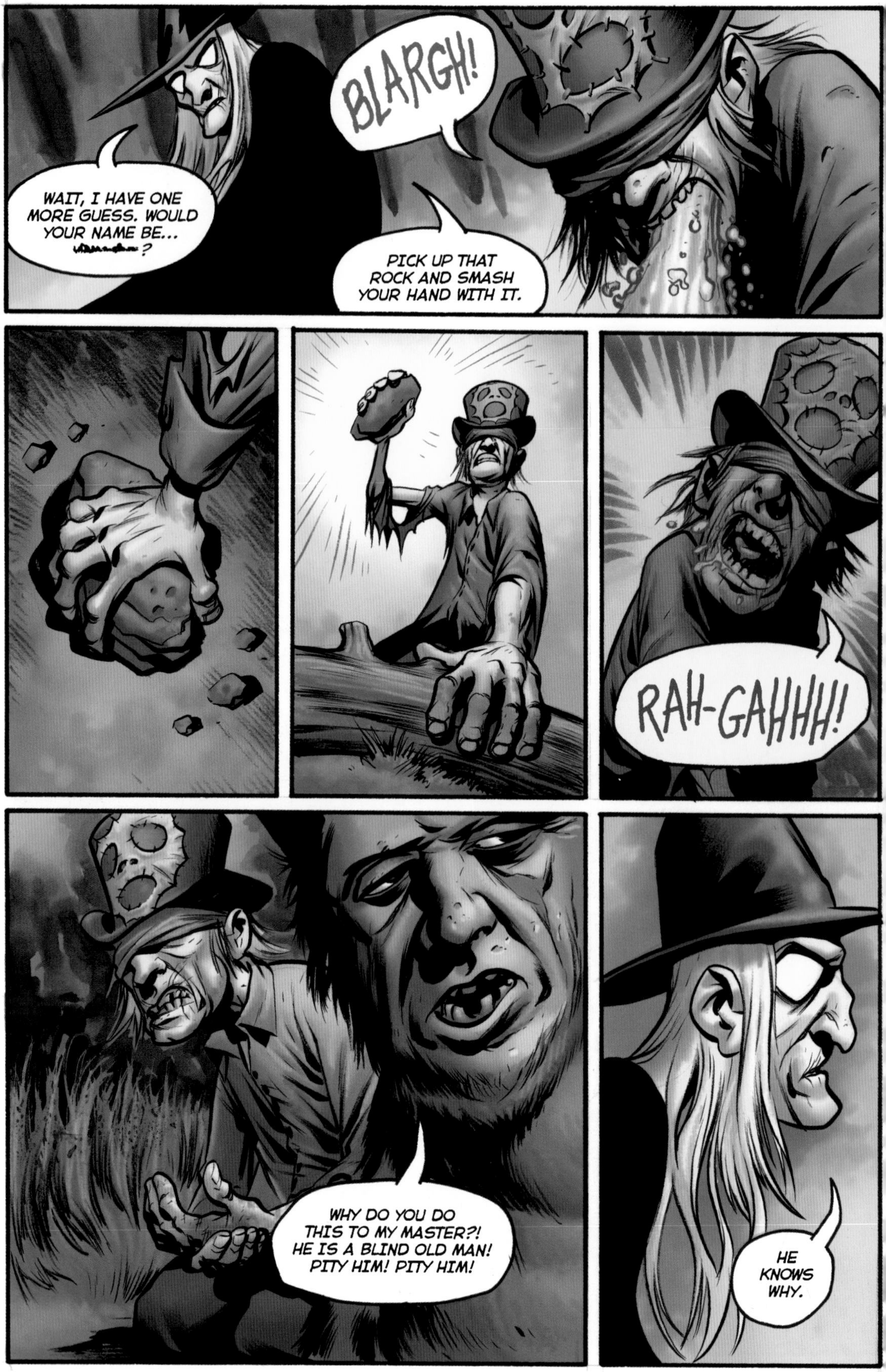

WAIT, I HAVE ONE MORE GUESS. WOULD YOUR NAME BE... ?
BLARGH!
PICK UP THAT ROCK AND SMASH YOUR HAND WITH IT.
RAH-GAHHH!
WHY DO YOU DO THIS TO MY MASTER?! HE IS A BLIND OLD MAN! PITY HIM! PITY HIM!
HE KNOWS WHY.

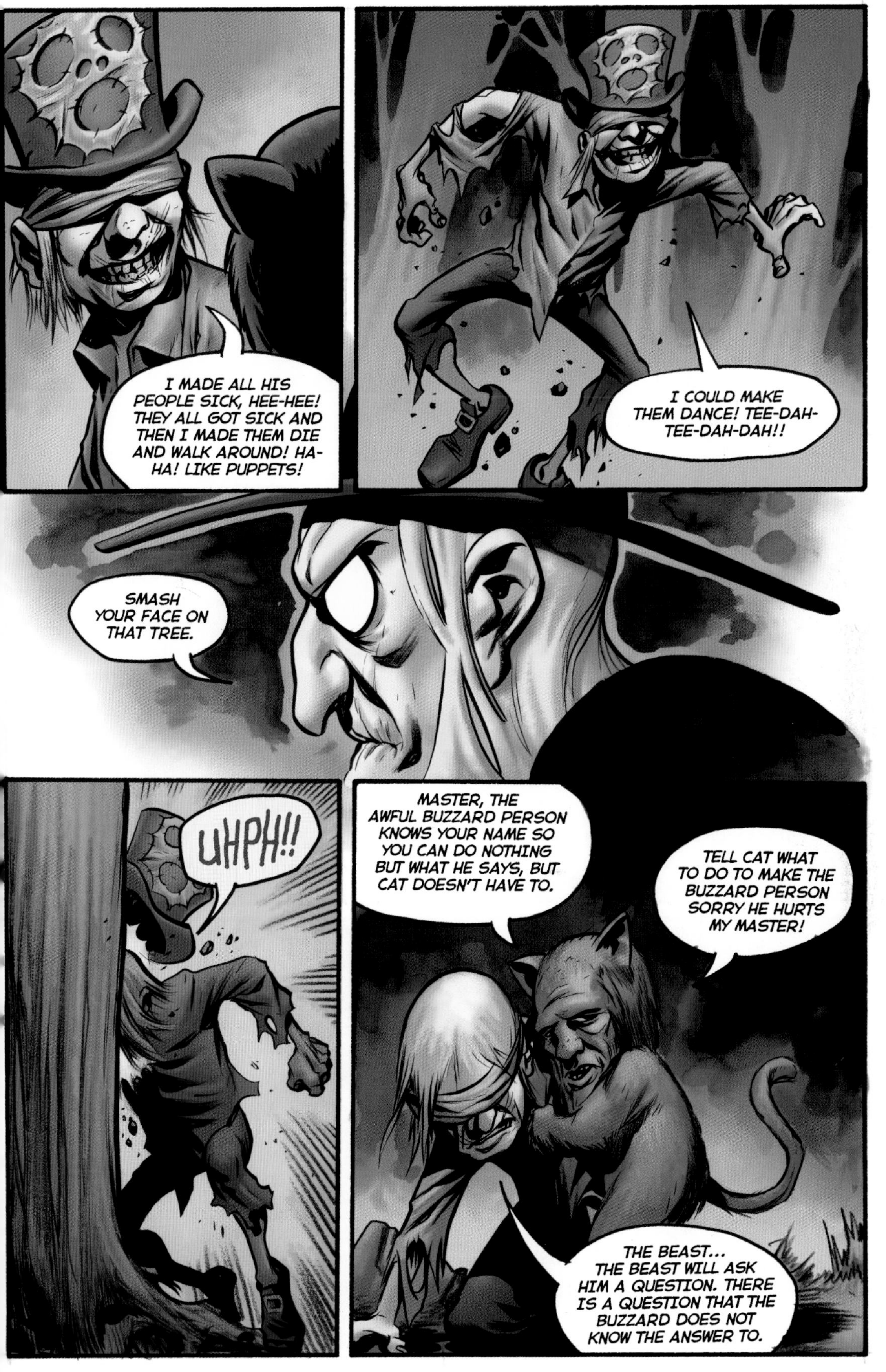
I MADE ALL HIS PEOPLE SICK, HEE-HEE! THEY ALL GOT SICK AND THEN I MADE THEM DIE AND WALK AROUND! HA-HA! LIKE PUPPETS!
I COULD MAKE THEM DANCE! TEE-DAH-TEE-DAH-DAH!!
SMASH YOUR FACE ON THAT TREE.
UHPH!!
MASTER, THE AWFUL BUZZARD PERSON KNOWS YOUR NAME SO YOU CAN DO NOTHING BUT WHAT HE SAYS, BUT CAT DOESN'T HAVE TO.
TELL CAT WHAT TO DO TO MAKE THE BUZZARD PERSON SORRY HE HURTS MY MASTER!
THE BEAST... THE BEAST WILL ASK HIM A QUESTION. THERE IS A QUESTION THAT THE BUZZARD DOES NOT KNOW THE ANSWER TO.

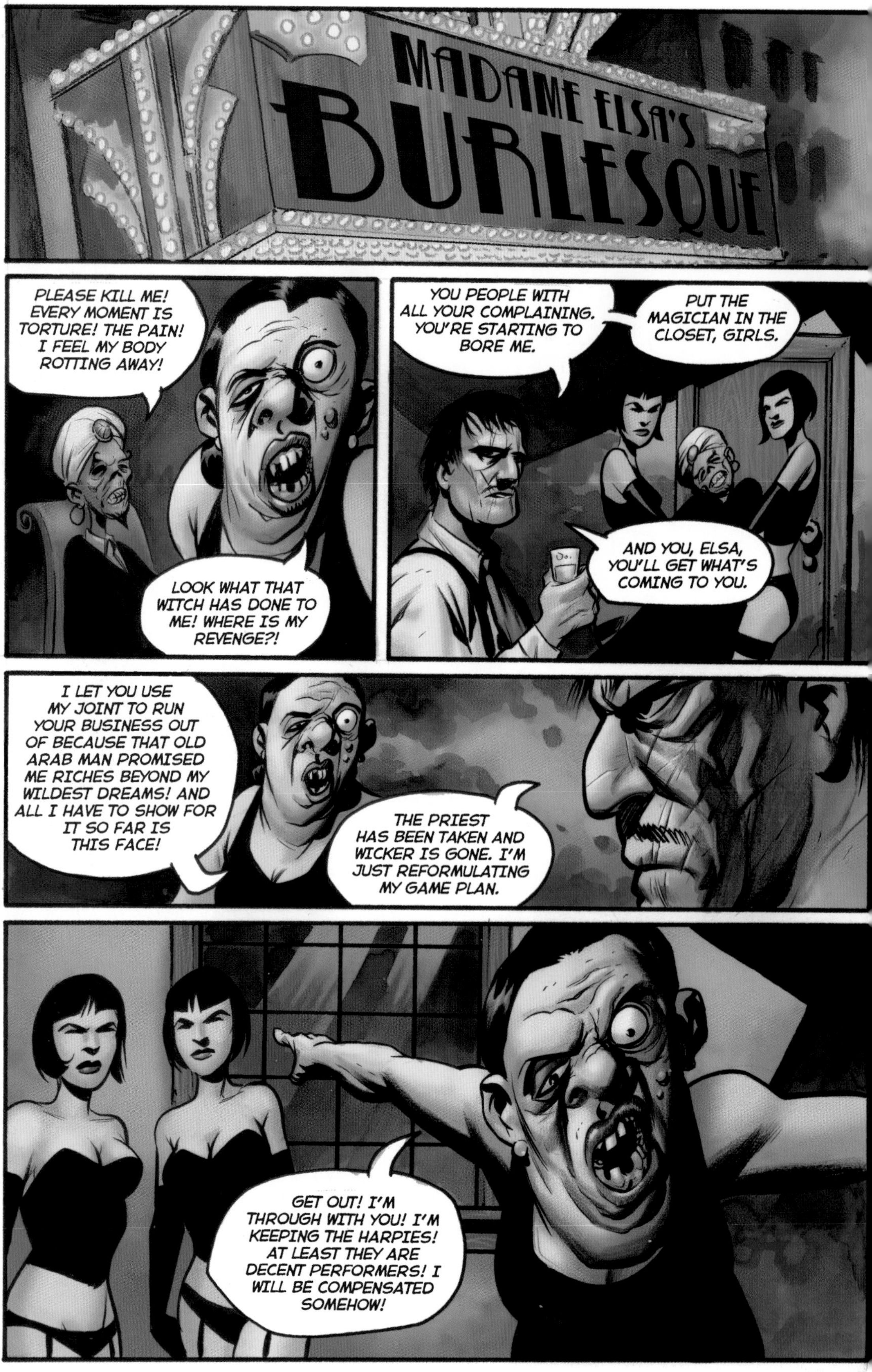
MADAME ELSA'S BURLESQUE
PLEASE KILL ME! EVERY MOMENT IS TORTURE! THE PAIN! I FEEL MY BODY ROTTING AWAY!
LOOK WHAT THAT WITCH HAS DONE TO ME! WHERE IS MY REVENGE?!
YOU PEOPLE WITH ALL YOUR COMPLAINING. YOU'RE STARTING TO BORE ME.
PUT THE MAGICIAN IN THE CLOSET, GIRLS.
AND YOU, ELSA, YOU'LL GET WHAT'S COMING TO YOU.
I LET YOU USE MY JOINT TO RUN YOUR BUSINESS OUT OF BECAUSE THAT OLD ARAB MAN PROMISED ME RICHES BEYOND MY WILDEST DREAMS! AND ALL I HAVE TO SHOW FOR IT SO FAR IS THIS FACE!
THE PRIEST HAS BEEN TAKEN AND WICKER IS GONE. I'M JUST REFORMULATING MY GAME PLAN.
GET OUT! I'M THROUGH WITH YOU! I'M KEEPING THE HARPIES! AT LEAST THEY ARE DECENT PERFORMERS! I WILL BE COMPENSATED SOMEHOW!

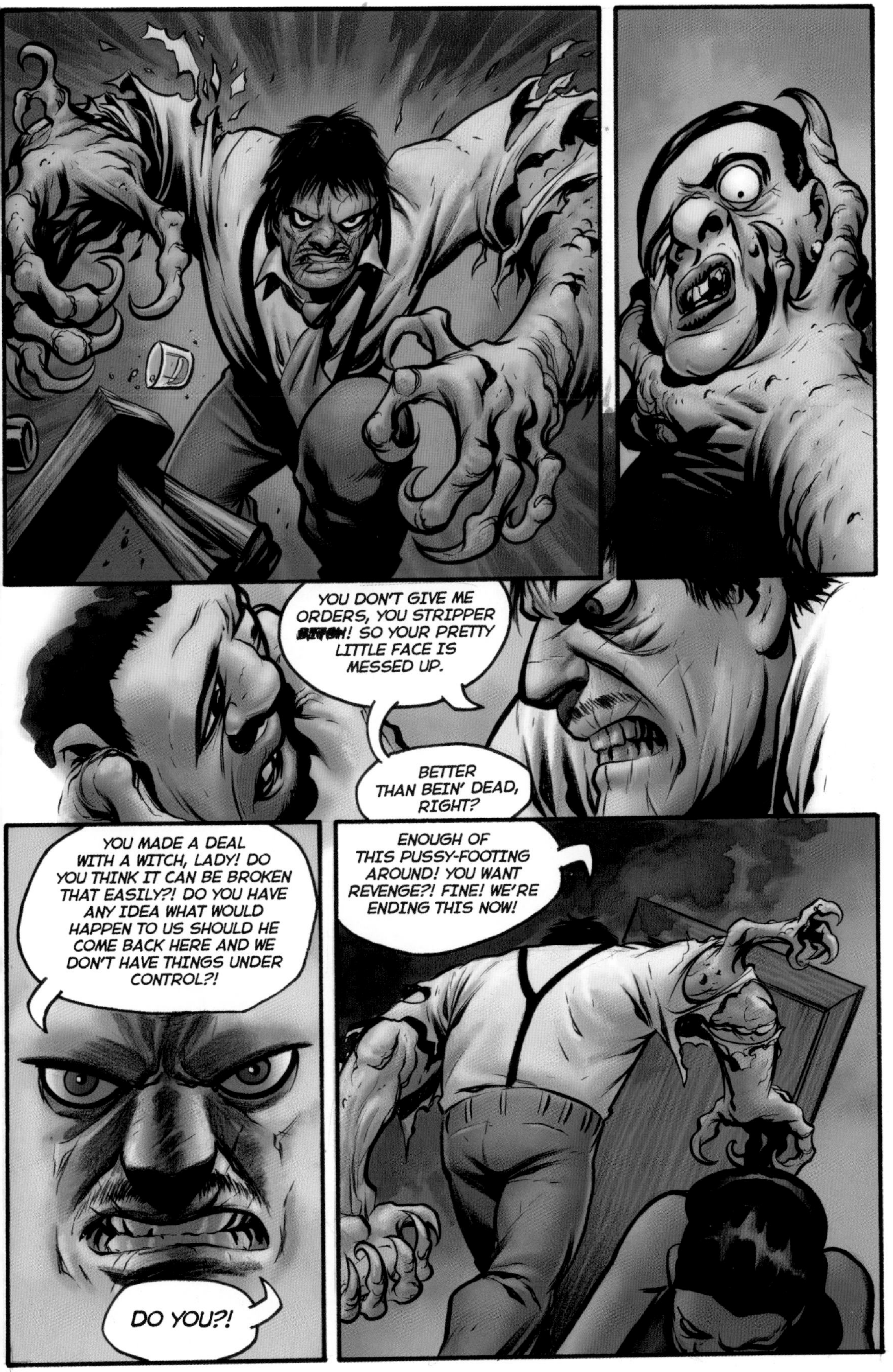
YOU DON'T GIVE ME ORDERS, YOU STRIPPER [redacted]! SO YOUR PRETTY LITTLE FACE IS MESSED UP.
BETTER THAN BEIN' DEAD, RIGHT?
YOU MADE A DEAL WITH A WITCH, LADY! DO YOU THINK IT CAN BE BROKEN THAT EASILY?! DO YOU HAVE ANY IDEA WHAT WOULD HAPPEN TO US SHOULD HE COME BACK HERE AND WE DON'T HAVE THINGS UNDER CONTROL?!
DO YOU?!
ENOUGH OF THIS PUSSY-FOOTING AROUND! YOU WANT REVENGE?! FINE! WE'RE ENDING THIS NOW!

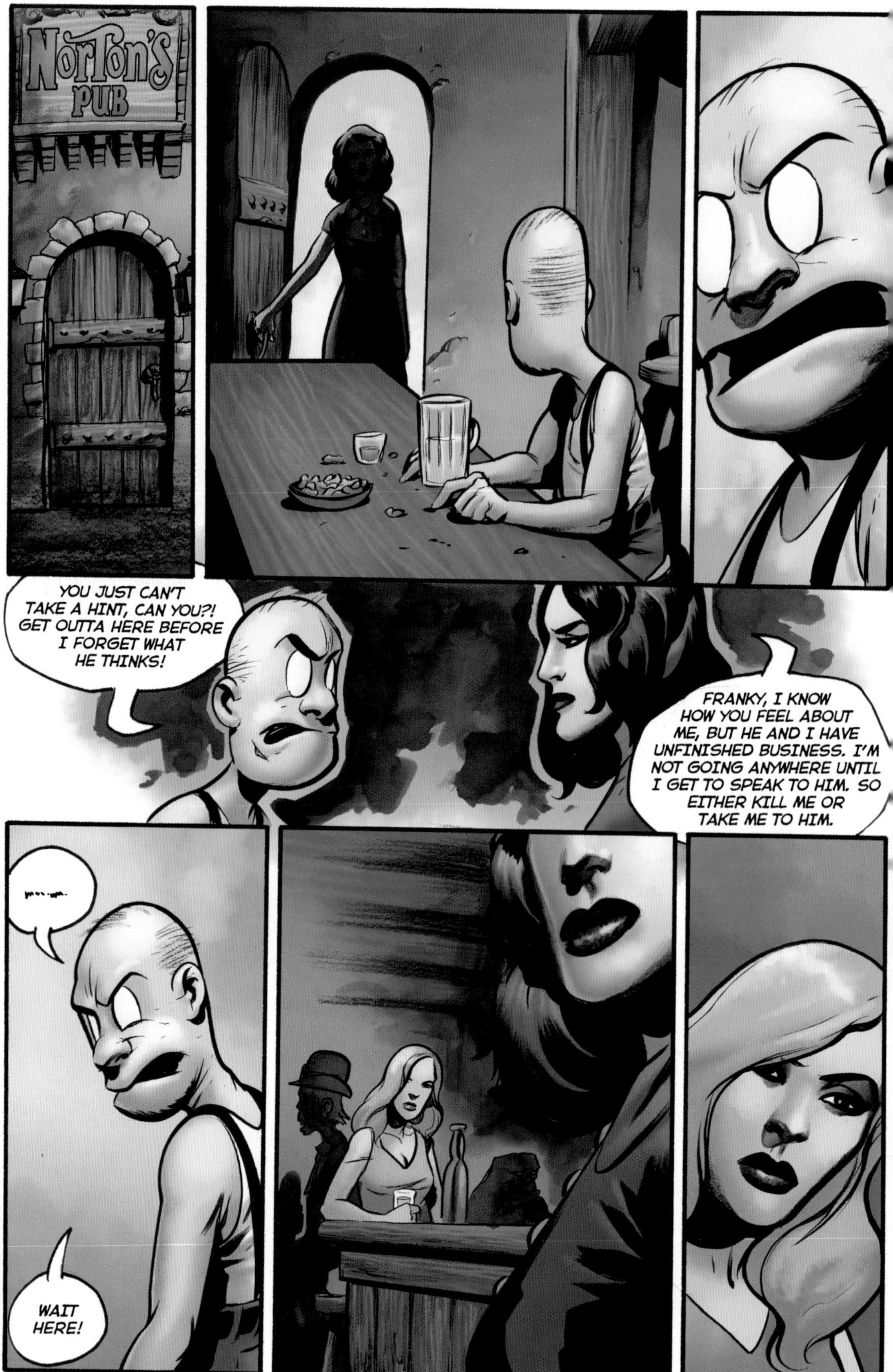

Norton's PUB
YOU JUST CAN'T TAKE A HINT, CAN YOU?! GET OUTTA HERE BEFORE I FORGET WHAT HE THINKS!
FRANKY, I KNOW HOW YOU FEEL ABOUT ME, BUT HE AND I HAVE UNFINISHED BUSINESS. I'M NOT GOING ANYWHERE UNTIL I GET TO SPEAK TO HIM. SO EITHER KILL ME OR TAKE ME TO HIM.
WAIT HERE!

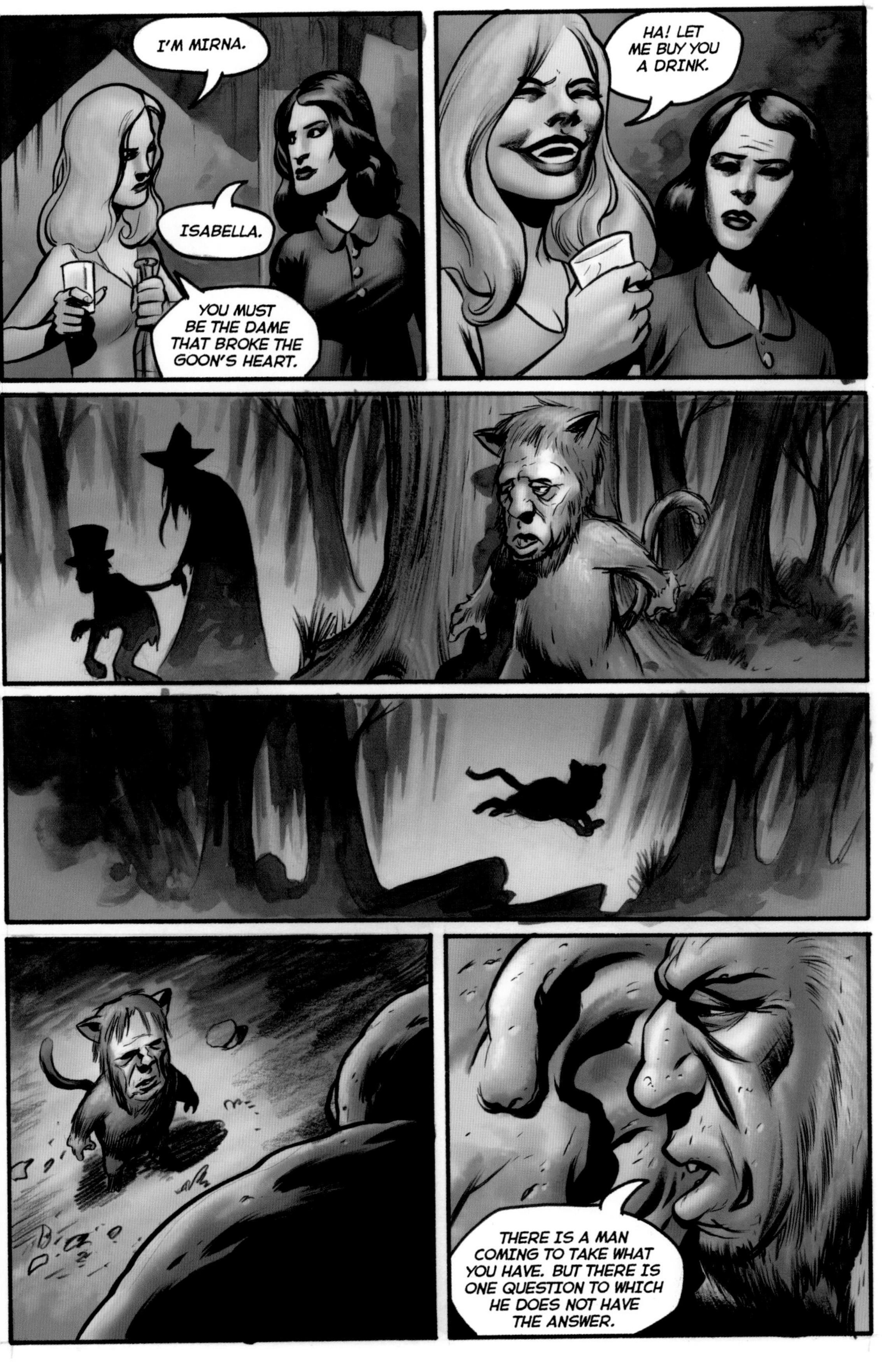

I'M MIRNA.
ISABELLA.
YOU MUST BE THE DAME THAT BROKE THE GOON'S HEART.
HA! LET ME BUY YOU A DRINK.
THERE IS A MAN COMING TO TAKE WHAT YOU HAVE. BUT THERE IS ONE QUESTION TO WHICH HE DOES NOT HAVE THE ANSWER.

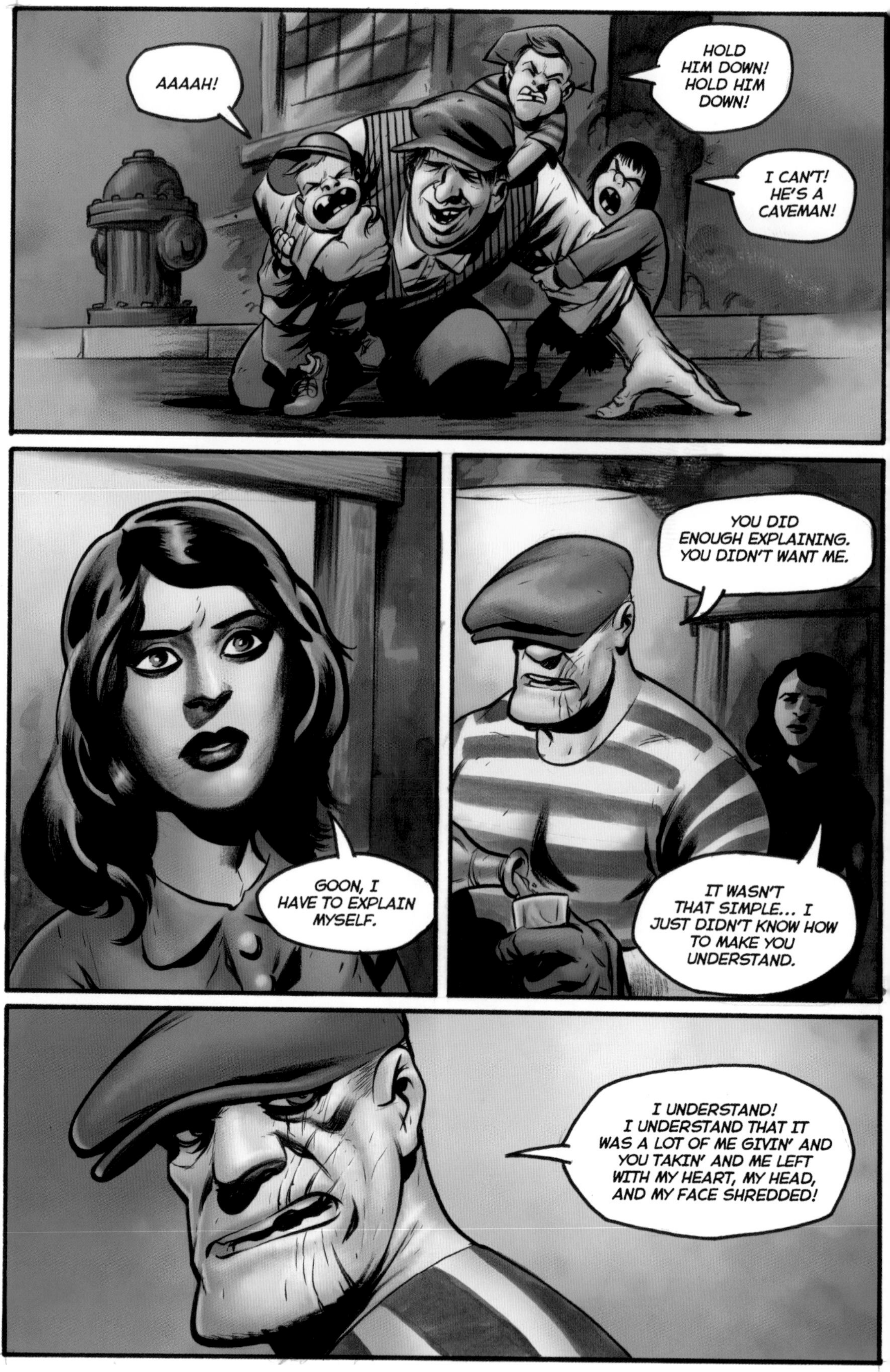
AAAAH!
HOLD HIM DOWN! HOLD HIM DOWN!
I CAN'T! HE'S A CAVEMAN!
GOON, I HAVE TO EXPLAIN MYSELF.
YOU DID ENOUGH EXPLAINING. YOU DIDN'T WANT ME.
IT WASN'T THAT SIMPLE... I JUST DIDN'T KNOW HOW TO MAKE YOU UNDERSTAND.
I UNDERSTAND! I UNDERSTAND THAT IT WAS A LOT OF ME GIVIN' AND YOU TAKIN' AND ME LEFT WITH MY HEART, MY HEAD, AND MY FACE SHREDDED!

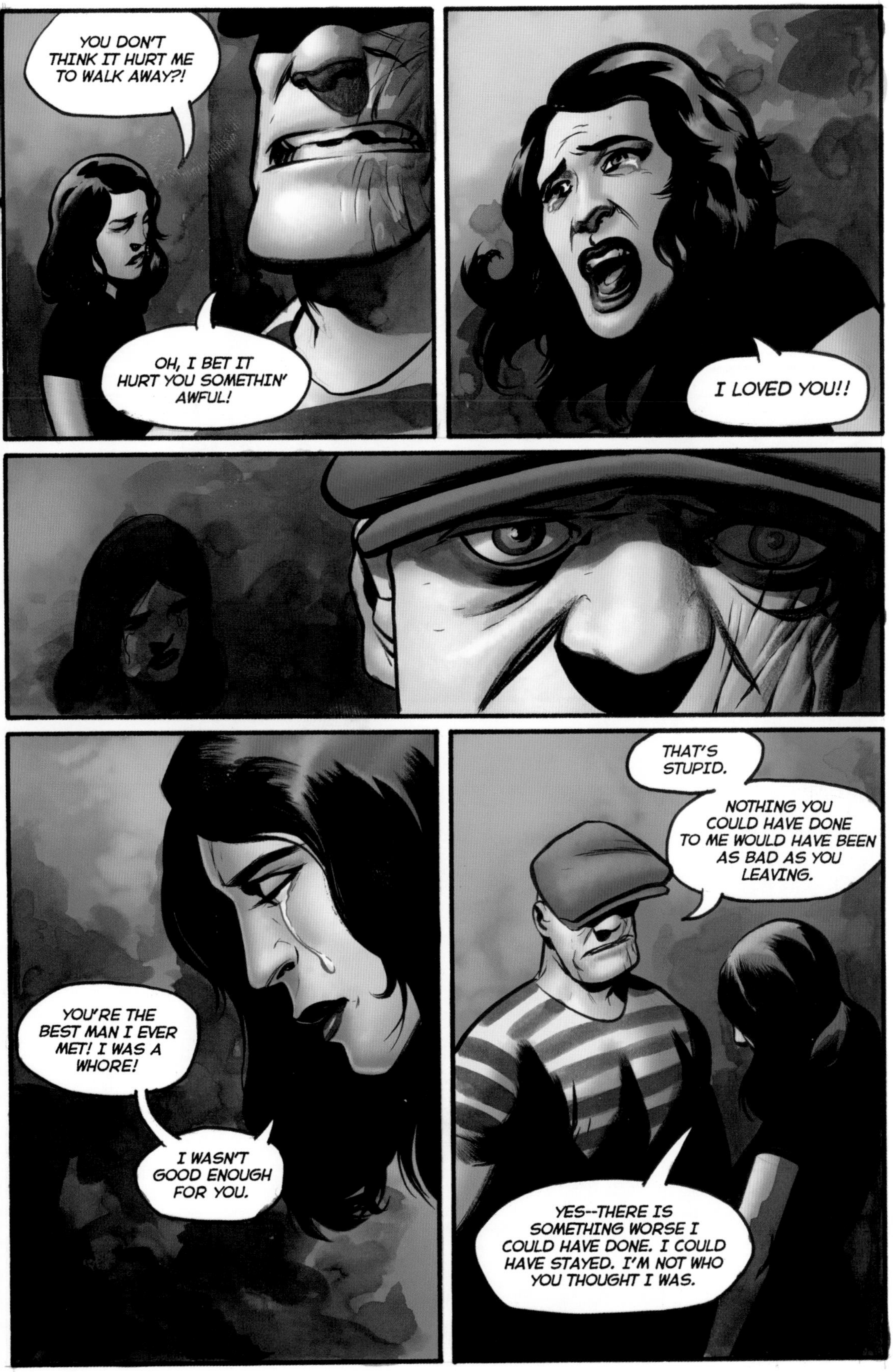
YOU DON'T THINK IT HURT ME TO WALK AWAY?!
OH, I BET IT HURT YOU SOMETHIN' AWFUL!
I LOVED YOU!!
YOU'RE THE BEST MAN I EVER MET! I WAS A WHORE!
I WASN'T GOOD ENOUGH FOR YOU.
THAT'S STUPID.
NOTHING YOU COULD HAVE DONE TO ME WOULD HAVE BEEN AS BAD AS YOU LEAVING.
YES--THERE IS SOMETHING WORSE I COULD HAVE DONE. I COULD HAVE STAYED. I'M NOT WHO YOU THOUGHT I WAS.

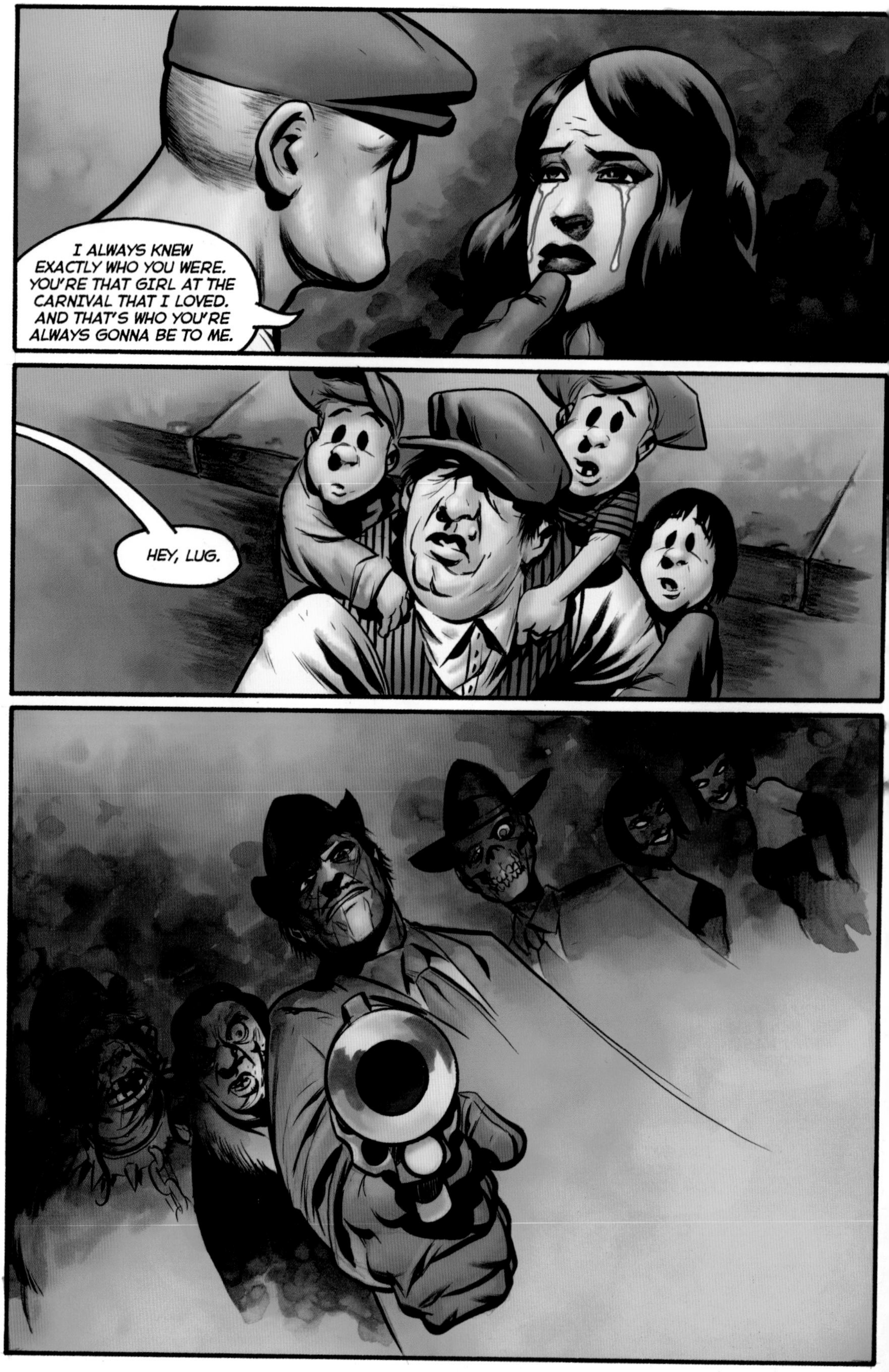
I ALWAYS KNEW EXACTLY WHO YOU WERE. YOU'RE THAT GIRL AT THE CARNIVAL THAT I LOVED. AND THAT'S WHO YOU'RE ALWAYS GONNA BE TO ME.
HEY, LUG.

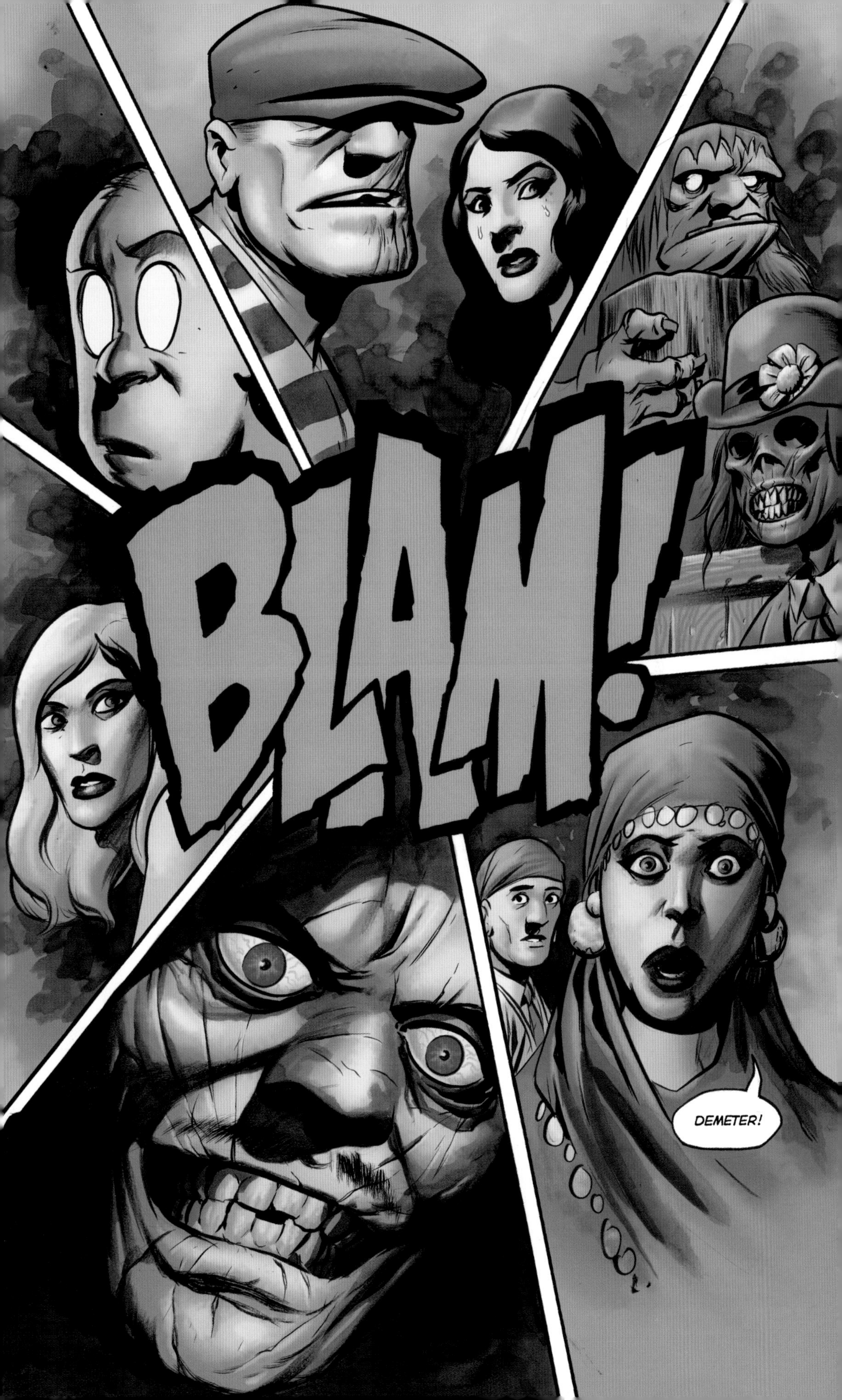
BLAM!
DEMETER!

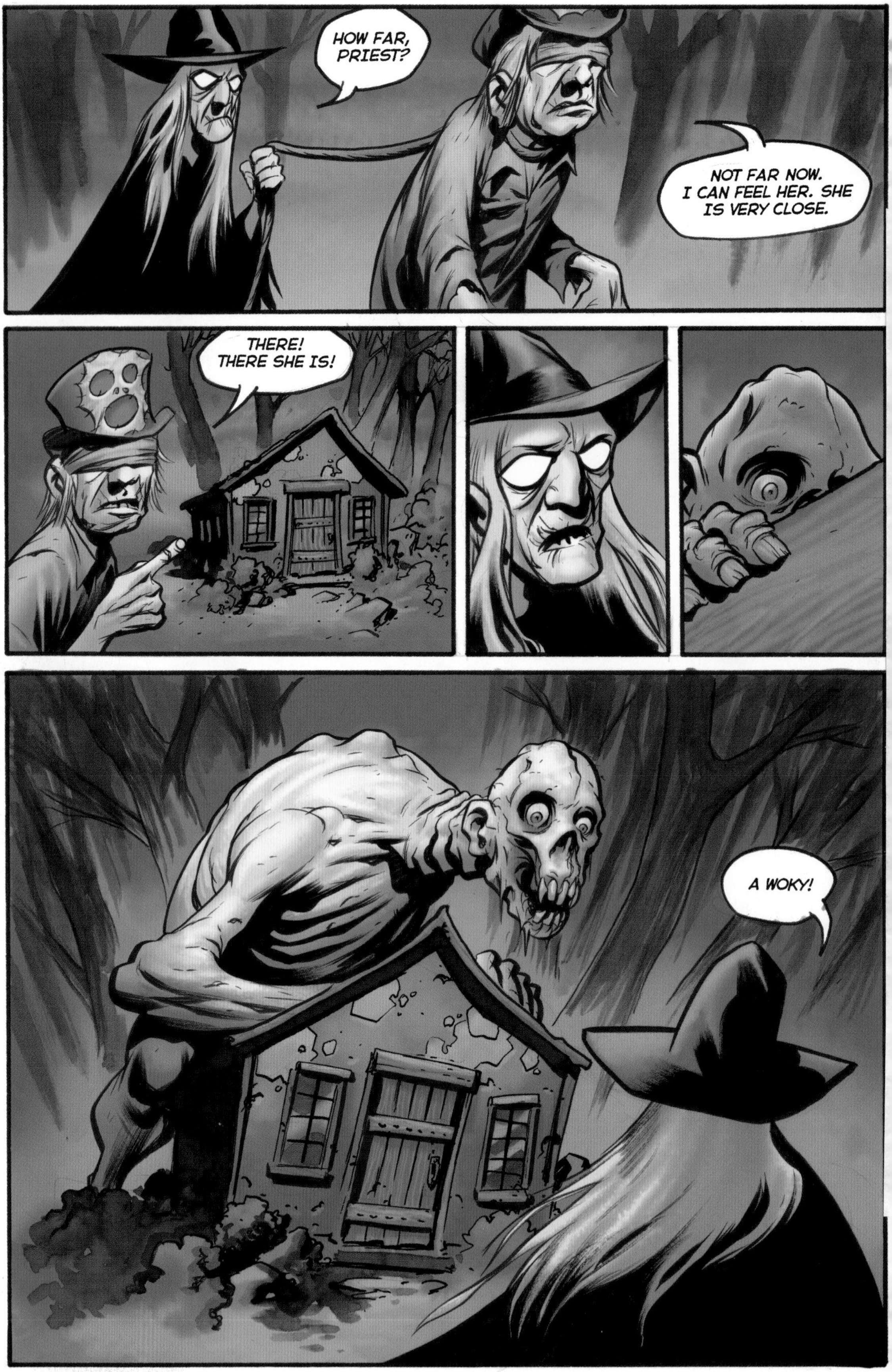
HOW FAR, PRIEST?
NOT FAR NOW. I CAN FEEL HER. SHE IS VERY CLOSE.
THERE! THERE SHE IS!
A WOKY!

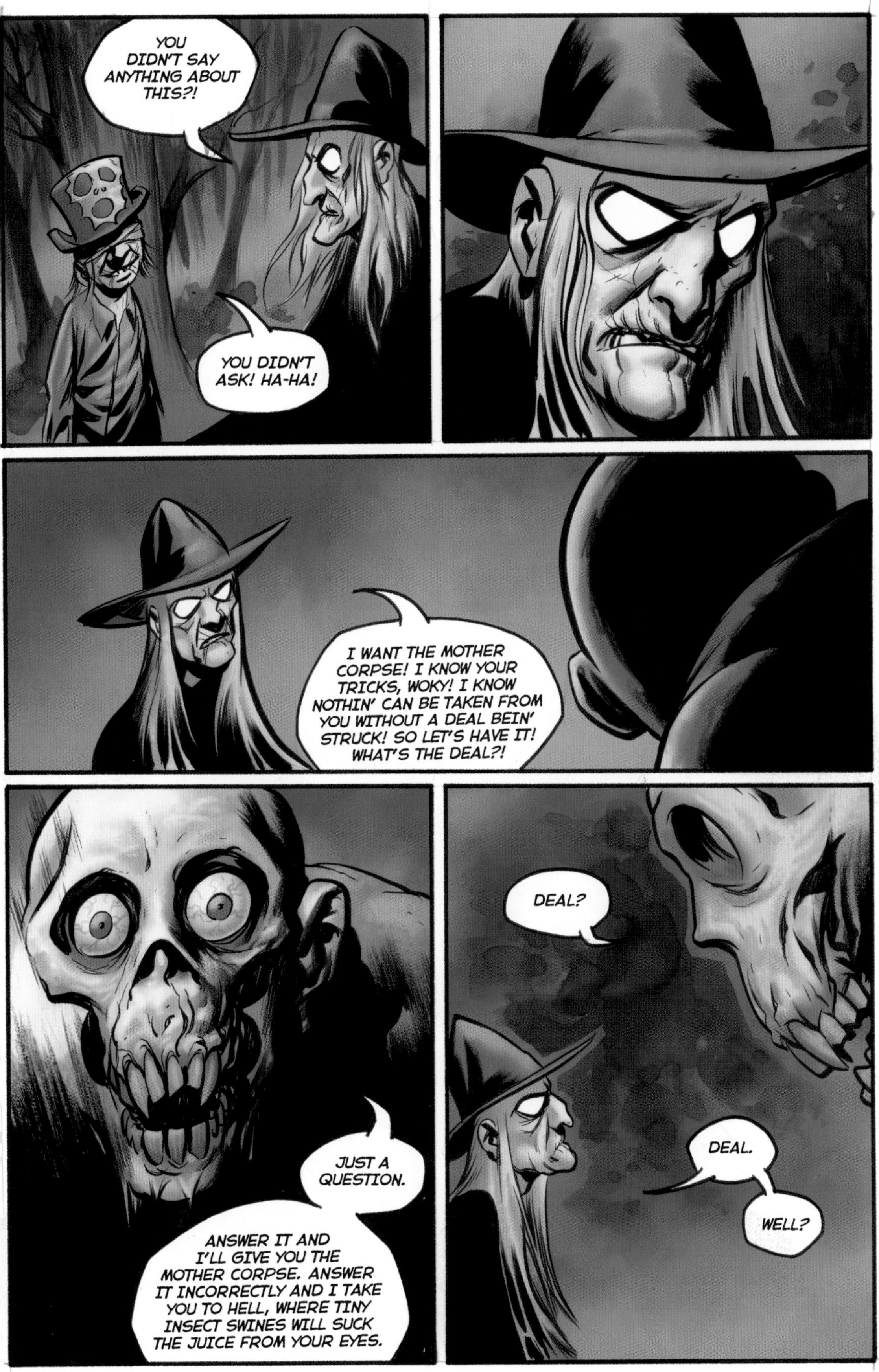
YOU DIDN'T SAY ANYTHING ABOUT THIS?!
YOU DIDN'T ASK! HA-HA!
I WANT THE MOTHER CORPSE! I KNOW YOUR TRICKS, WOKY! I KNOW NOTHIN' CAN BE TAKEN FROM YOU WITHOUT A DEAL BEIN' STRUCK! SO LET'S HAVE IT! WHAT'S THE DEAL?!
JUST A QUESTION.
ANSWER IT AND I'LL GIVE YOU THE MOTHER CORPSE. ANSWER IT INCORRECTLY AND I TAKE YOU TO HELL, WHERE TINY INSECT SWINES WILL SUCK THE JUICE FROM YOUR EYES.
DEAL?
DEAL.
WELL?

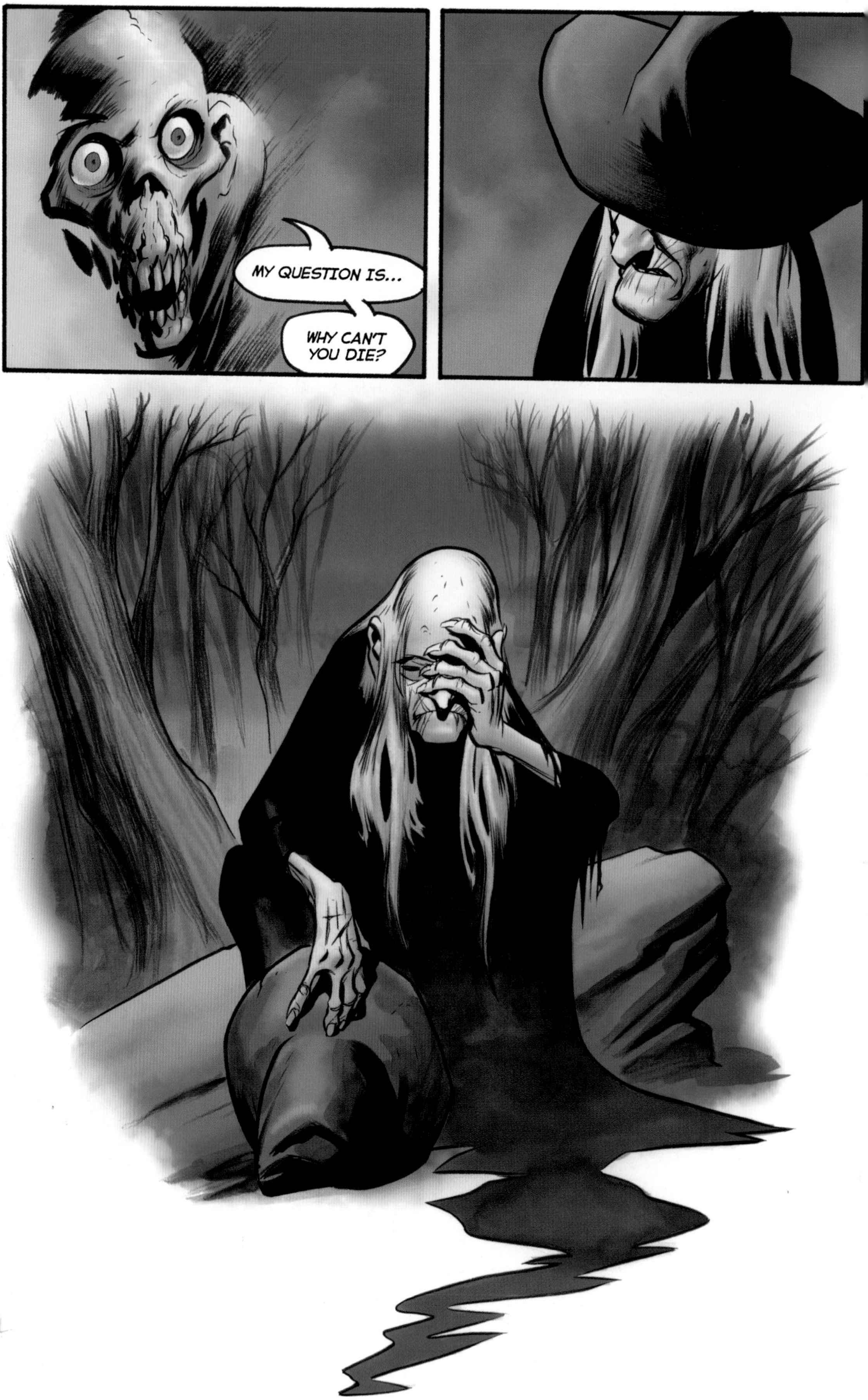
MY QUESTION IS...
WHY CAN'T YOU DIE?

CHAPTER 4

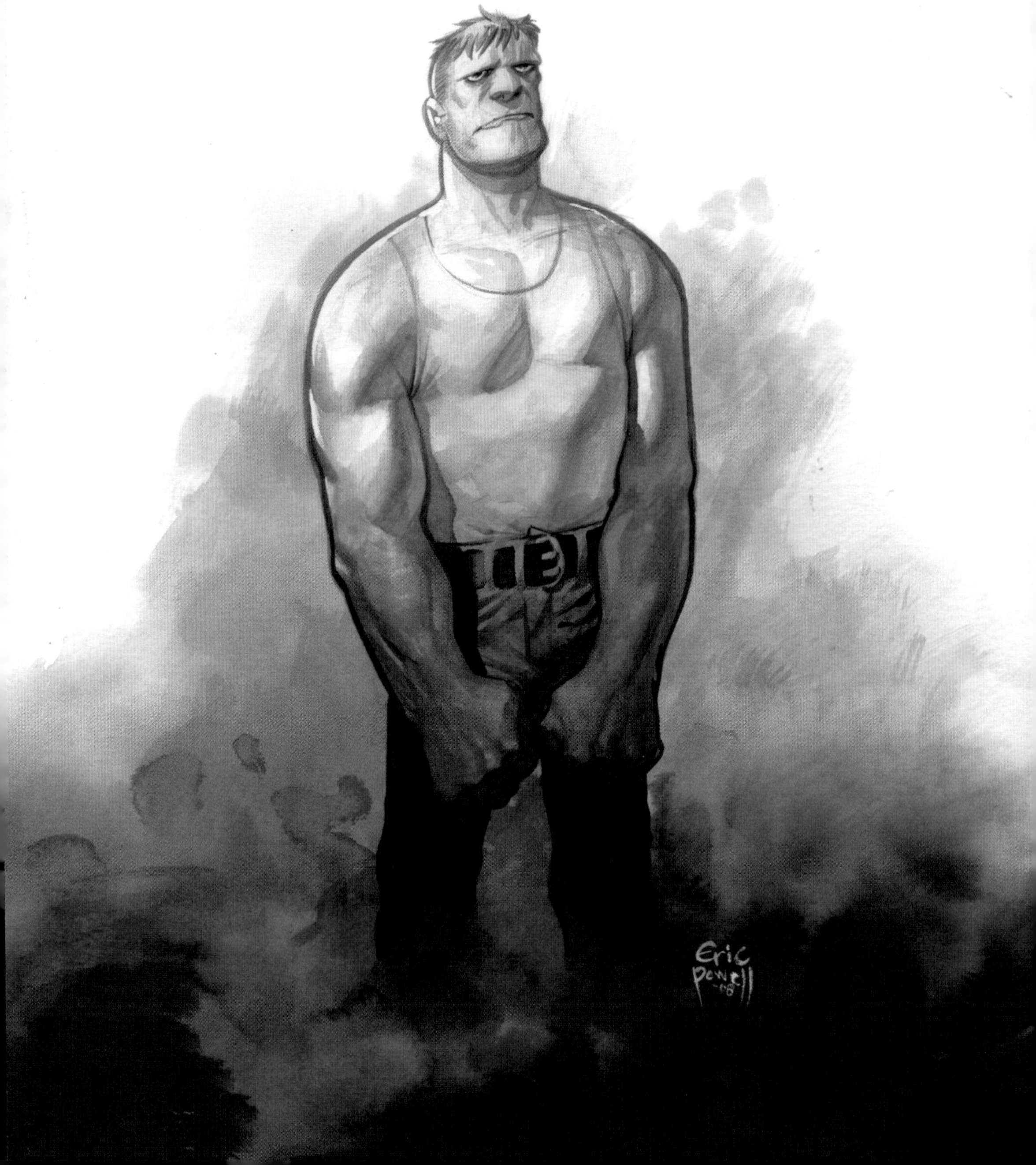
Eric Powell -08

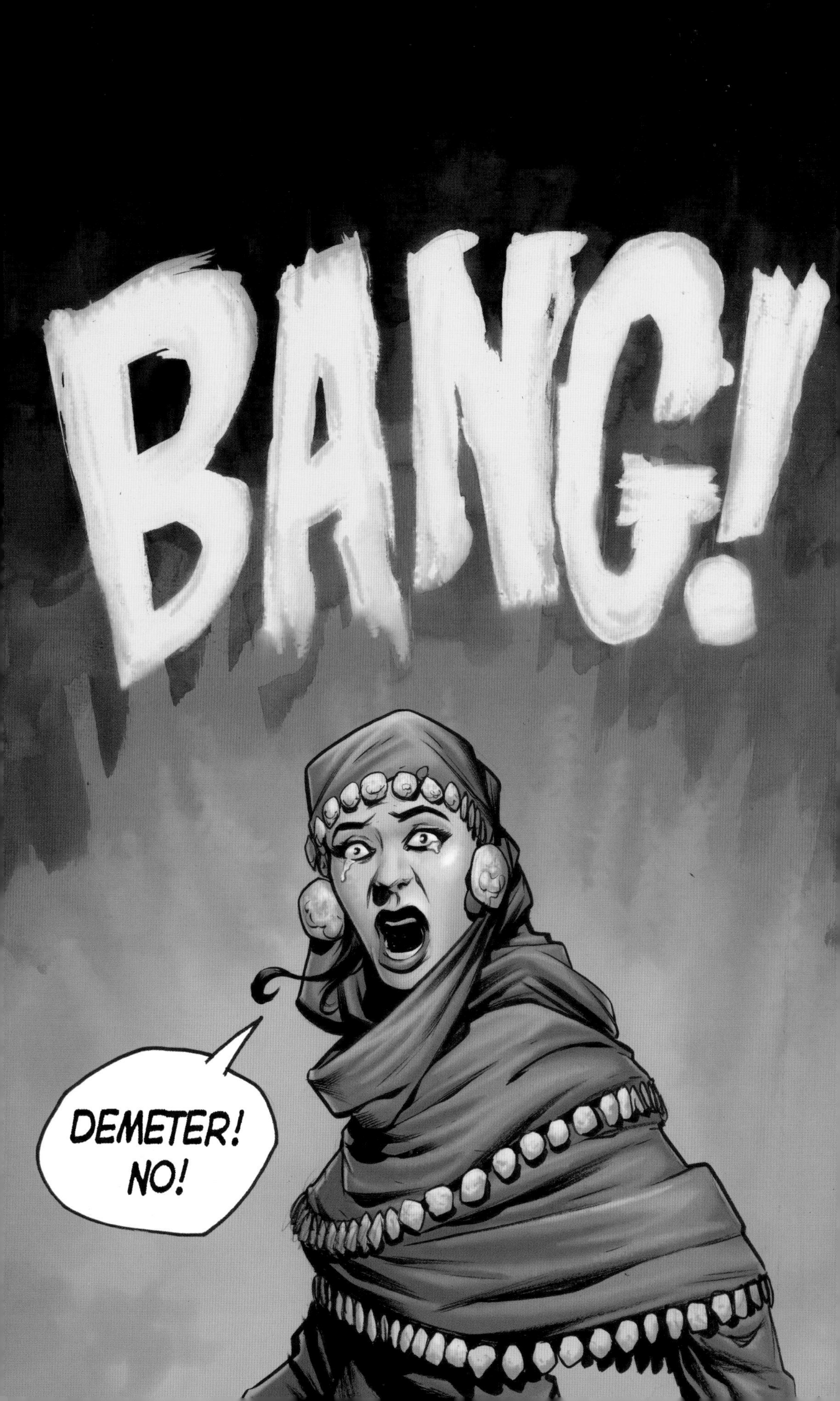
BANG!
DEMETER! NO!

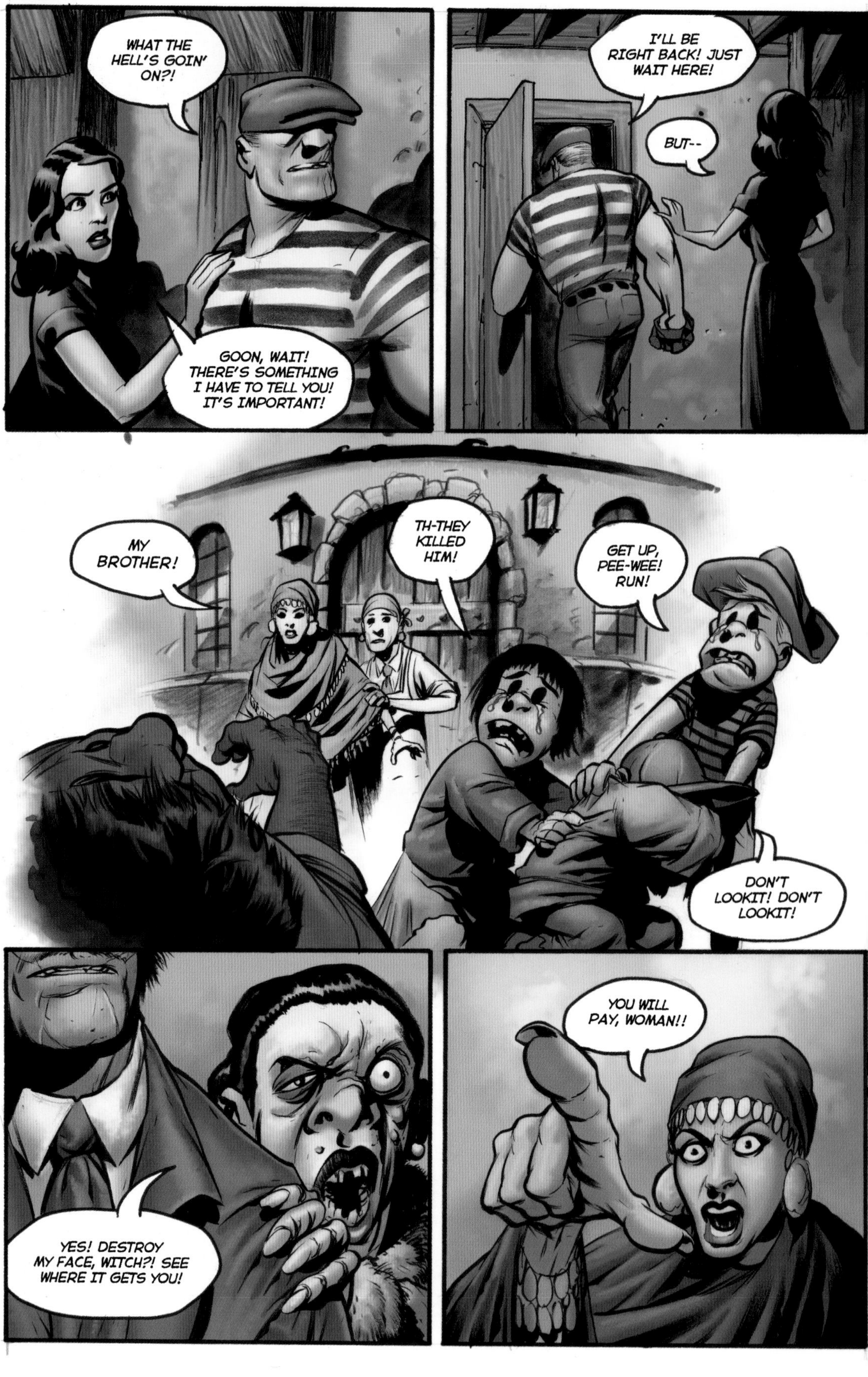
WHAT THE HELL'S GOIN' ON?!
GOON, WAIT! THERE'S SOMETHING I HAVE TO TELL YOU! IT'S IMPORTANT!
I'LL BE RIGHT BACK! JUST WAIT HERE!
BUT--
MY BROTHER!
TH-THEY KILLED HIM!
GET UP, PEE-WEE! RUN!
DON'T LOOKIT! DON'T LOOKIT!
YES! DESTROY MY FACE, WITCH?! SEE WHERE IT GETS YOU!
YOU WILL PAY, WOMAN!!

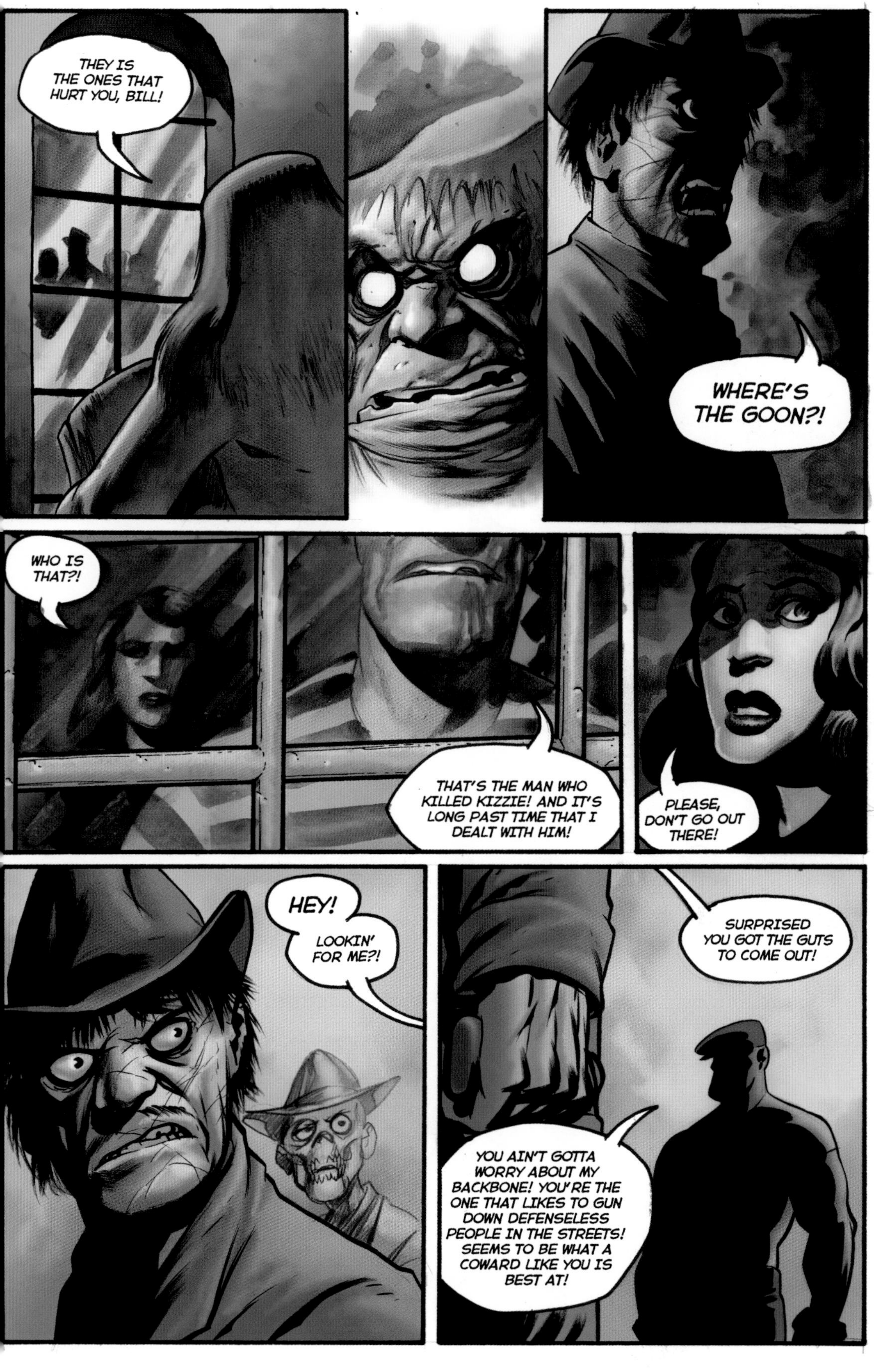

THEY IS THE ONES THAT HURT YOU, BILL!
WHERE'S THE GOON?!
WHO IS THAT?!
THAT'S THE MAN WHO KILLED KIZZIE! AND IT'S LONG PAST TIME THAT I DEALT WITH HIM!
PLEASE, DON'T GO OUT THERE!
HEY!
LOOKIN' FOR ME?!
SURPRISED YOU GOT THE GUTS TO COME OUT!
YOU AIN'T GOTTA WORRY ABOUT MY BACKBONE! YOU'RE THE ONE THAT LIKES TO GUN DOWN DEFENSELESS PEOPLE IN THE STREETS! SEEMS TO BE WHAT A COWARD LIKE YOU IS BEST AT!

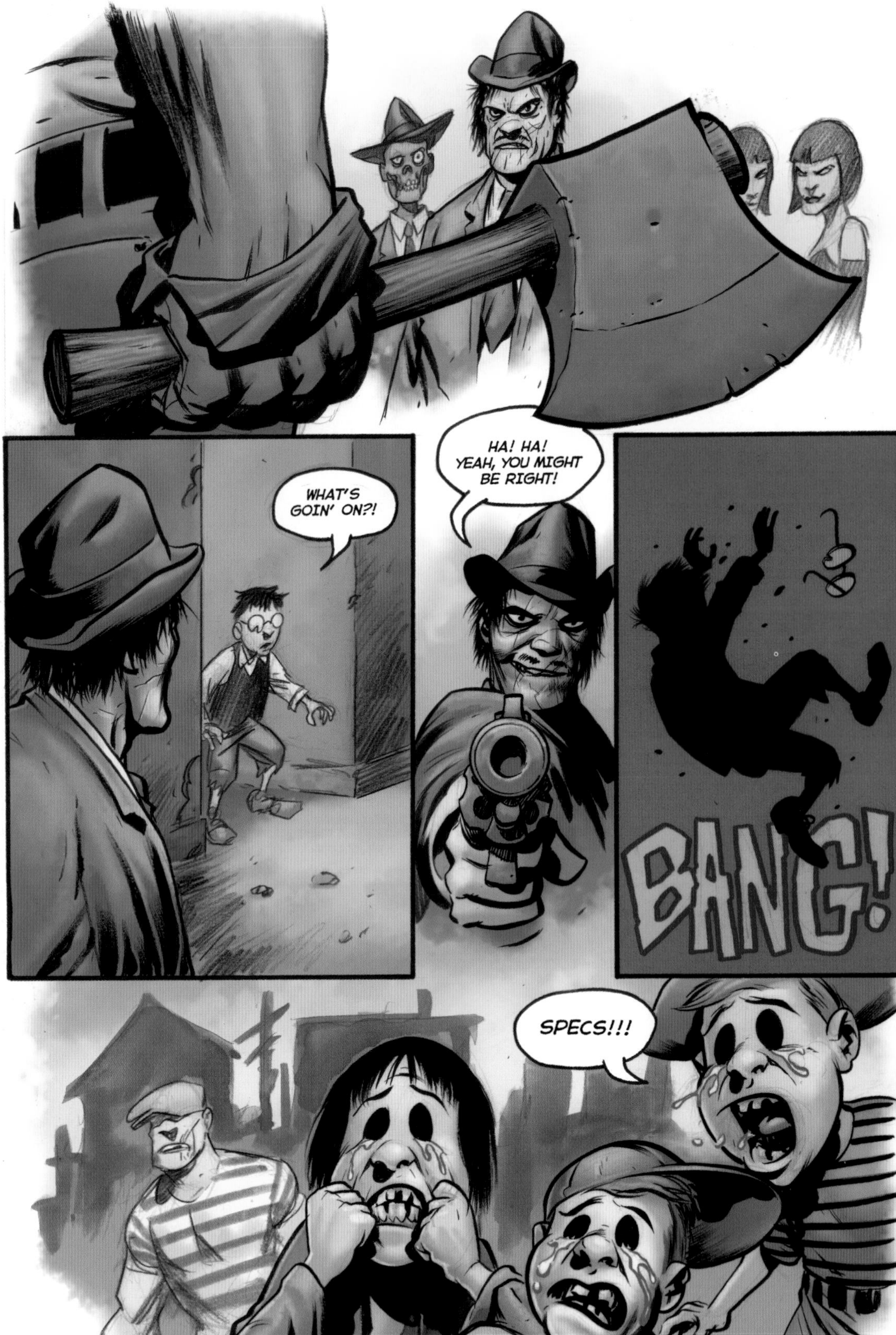
WHAT'S GOIN' ON?!
HA! HA! YEAH, YOU MIGHT BE RIGHT!
BANG!
SPECS!!!

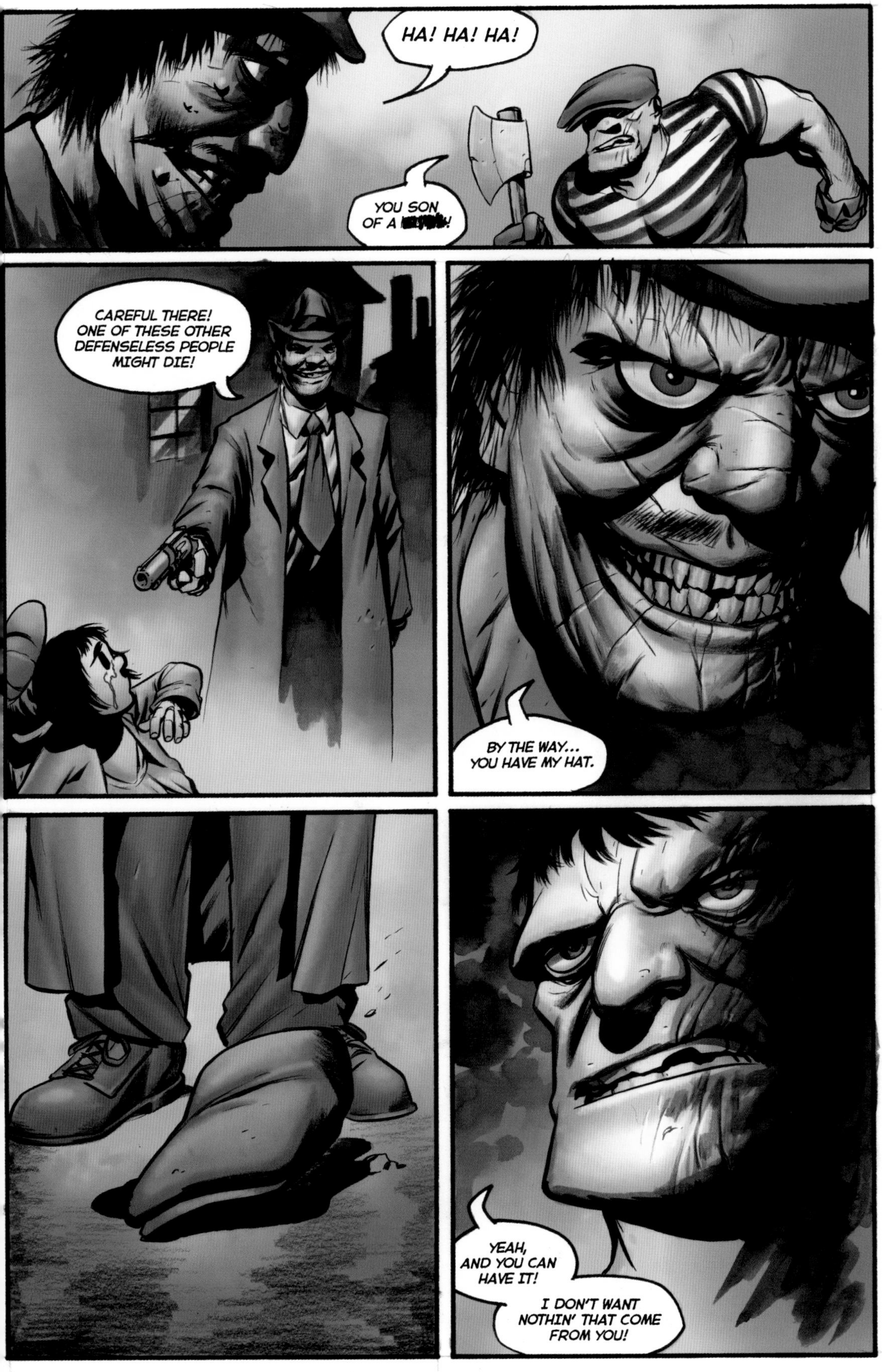

HA! HA! HA!
YOU SON OF A [redacted]!
CAREFUL THERE! ONE OF THESE OTHER DEFENSELESS PEOPLE MIGHT DIE!
BY THE WAY... YOU HAVE MY HAT.
YEAH, AND YOU CAN HAVE IT!
I DON'T WANT NOTHIN' THAT COME FROM YOU!

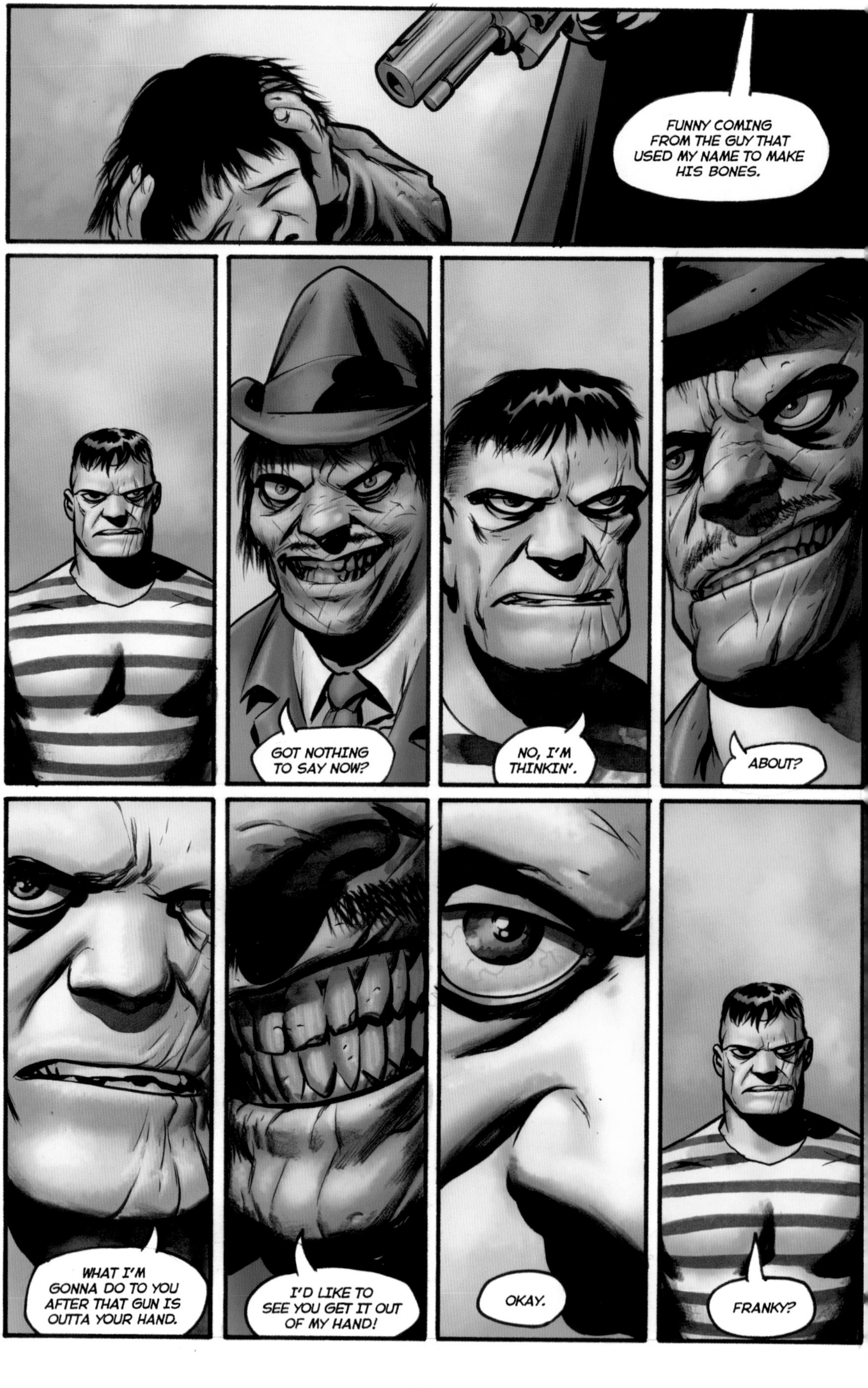
FUNNY COMING FROM THE GUY THAT USED MY NAME TO MAKE HIS BONES.
GOT NOTHING TO SAY NOW?
NO, I'M THINKIN'.
ABOUT?
WHAT I'M GONNA DO TO YOU AFTER THAT GUN IS OUTTA YOUR HAND.
I'D LIKE TO SEE YOU GET IT OUT OF MY HAND!
OKAY.
FRANKY?

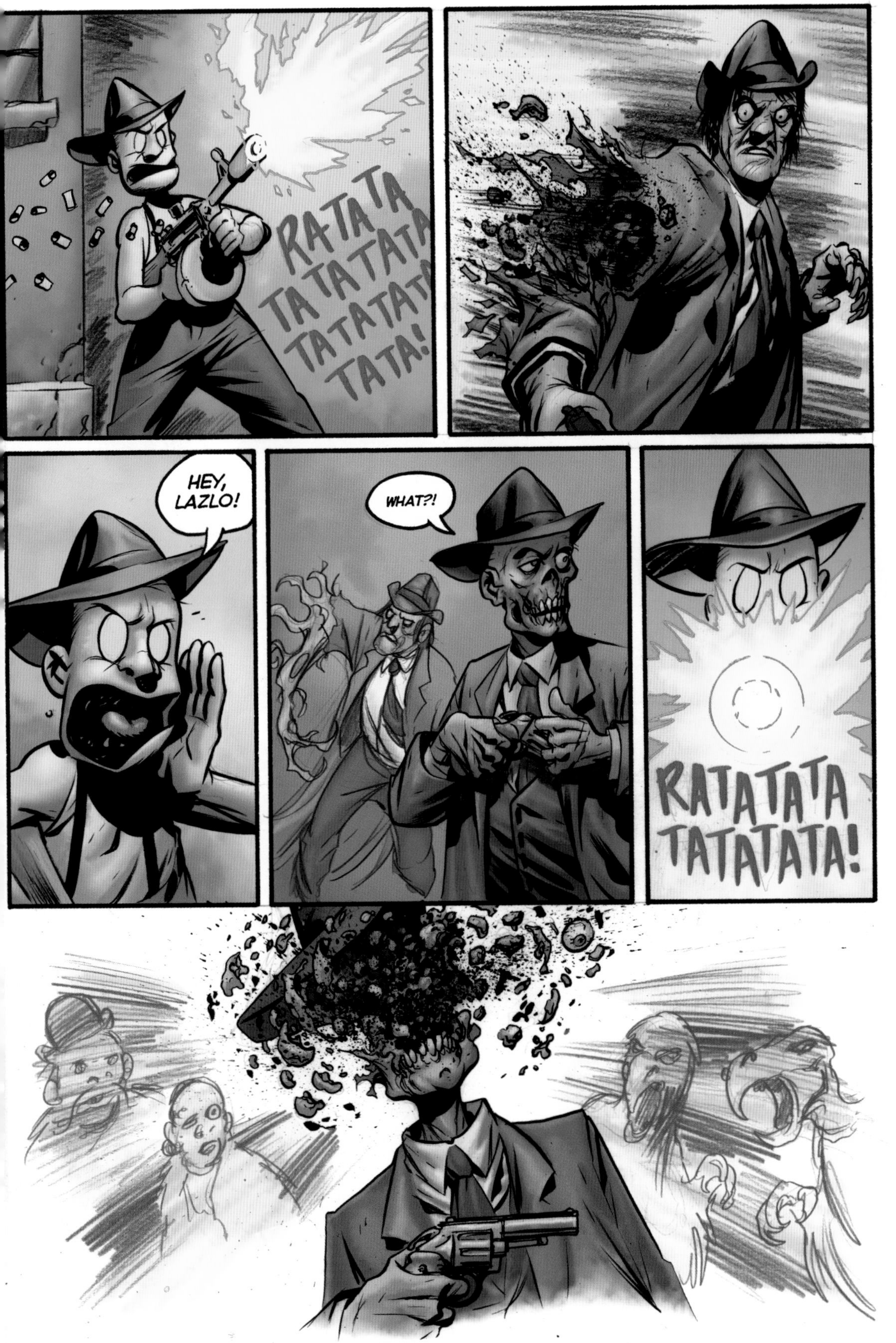
RATATA TATATATA TATATATA TATATATA TATA!
HEY, LAZLO!
WHAT?!
RATATATA TATATATA!

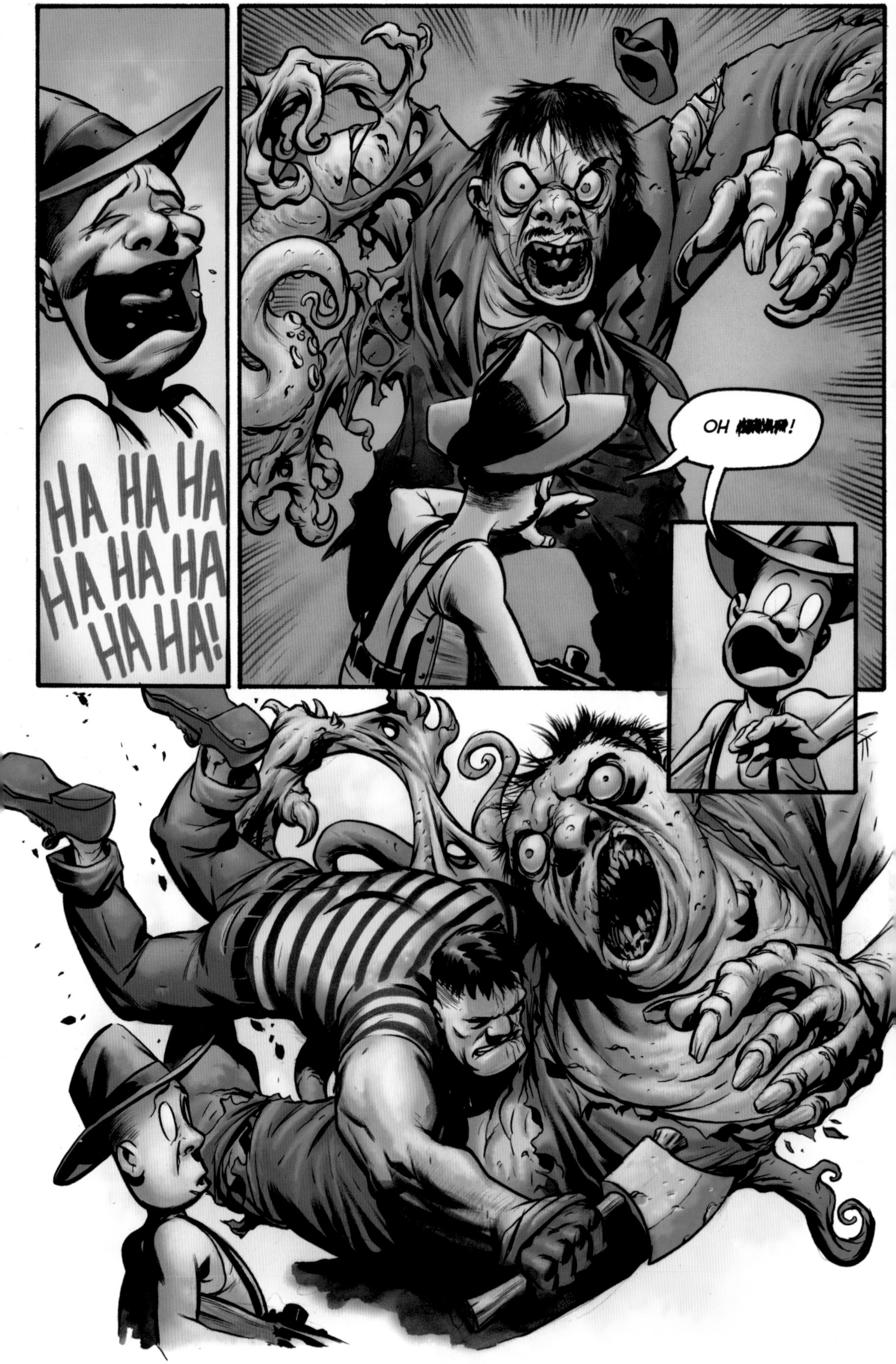
HA HA HA
HA HA HA
HA HA!
OH [redacted]!

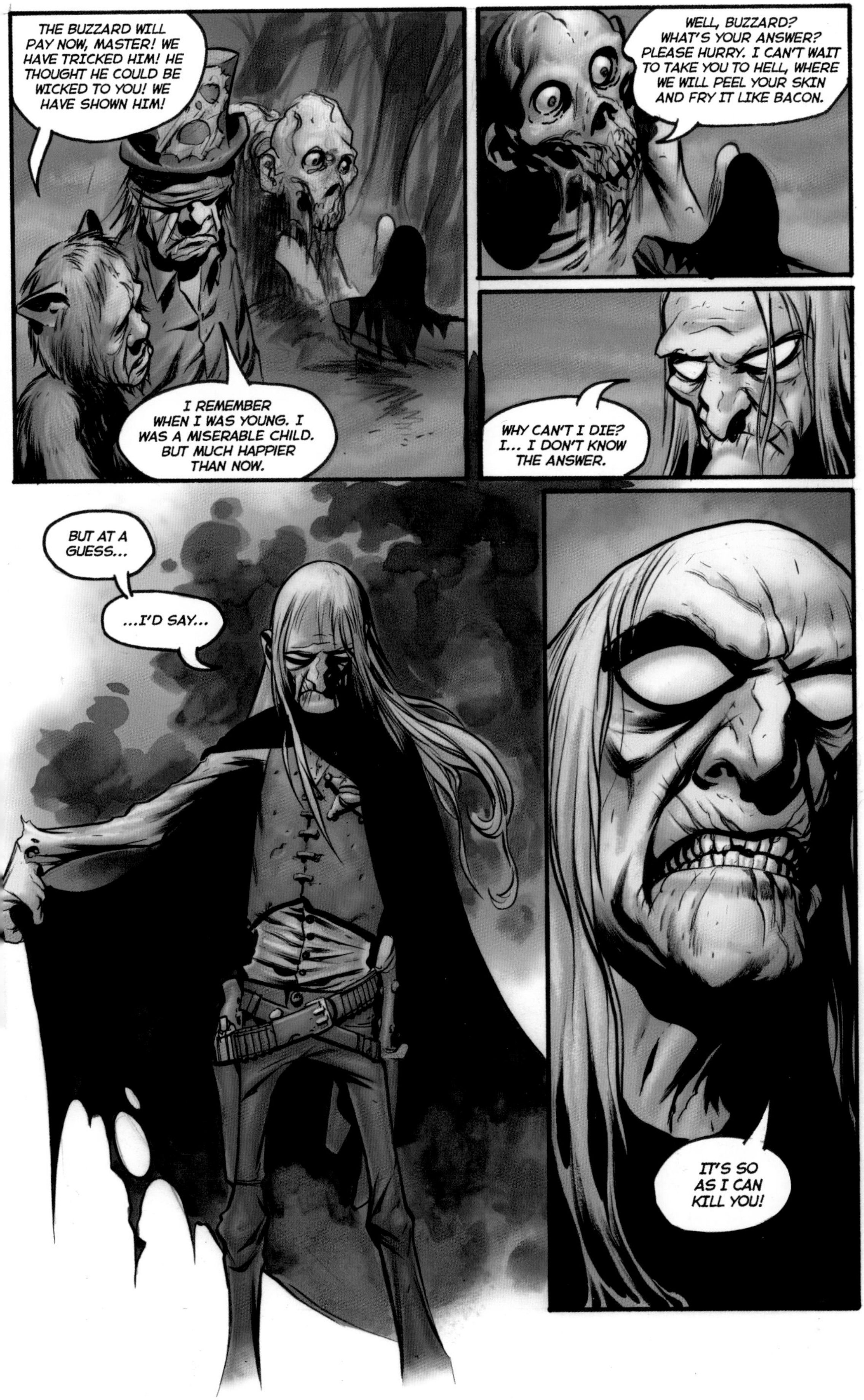
THE BUZZARD WILL PAY NOW, MASTER! WE HAVE TRICKED HIM! HE THOUGHT HE COULD BE WICKED TO YOU! WE HAVE SHOWN HIM!
I REMEMBER WHEN I WAS YOUNG. I WAS A MISERABLE CHILD. BUT MUCH HAPPIER THAN NOW.
WELL, BUZZARD? WHAT'S YOUR ANSWER? PLEASE HURRY. I CAN'T WAIT TO TAKE YOU TO HELL, WHERE WE WILL PEEL YOUR SKIN AND FRY IT LIKE BACON.
WHY CAN'T I DIE? I... I DON'T KNOW THE ANSWER.
BUT AT A GUESS...
...I'D SAY...
IT'S SO AS I CAN KILL YOU!

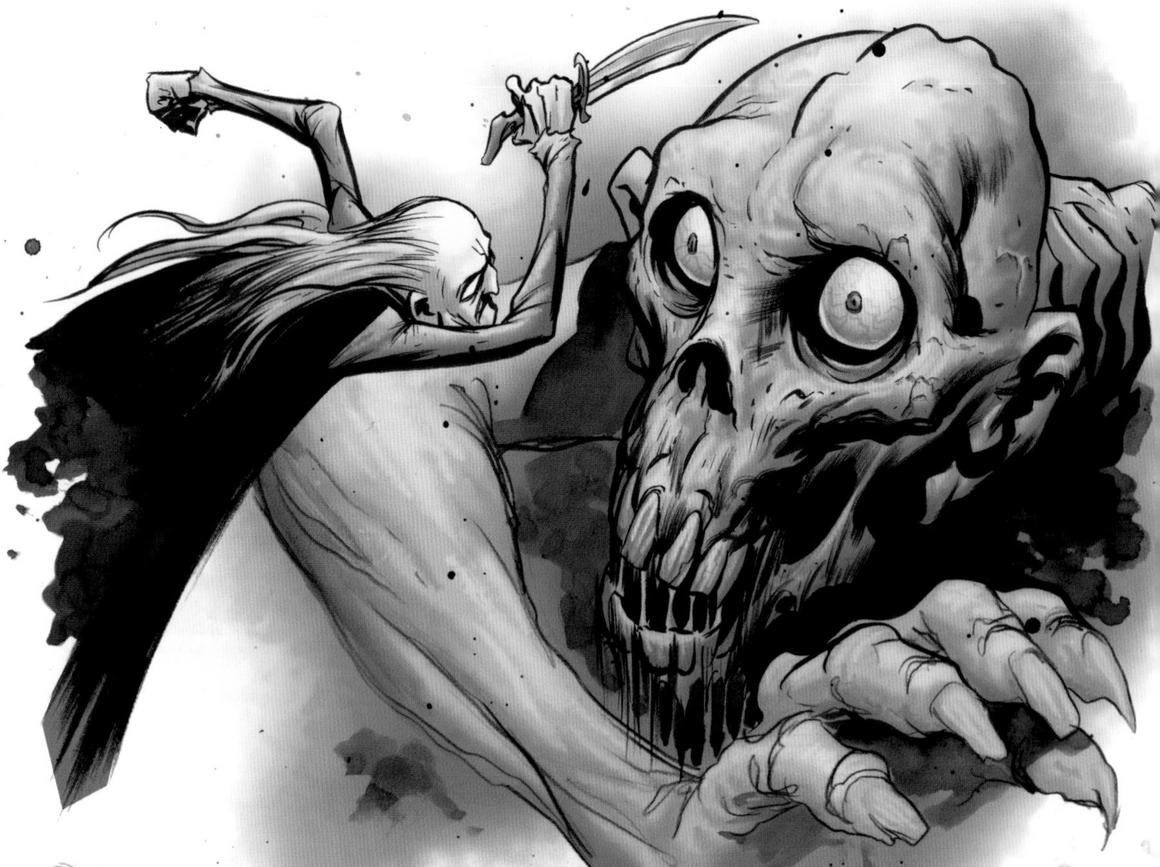

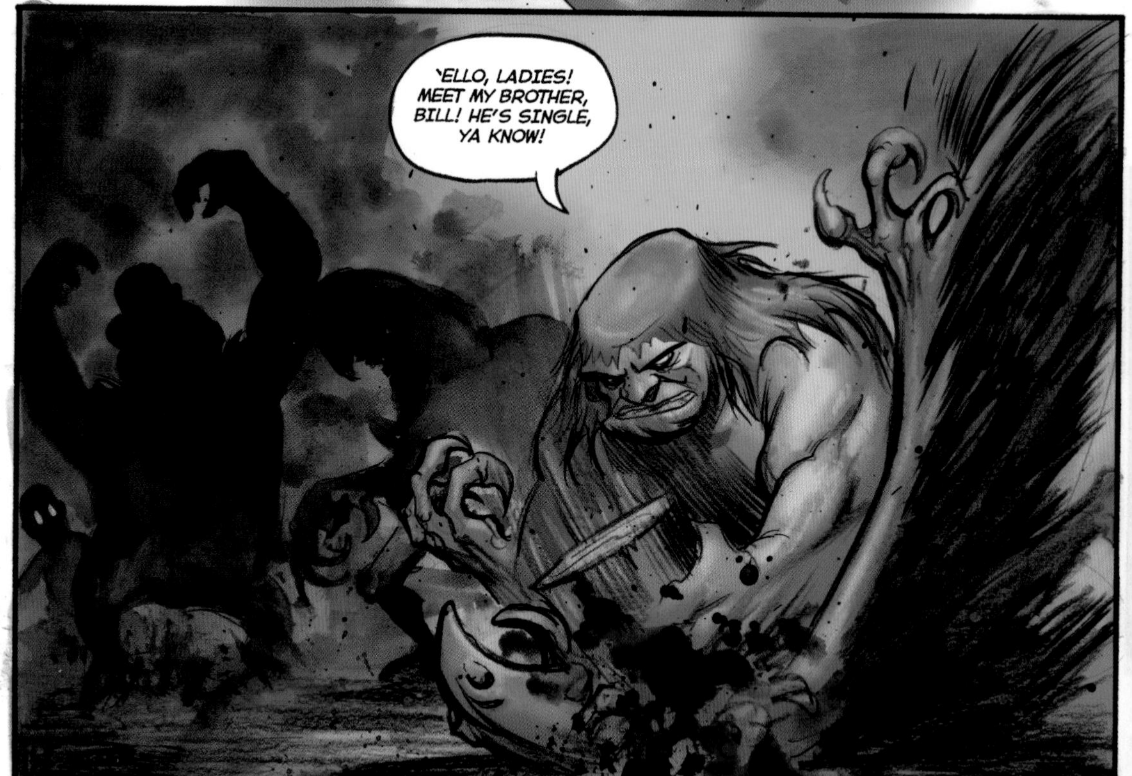
'ELLO, LADIES! MEET MY BROTHER, BILL! HE'S SINGLE, YA KNOW!

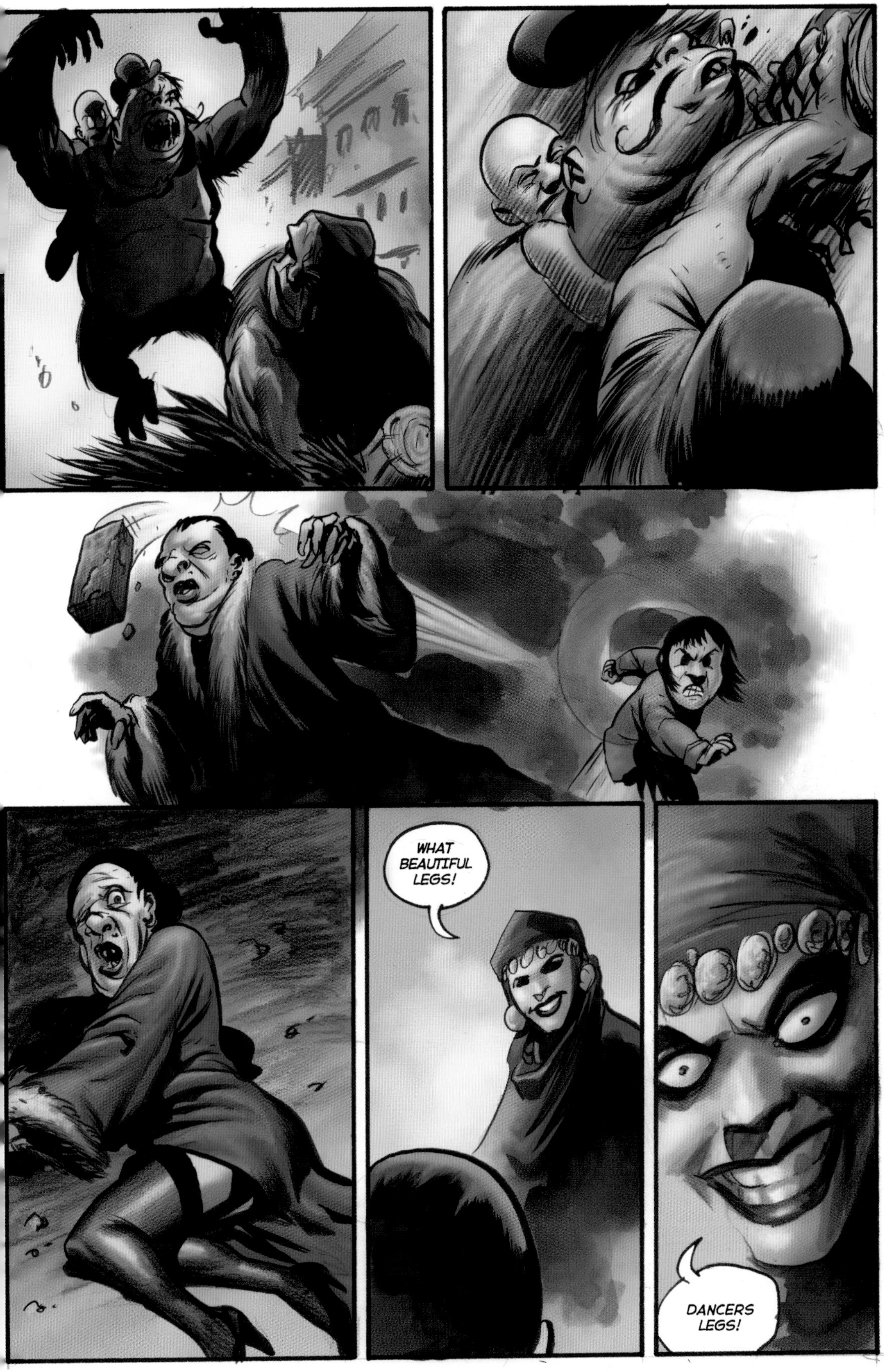
WHAT BEAUTIFUL LEGS!
DANCERS LEGS!

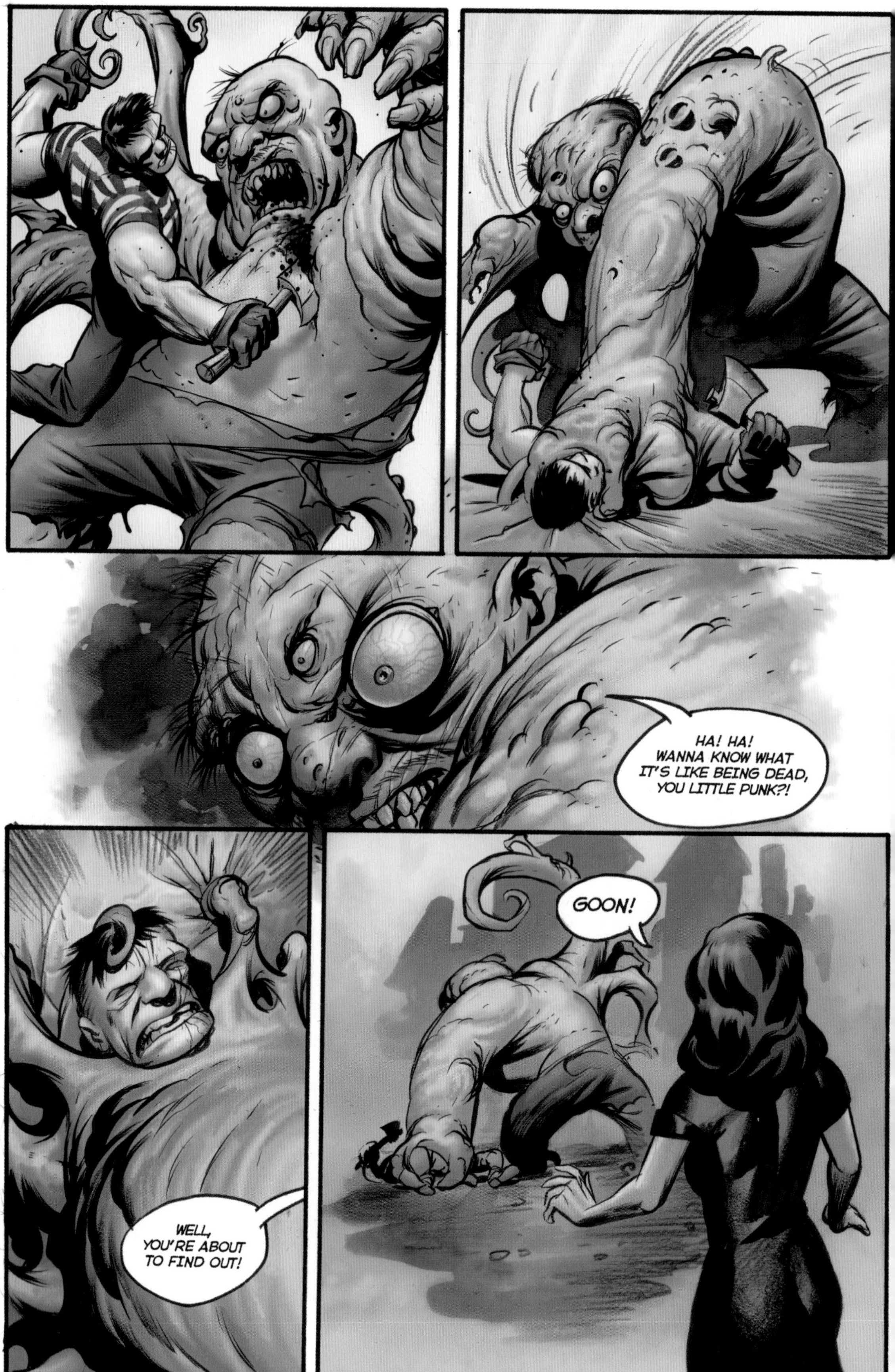
HA! HA! WANNA KNOW WHAT IT'S LIKE BEING DEAD, YOU LITTLE PUNK?!
WELL, YOU'RE ABOUT TO FIND OUT!
GOON!

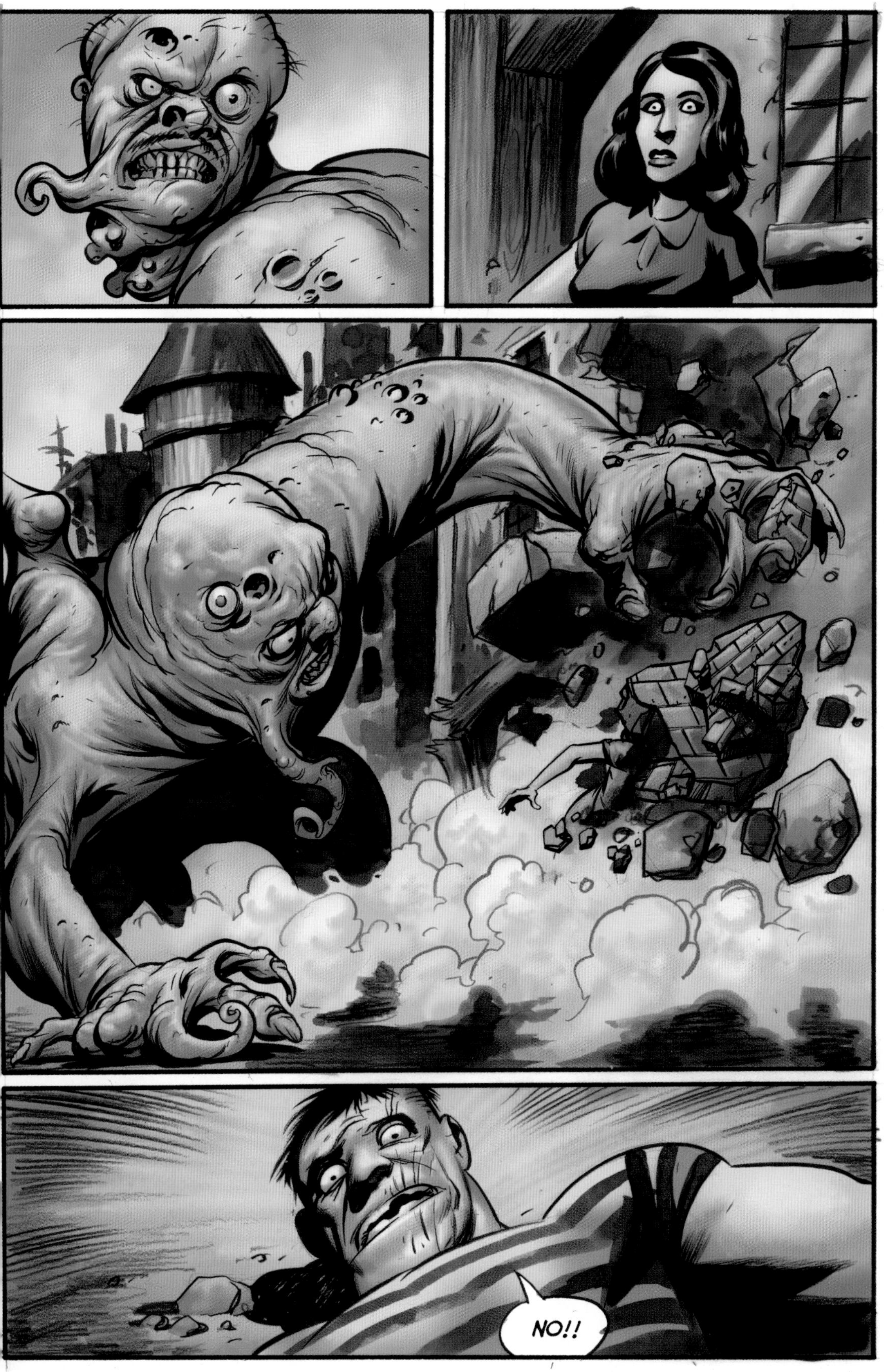
NO!!

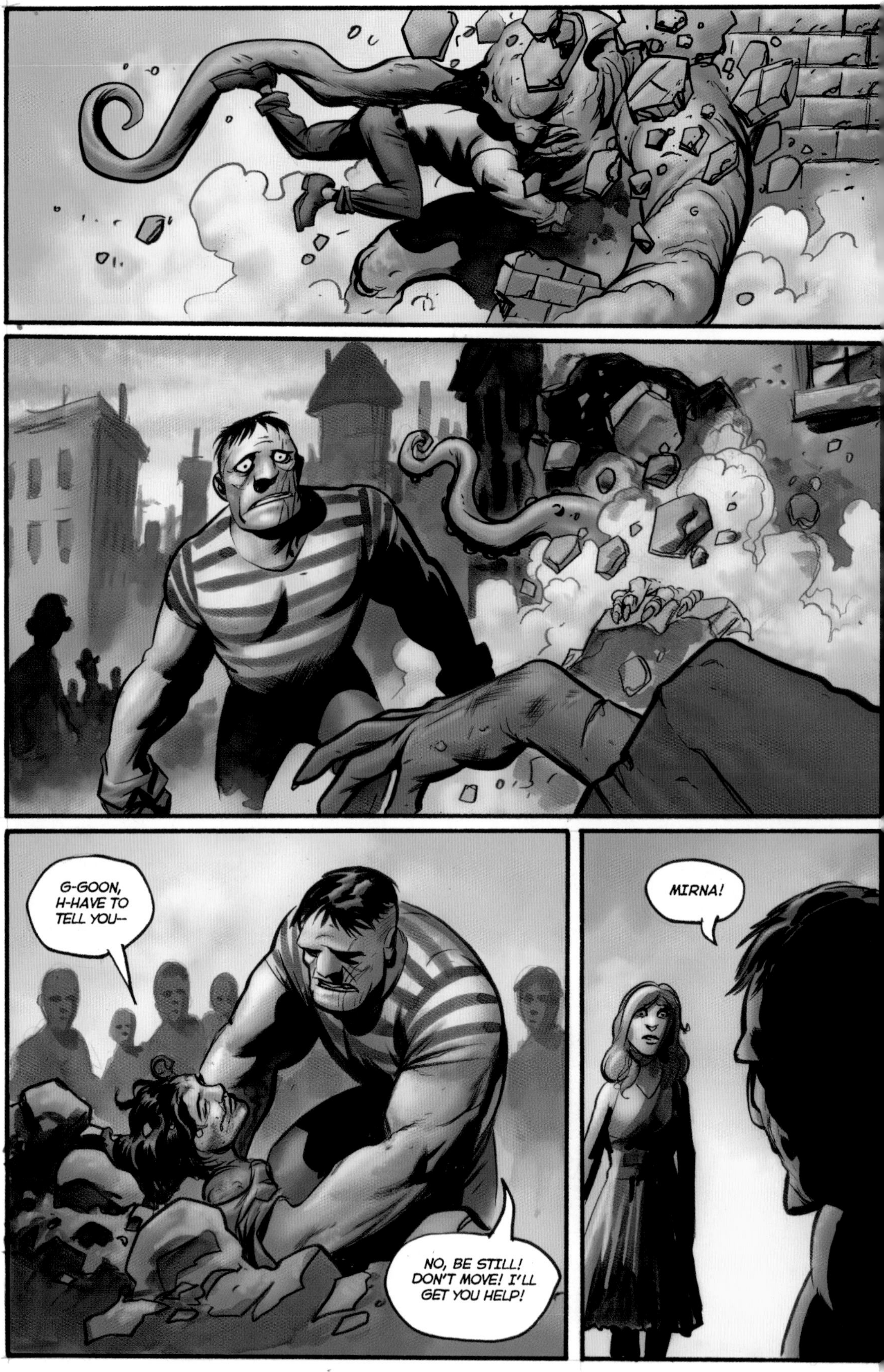
G-GOON, H-HAVE TO TELL YOU--
NO, BE STILL! DON'T MOVE! I'LL GET YOU HELP!
MIRNA!

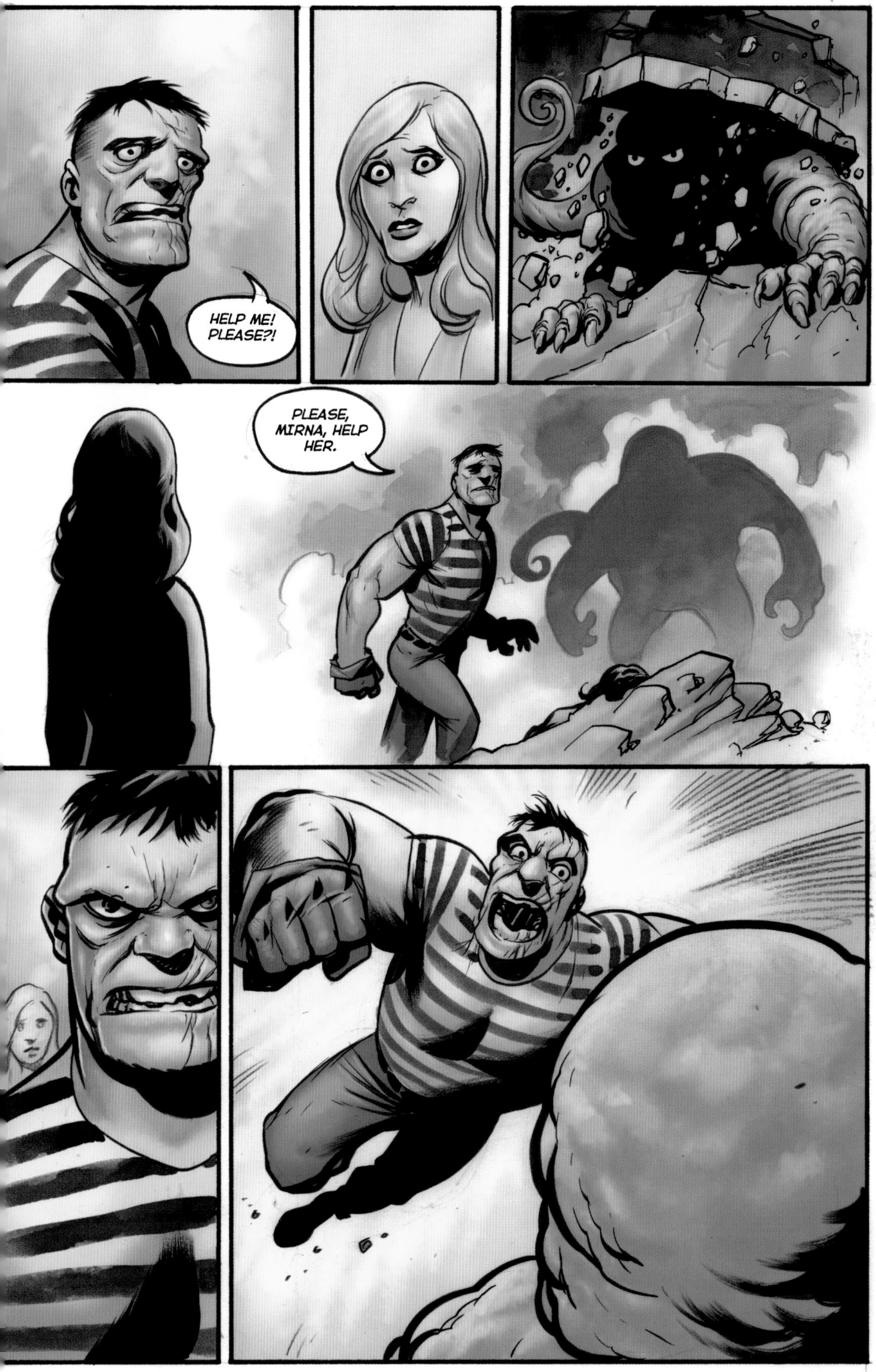
HELP ME! PLEASE?!
PLEASE, MIRNA, HELP HER.

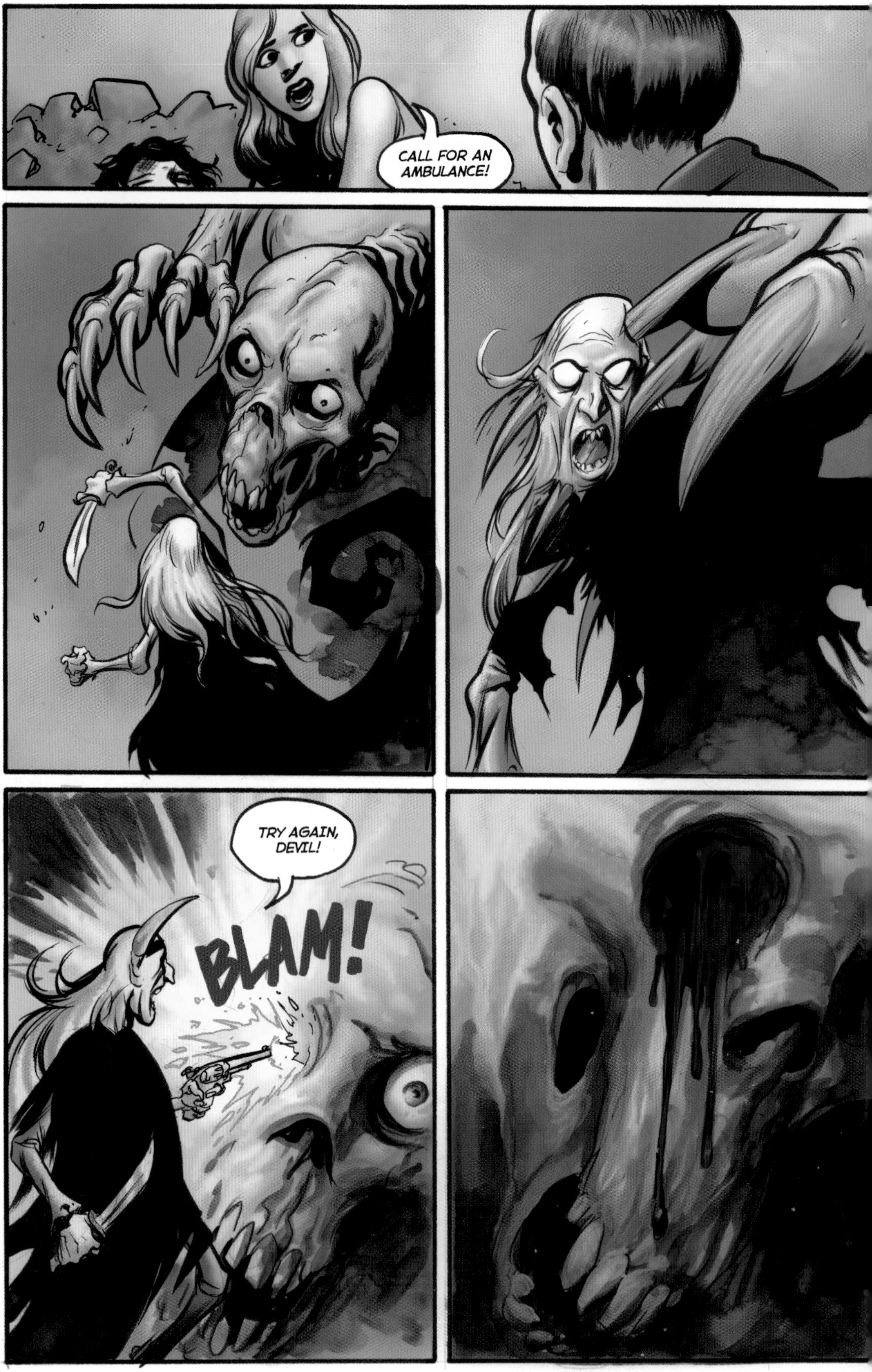
CALL FOR AN AMBULANCE!
TRY AGAIN, DEVIL!
BLAM!

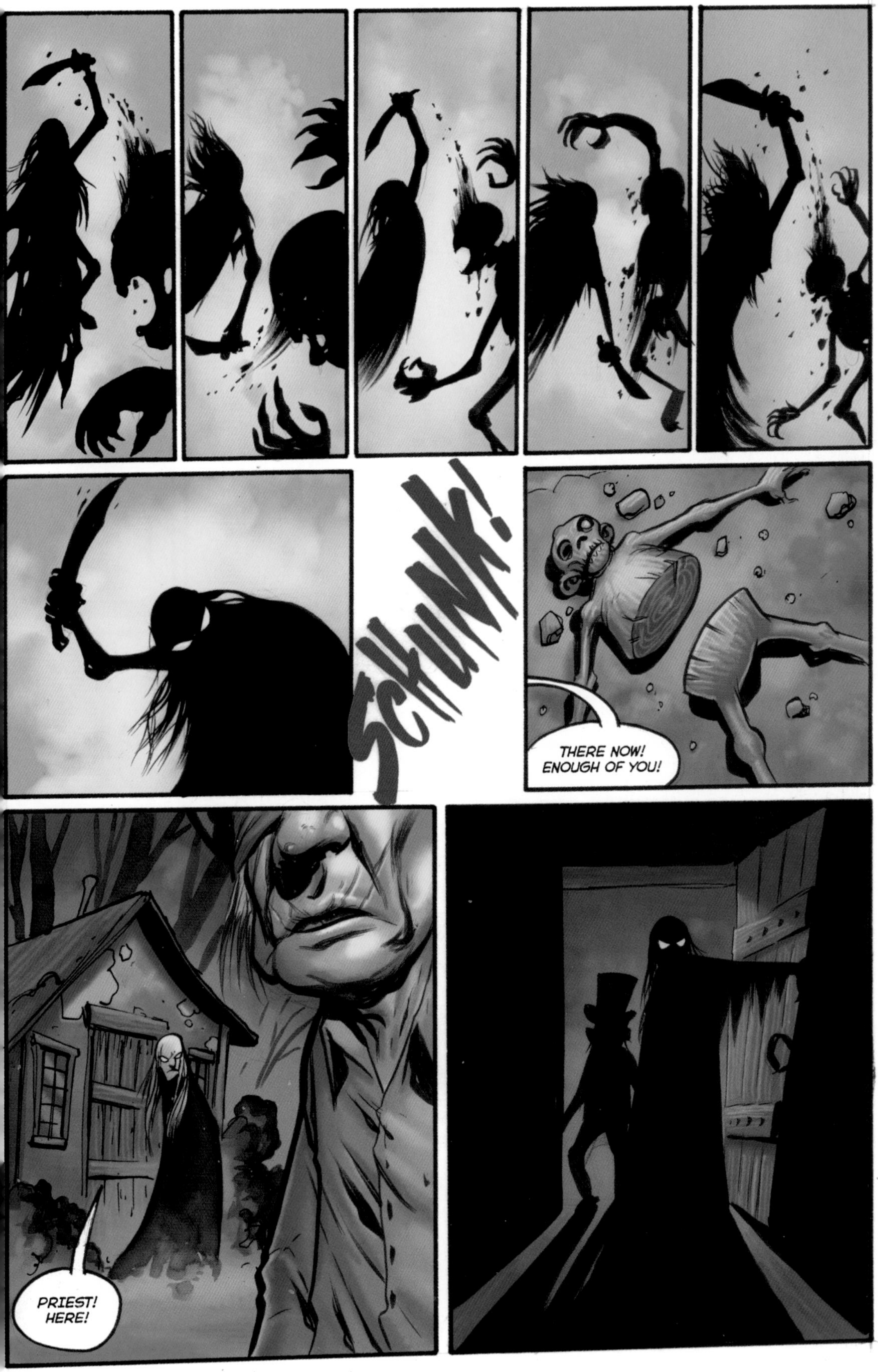
SCHUNK!
THERE NOW! ENOUGH OF YOU!
PRIEST! HERE!

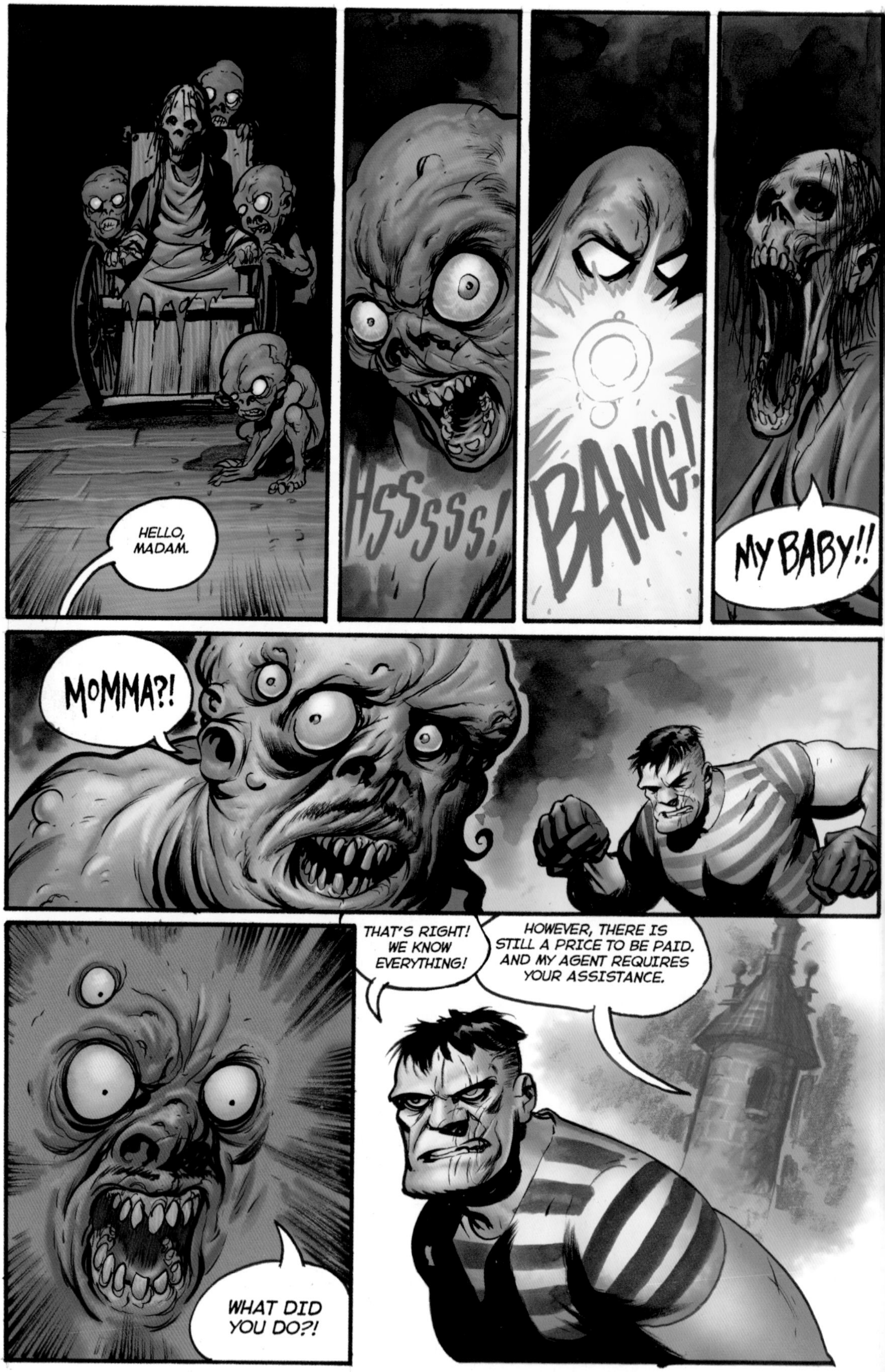
HELLO, MADAM.
HSSSSS!
BANG!
MY BABY!!
MOMMA?!
WHAT DID YOU DO?!
THAT'S RIGHT! WE KNOW EVERYTHING!
HOWEVER, THERE IS STILL A PRICE TO BE PAID. AND MY AGENT REQUIRES YOUR ASSISTANCE.

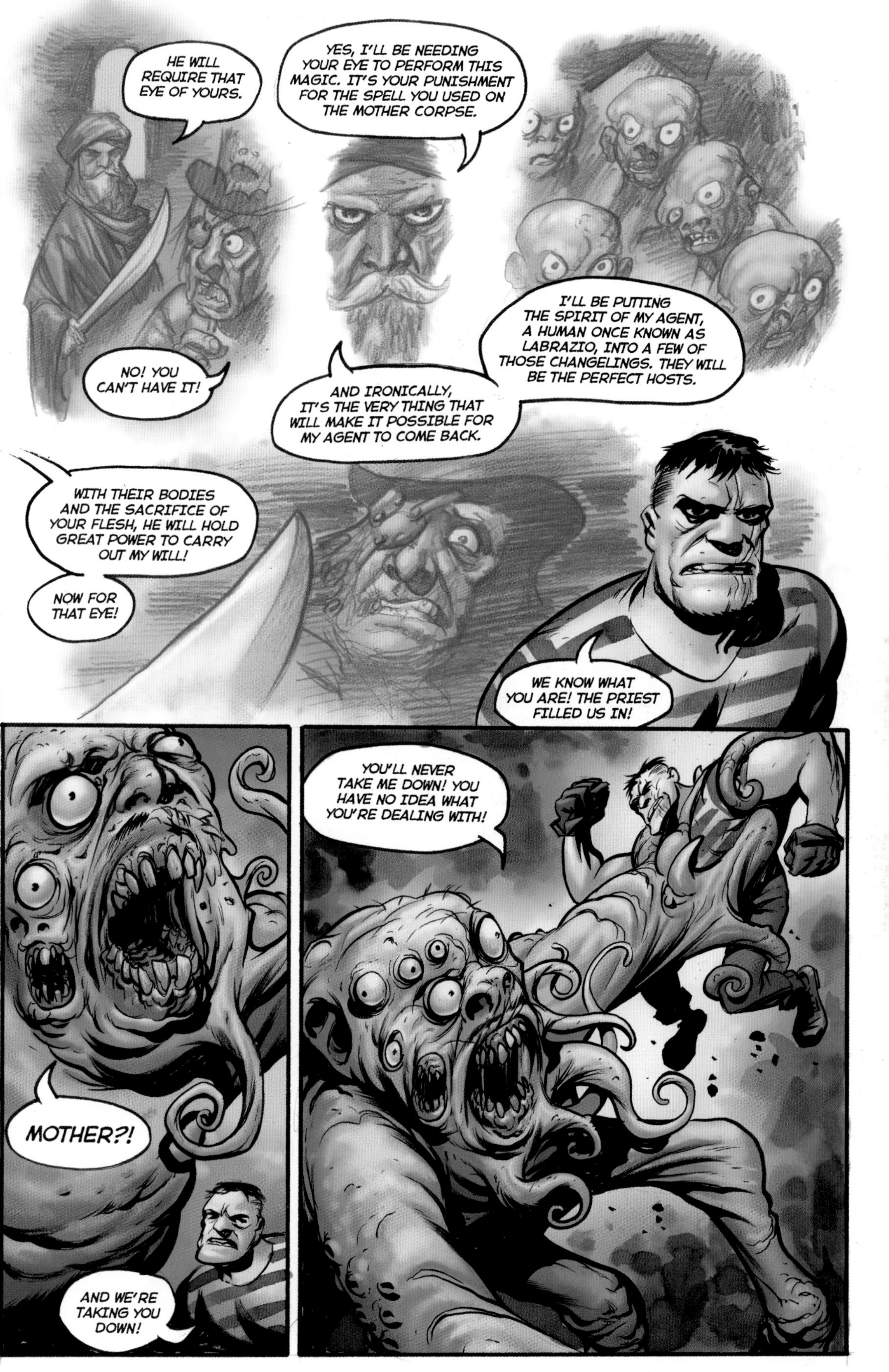
HE WILL REQUIRE THAT EYE OF YOURS.
YES, I'LL BE NEEDING YOUR EYE TO PERFORM THIS MAGIC. IT'S YOUR PUNISHMENT FOR THE SPELL YOU USED ON THE MOTHER CORPSE.
NO! YOU CAN'T HAVE IT!
AND IRONICALLY, IT'S THE VERY THING THAT WILL MAKE IT POSSIBLE FOR MY AGENT TO COME BACK.
I'LL BE PUTTING THE SPIRIT OF MY AGENT, A HUMAN ONCE KNOWN AS LABRAZIO, INTO A FEW OF THOSE CHANGELINGS. THEY WILL BE THE PERFECT HOSTS.
WITH THEIR BODIES AND THE SACRIFICE OF YOUR FLESH, HE WILL HOLD GREAT POWER TO CARRY OUT MY WILL!
NOW FOR THAT EYE!
WE KNOW WHAT YOU ARE! THE PRIEST FILLED US IN!
MOTHER?!
AND WE'RE TAKING YOU DOWN!
YOU'LL NEVER TAKE ME DOWN! YOU HAVE NO IDEA WHAT YOU'RE DEALING WITH!

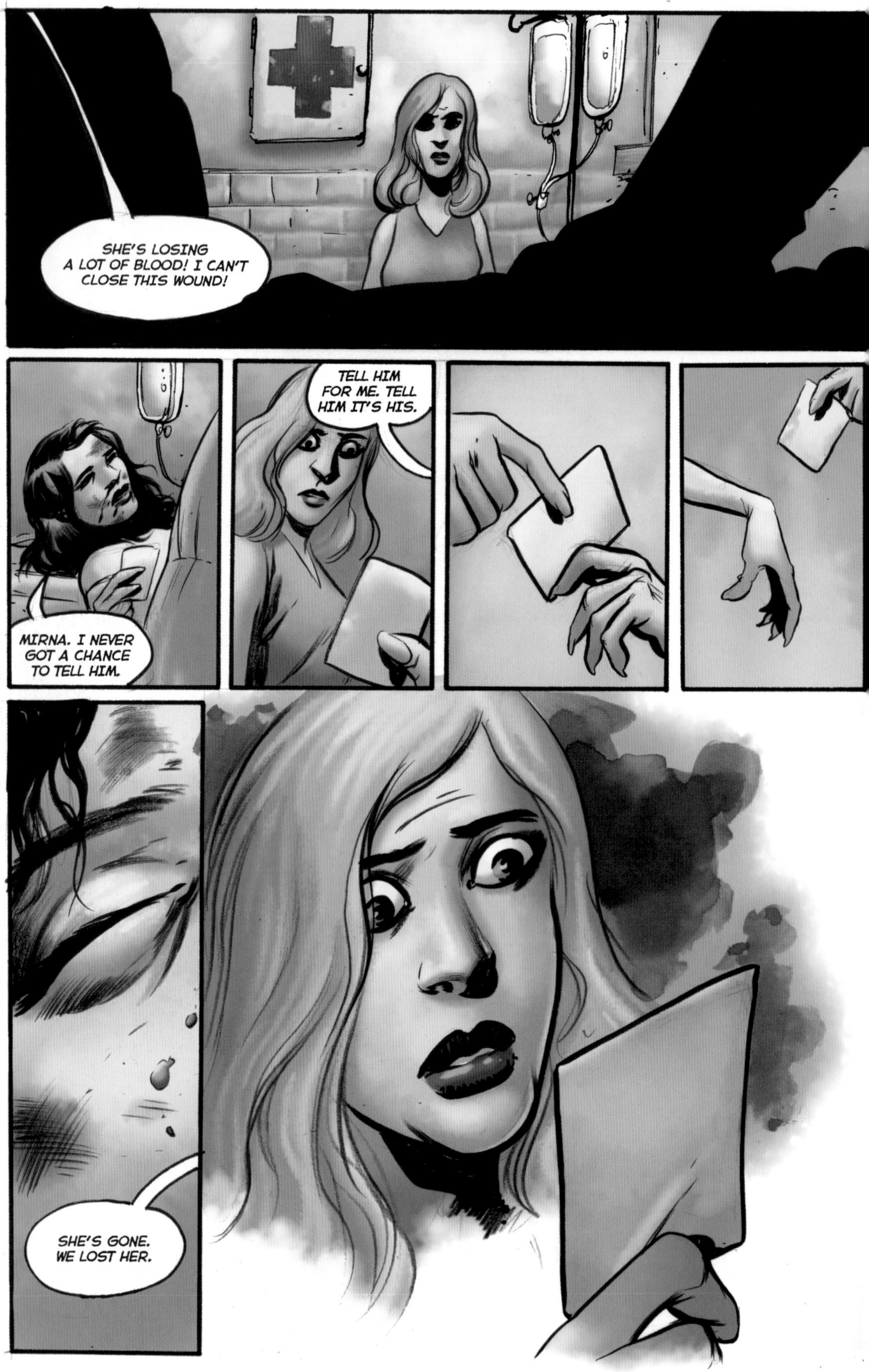
SHE'S LOSING A LOT OF BLOOD! I CAN'T CLOSE THIS WOUND!
MIRNA. I NEVER GOT A CHANCE TO TELL HIM.
TELL HIM FOR ME. TELL HIM IT'S HIS.
SHE'S GONE. WE LOST HER.

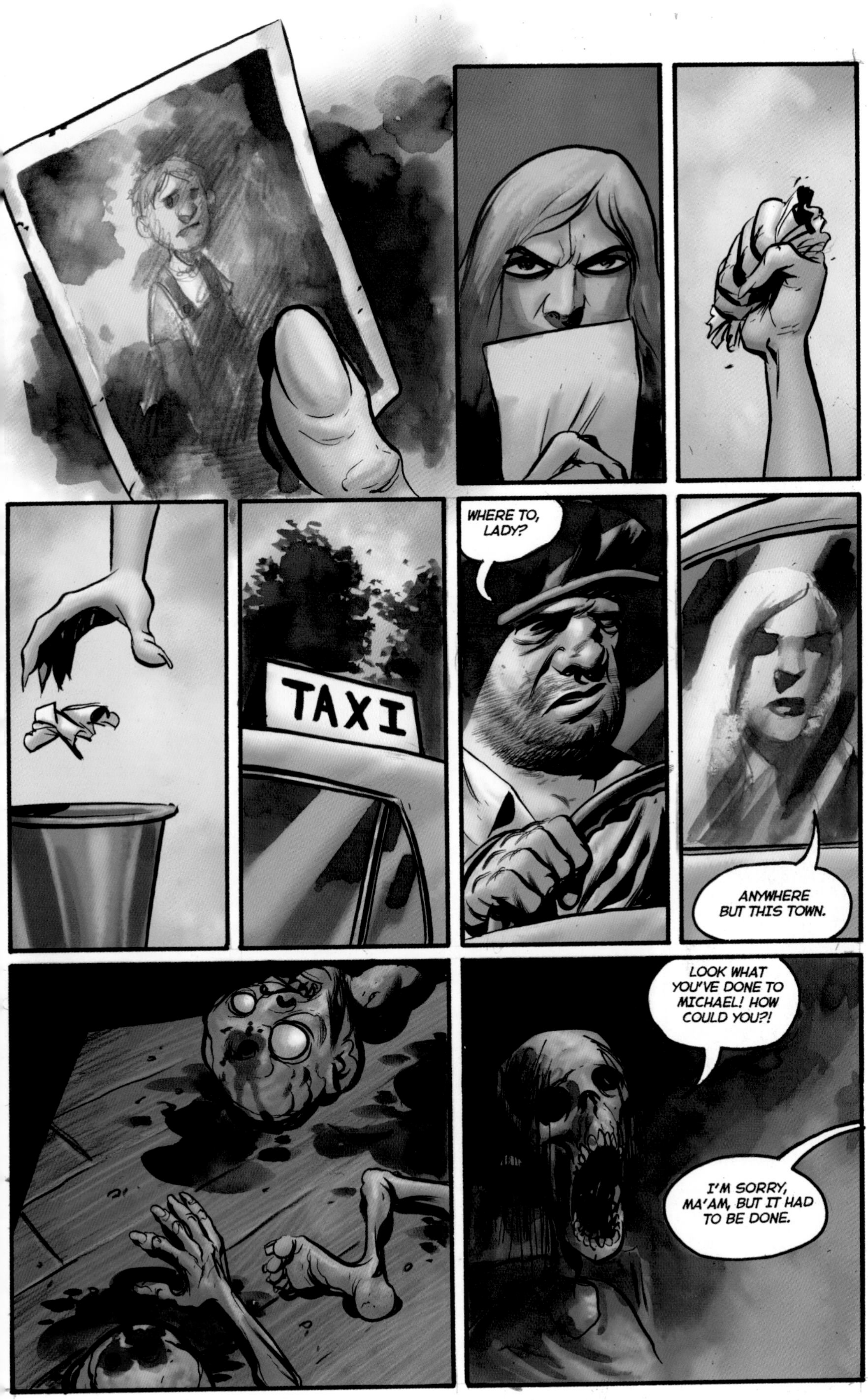

TAXI
WHERE TO, LADY?
ANYWHERE BUT THIS TOWN.
LOOK WHAT YOU'VE DONE TO MICHAEL! HOW COULD YOU?!
I'M SORRY, MA'AM, BUT IT HAD TO BE DONE.

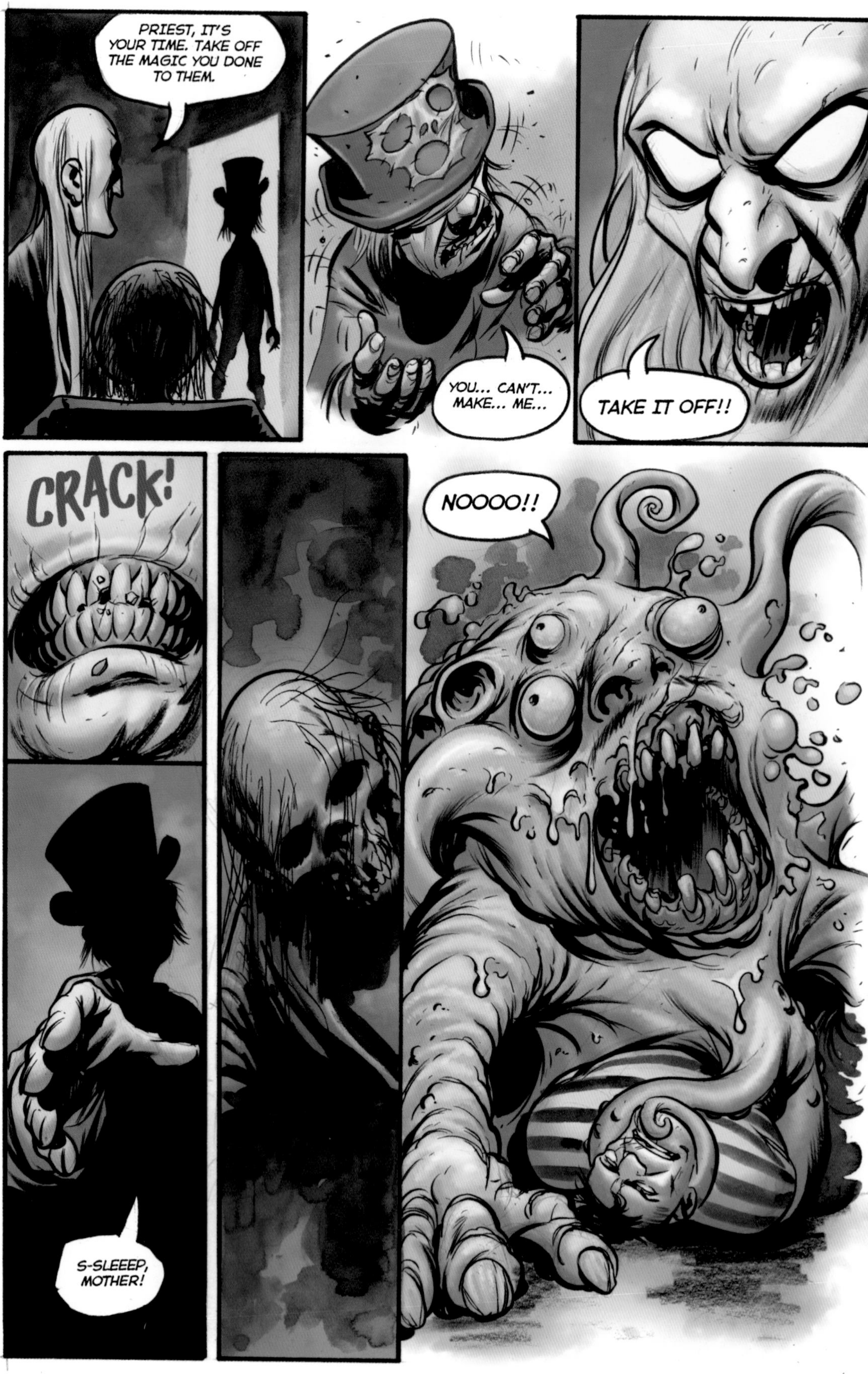
PRIEST, IT'S YOUR TIME. TAKE OFF THE MAGIC YOU DONE TO THEM.
YOU... CAN'T... MAKE... ME...
TAKE IT OFF!!
CRACK!
S-SLEEEP, MOTHER!
NOOOO!!

THAT'S RIGHT! YOU SON OF A [redacted]!
DIE!!
YOU THINK YOU'VE WON?!
THEY'RE COMING FOR THIS PLACE! HA! I'D RATHER BE DEAD THAN BE YOU!

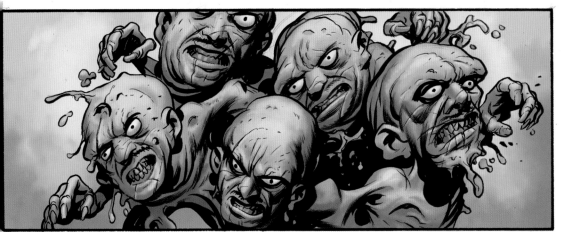

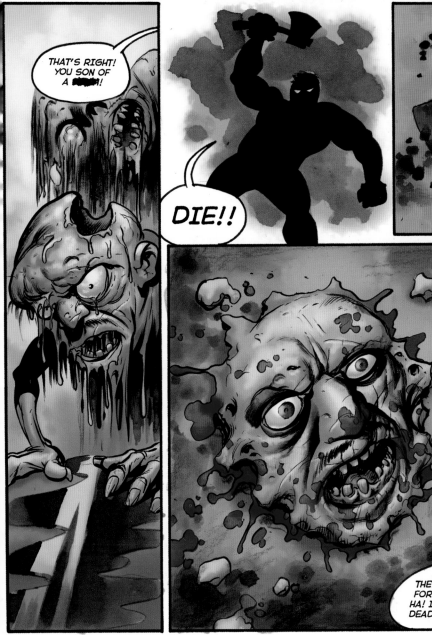

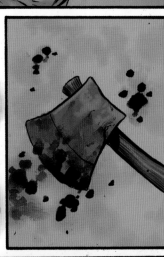

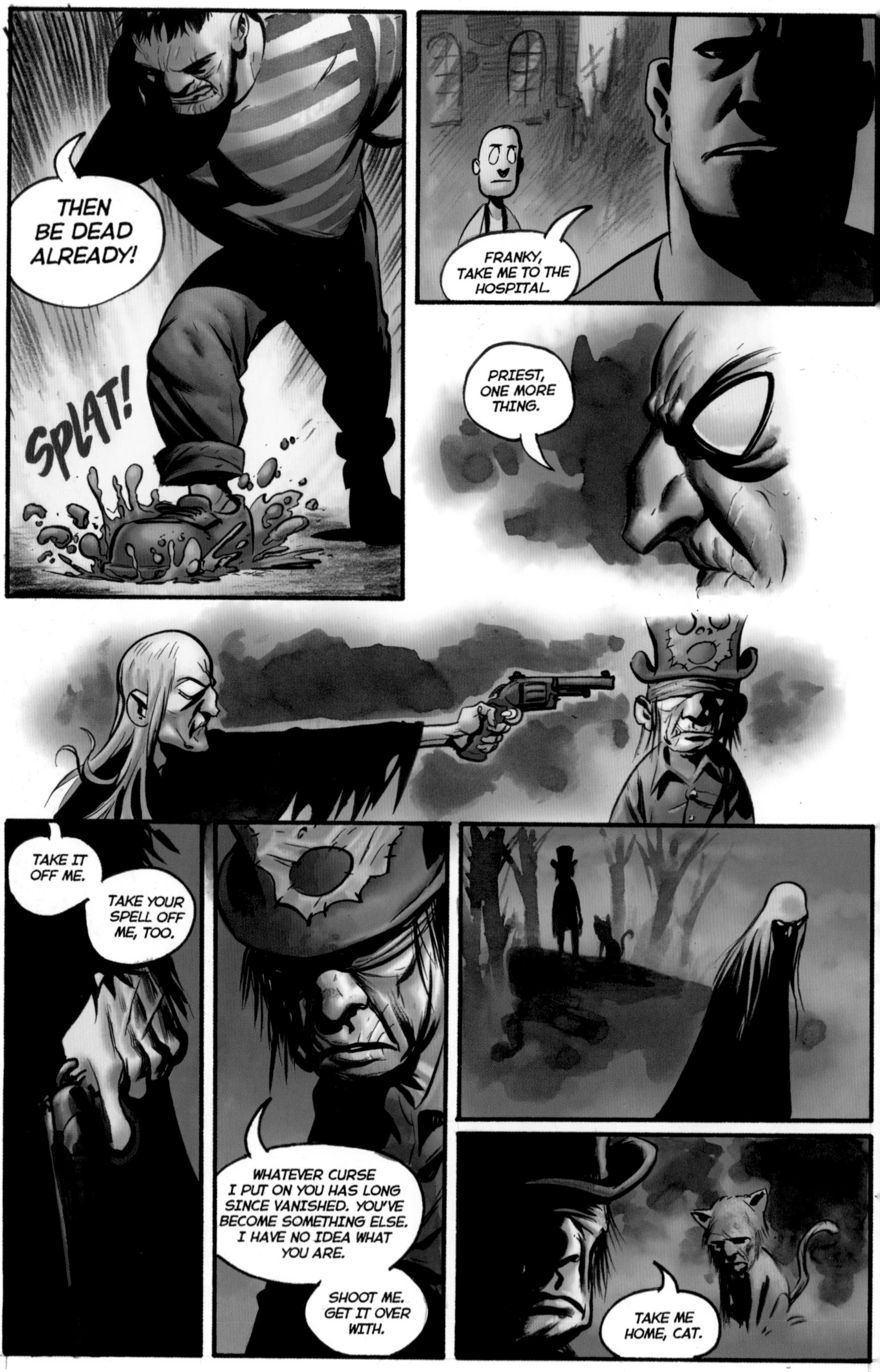
THEN BE DEAD ALREADY!
SPLAT!
FRANKY, TAKE ME TO THE HOSPITAL.
PRIEST, ONE MORE THING.
TAKE IT OFF ME.
TAKE YOUR SPELL OFF ME, TOO.
WHATEVER CURSE I PUT ON YOU HAS LONG SINCE VANISHED. YOU'VE BECOME SOMETHING ELSE. I HAVE NO IDEA WHAT YOU ARE.
SHOOT ME. GET IT OVER WITH.
TAKE ME HOME, CAT.

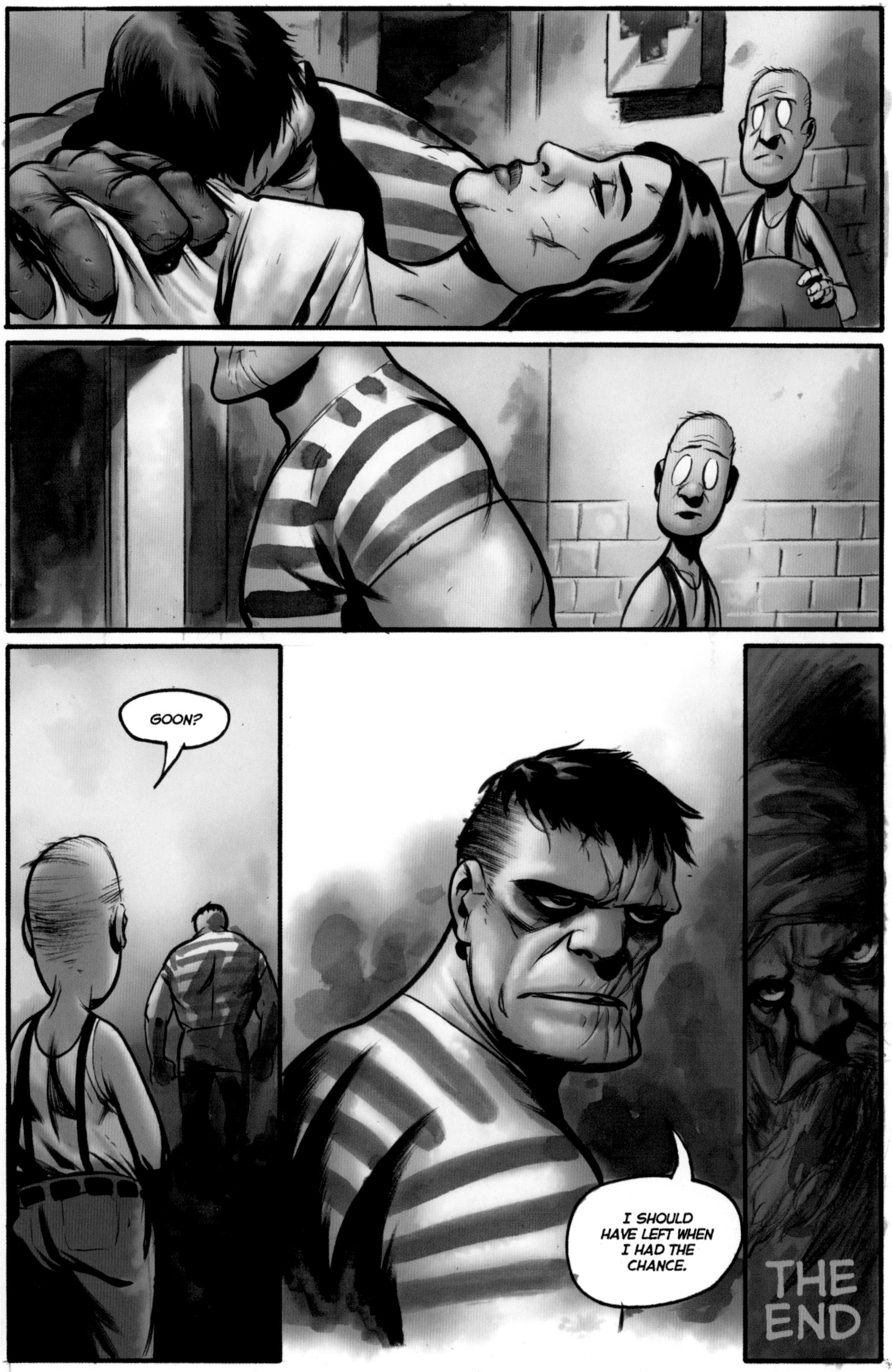
GOON?
I SHOULD HAVE LEFT WHEN I HAD THE CHANCE.
THE END

THE GOON ™

BLACK AND WHITE VERSUS COLOR

Starting with the yearlong monthly run of *The Goon* we had going in 2008, I began collaborating with one of the best colorists in the business: Dave Stewart. Without a doubt he made my illustrations look better. As the douche bags say, Dave is the man—and on top of that, one of the nicest people in comics. So don't think I have anything against Stewart's work when I say that sometimes I wish *The Goon* were a black-and-white comic. When I started *The Goon* I wanted it to just be a black-and-white comic. The shades of gray I put in the first two series were there not only because of a lack of funds but also because I love the pulpy feel of the grays. I can't put my finger on it, but there's just a vividness that comes out from a subdued palette. But the move to Dark Horse also brought on the argument that it would be a lot easier to get people to buy this book if it was in color. A sad fact that I have a hard time understanding. Anyway, I switched to color, but sometimes I wish the book were still gray. I thought it might be fun to show you some random pages from Goon Year devoid of color. Just for poops and chuckles.

Eric

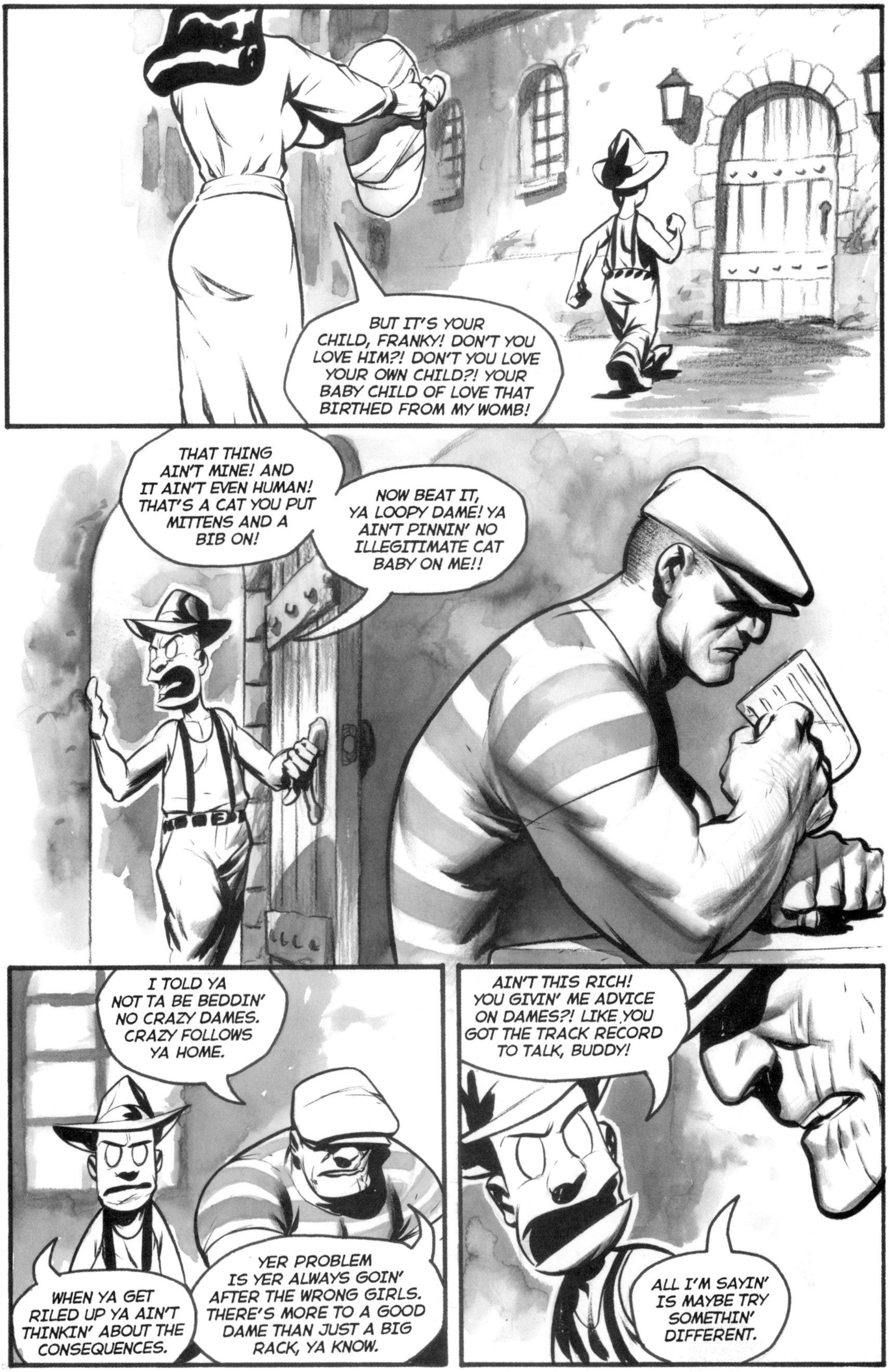
BUT IT'S YOUR CHILD, FRANKY! DON'T YOU LOVE HIM?! DON'T YOU LOVE YOUR OWN CHILD?! YOUR BABY CHILD OF LOVE THAT BIRTHED FROM MY WOMB!
THAT THING AIN'T MINE! AND IT AIN'T EVEN HUMAN! THAT'S A CAT YOU PUT MITTENS AND A BIB ON!
NOW BEAT IT, YA LOOPY DAME! YA AIN'T PINNIN' NO ILLEGITIMATE CAT BABY ON ME!!
I TOLD YA NOT TA BE BEDDIN' NO CRAZY DAMES. CRAZY FOLLOWS YA HOME.
WHEN YA GET RILED UP YA AIN'T THINKIN' ABOUT THE CONSEQUENCES.
YER PROBLEM IS YER ALWAYS GOIN' AFTER THE WRONG GIRLS. THERE'S MORE TO A GOOD DAME THAN JUST A BIG RACK, YA KNOW.
AIN'T THIS RICH! YOU GIVIN' ME ADVICE ON DAMES?! LIKE YOU GOT THE TRACK RECORD TO TALK, BUDDY!
ALL I'M SAYIN' IS MAYBE TRY SOMETHIN' DIFFERENT.

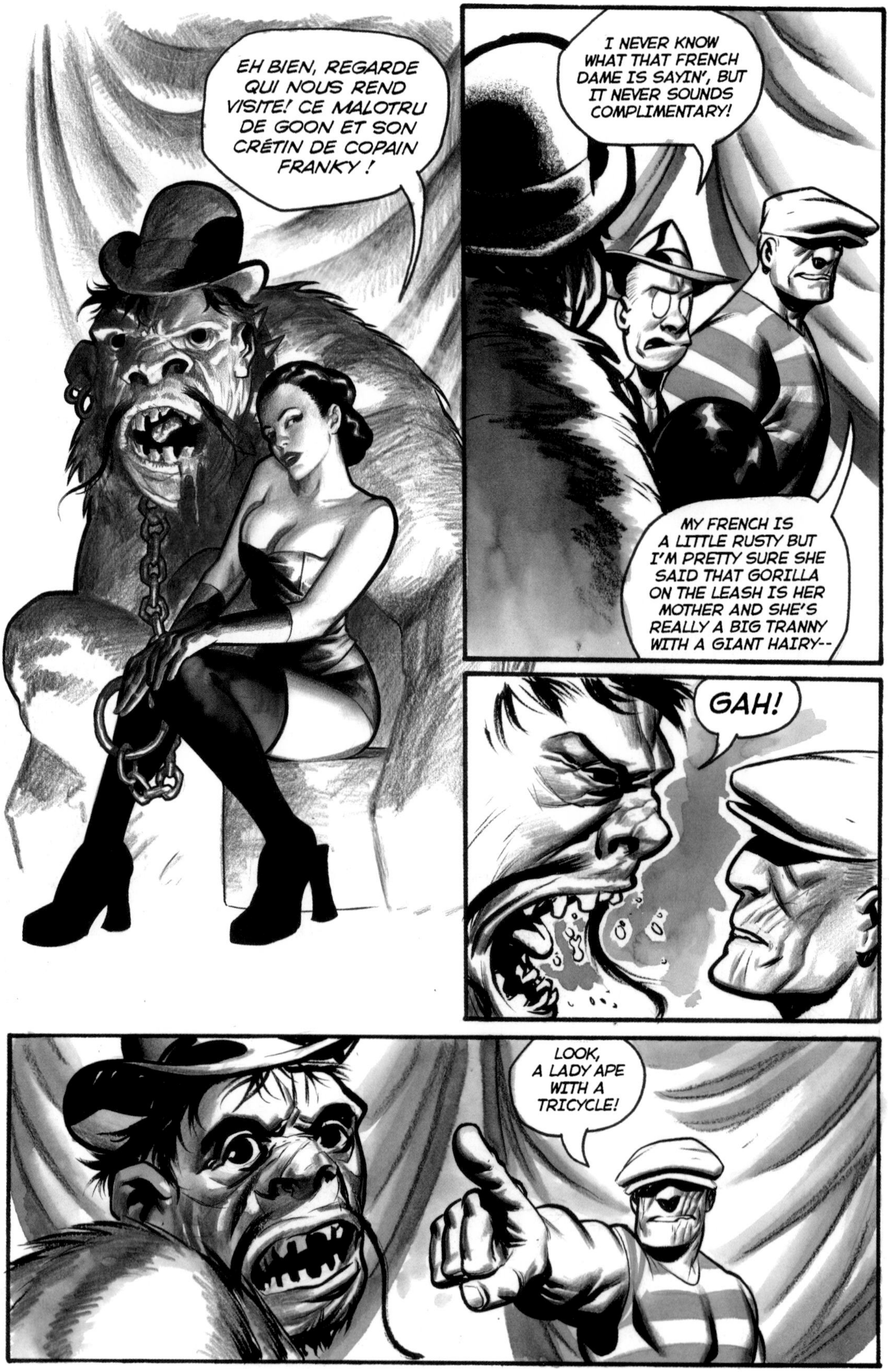
EH BIEN, REGARDE QUI NOUS REND VISITE! CE MALOTRU DE GOON ET SON CRÉTIN DE COPAIN FRANKY !
I NEVER KNOW WHAT THAT FRENCH DAME IS SAYIN', BUT IT NEVER SOUNDS COMPLIMENTARY!
MY FRENCH IS A LITTLE RUSTY BUT I'M PRETTY SURE SHE SAID THAT GORILLA ON THE LEASH IS HER MOTHER AND SHE'S REALLY A BIG TRANNY WITH A GIANT HAIRY--
GAH!
LOOK, A LADY APE WITH A TRICYCLE!

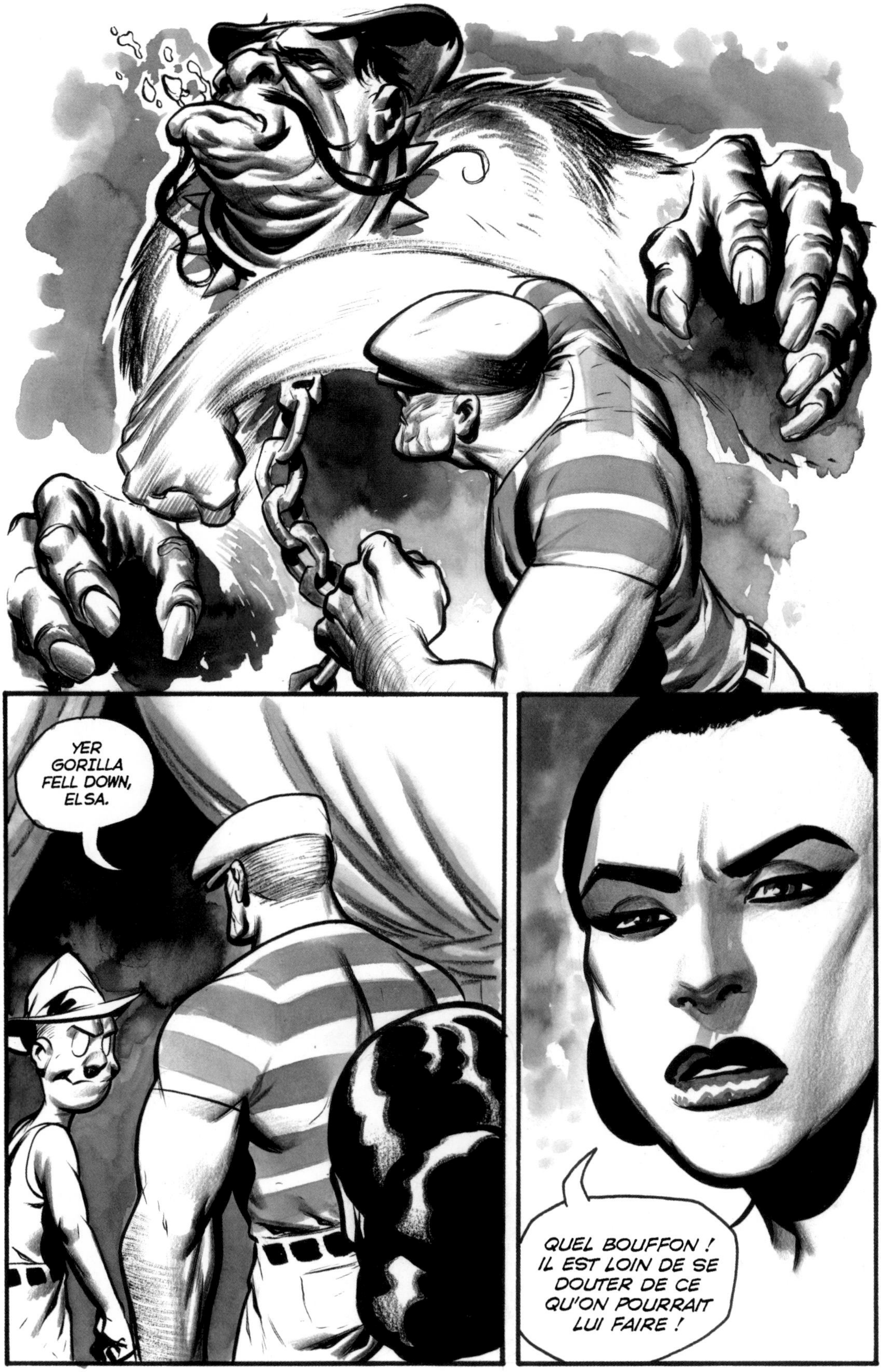
YER GORILLA FELL DOWN, ELSA.
QUEL BOUFFON ! IL EST LOIN DE SE DOUTER DE CE QU'ON POURRAIT LUI FAIRE !

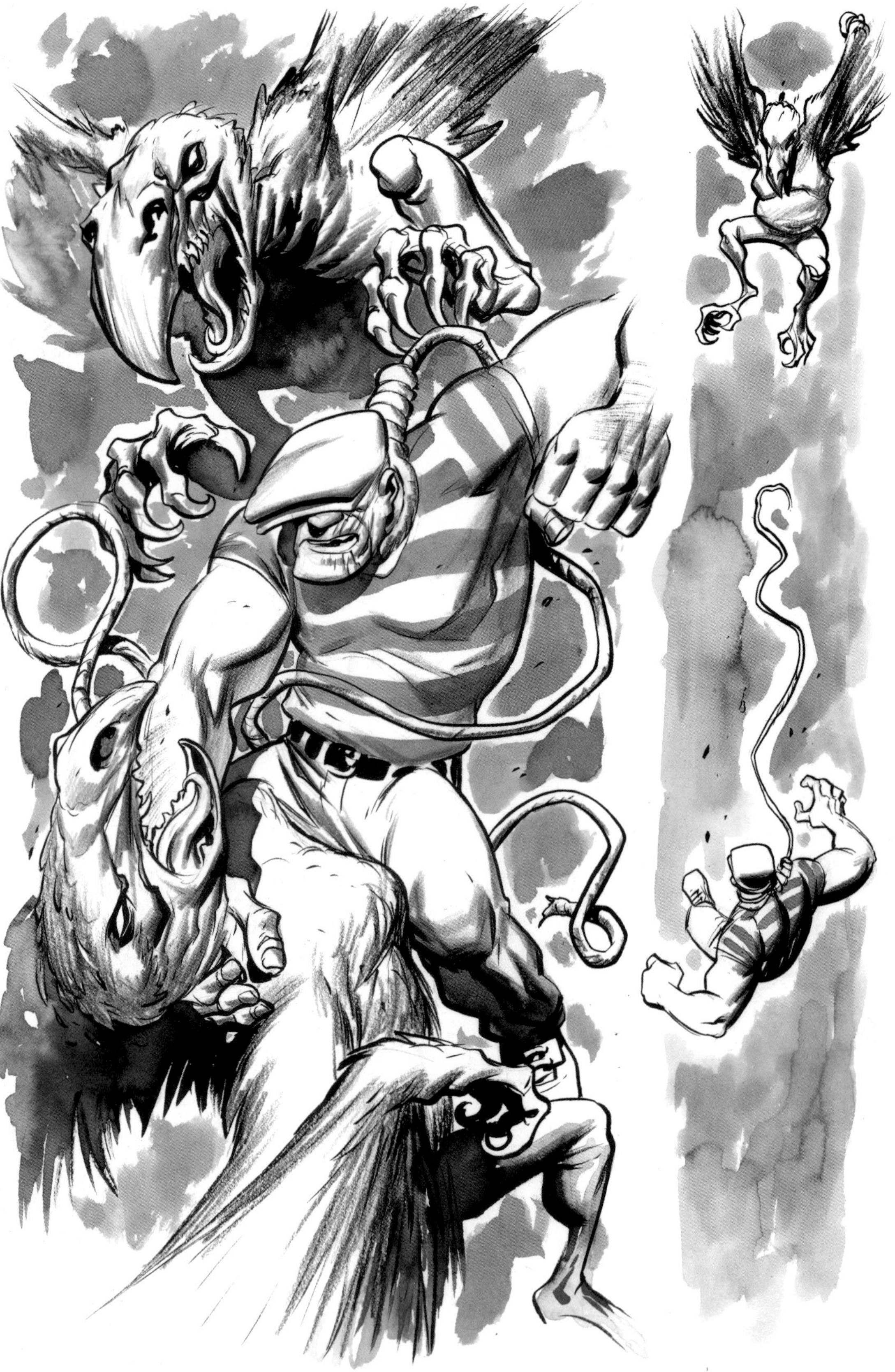

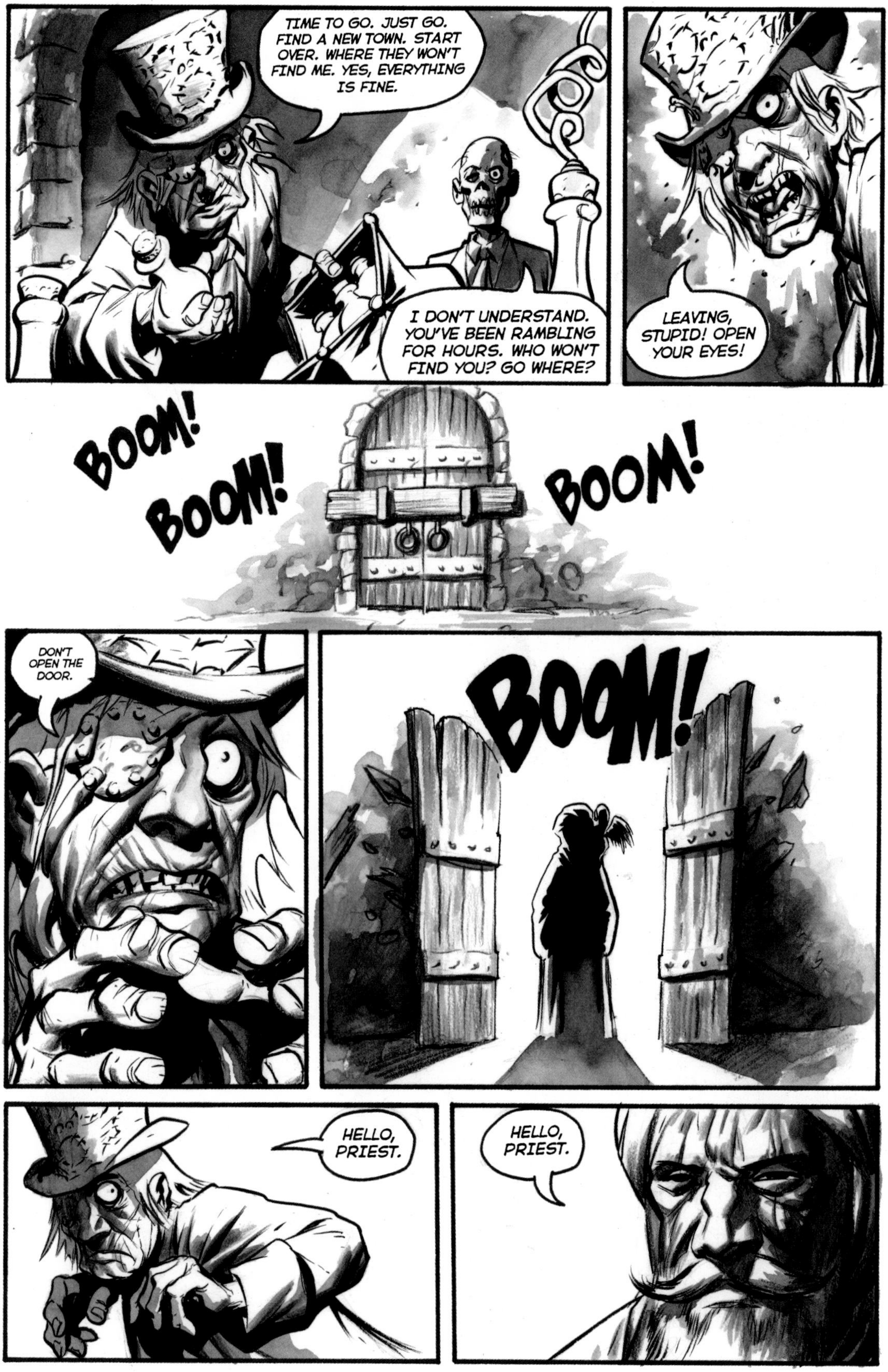
TIME TO GO. JUST GO. FIND A NEW TOWN. START OVER. WHERE THEY WON'T FIND ME. YES, EVERYTHING IS FINE.
I DON'T UNDERSTAND. YOU'VE BEEN RAMBLING FOR HOURS. WHO WON'T FIND YOU? GO WHERE?
LEAVING, STUPID! OPEN YOUR EYES!
BOOM!
BOOM!
BOOM!
DON'T OPEN THE DOOR.
BOOM!
HELLO, PRIEST.
HELLO, PRIEST.

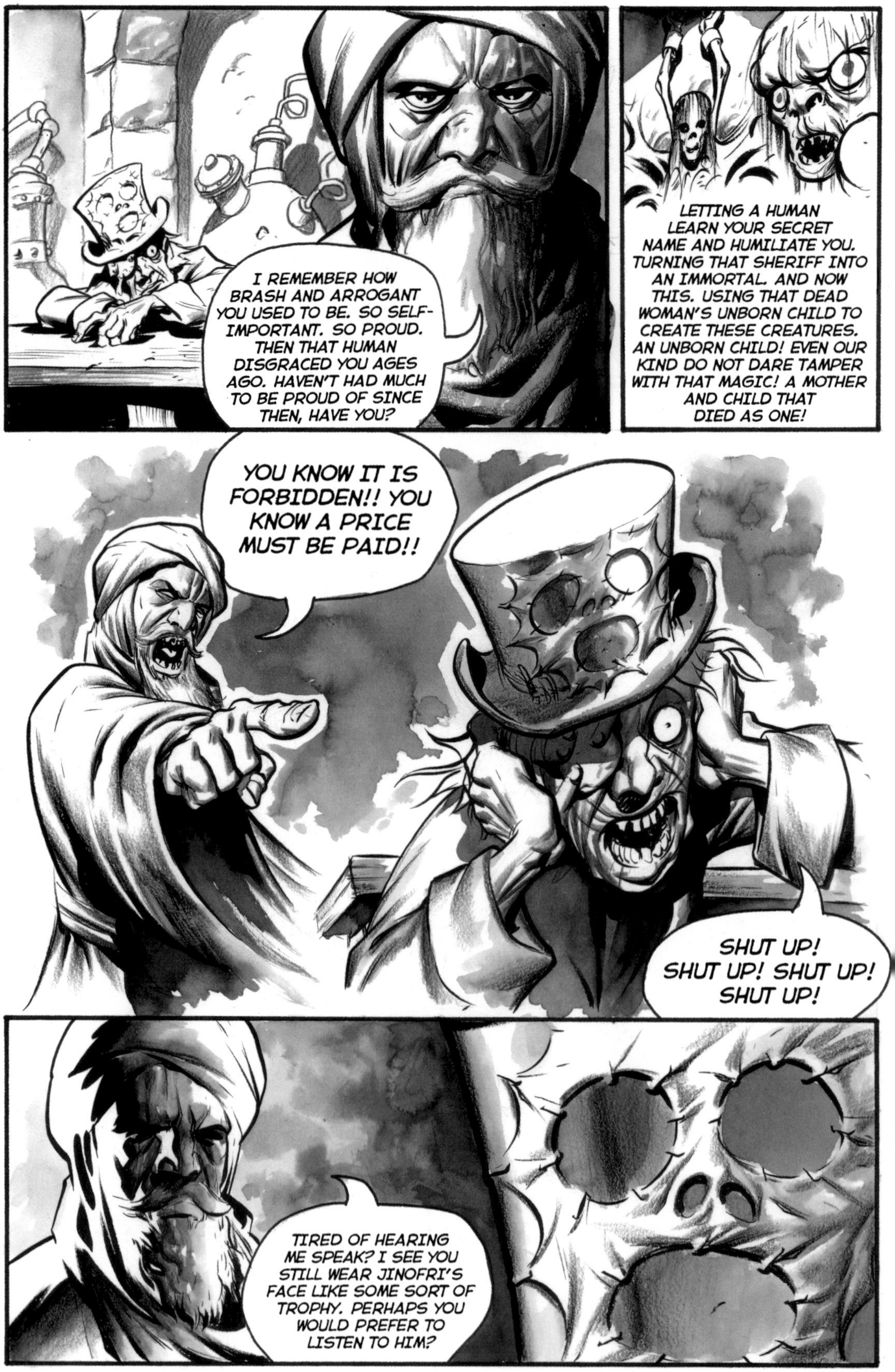
I REMEMBER HOW BRASH AND ARROGANT YOU USED TO BE. SO SELF-IMPORTANT. SO PROUD. THEN THAT HUMAN DISGRACED YOU AGES AGO. HAVEN'T HAD MUCH TO BE PROUD OF SINCE THEN, HAVE YOU?
LETTING A HUMAN LEARN YOUR SECRET NAME AND HUMILIATE YOU. TURNING THAT SHERIFF INTO AN IMMORTAL. AND NOW THIS. USING THAT DEAD WOMAN'S UNBORN CHILD TO CREATE THESE CREATURES. AN UNBORN CHILD! EVEN OUR KIND DO NOT DARE TAMPER WITH THAT MAGIC! A MOTHER AND CHILD THAT DIED AS ONE!
YOU KNOW IT IS FORBIDDEN!! YOU KNOW A PRICE MUST BE PAID!!
SHUT UP! SHUT UP! SHUT UP! SHUT UP!
TIRED OF HEARING ME SPEAK? I SEE YOU STILL WEAR JINOFRI'S FACE LIKE SOME SORT OF TROPHY. PERHAPS YOU WOULD PREFER TO LISTEN TO HIM?

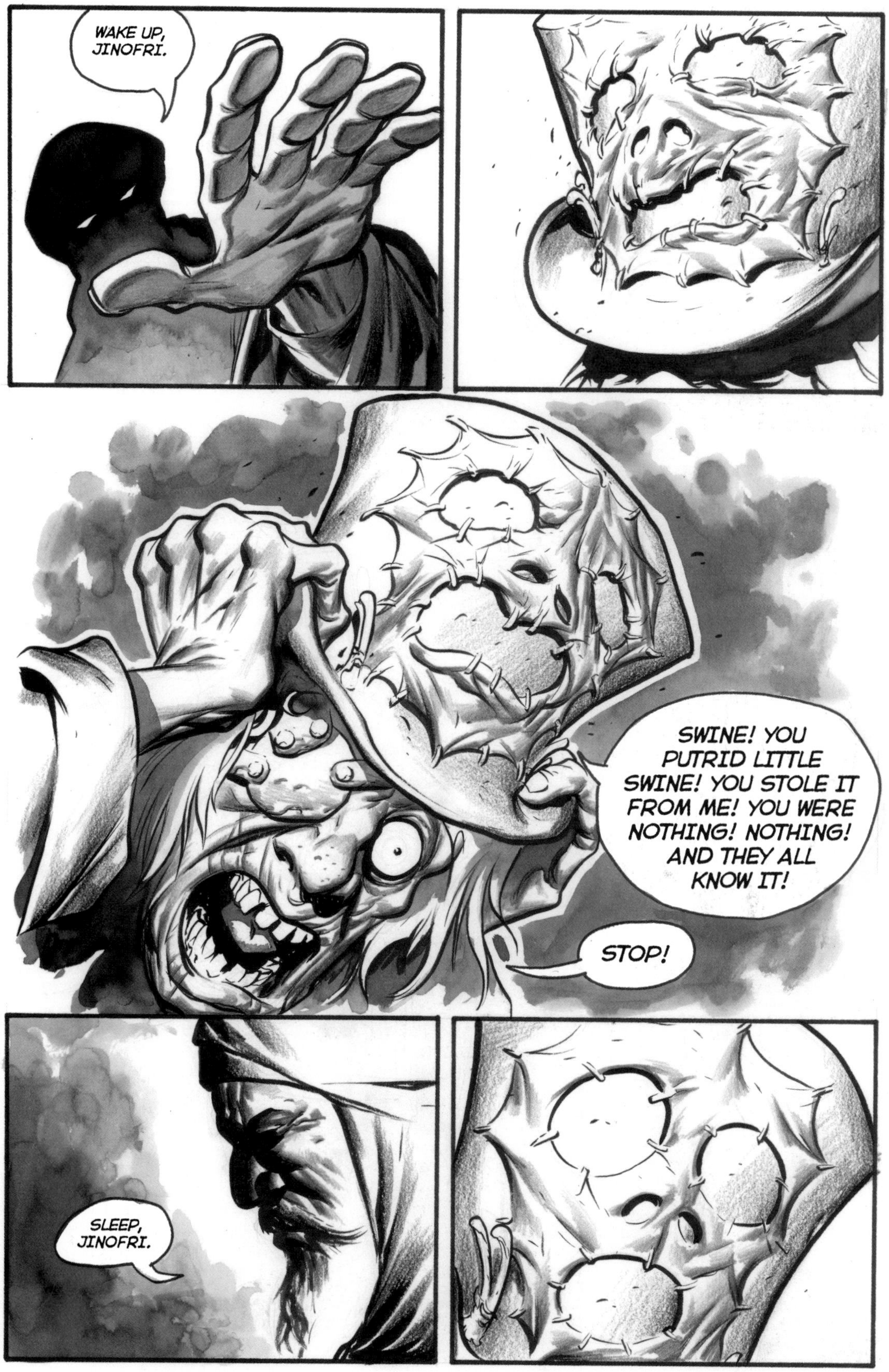
WAKE UP, JINOFRI.
SWINE! YOU PUTRID LITTLE SWINE! YOU STOLE IT FROM ME! YOU WERE NOTHING! NOTHING! AND THEY ALL KNOW IT!
STOP!
SLEEP, JINOFRI.

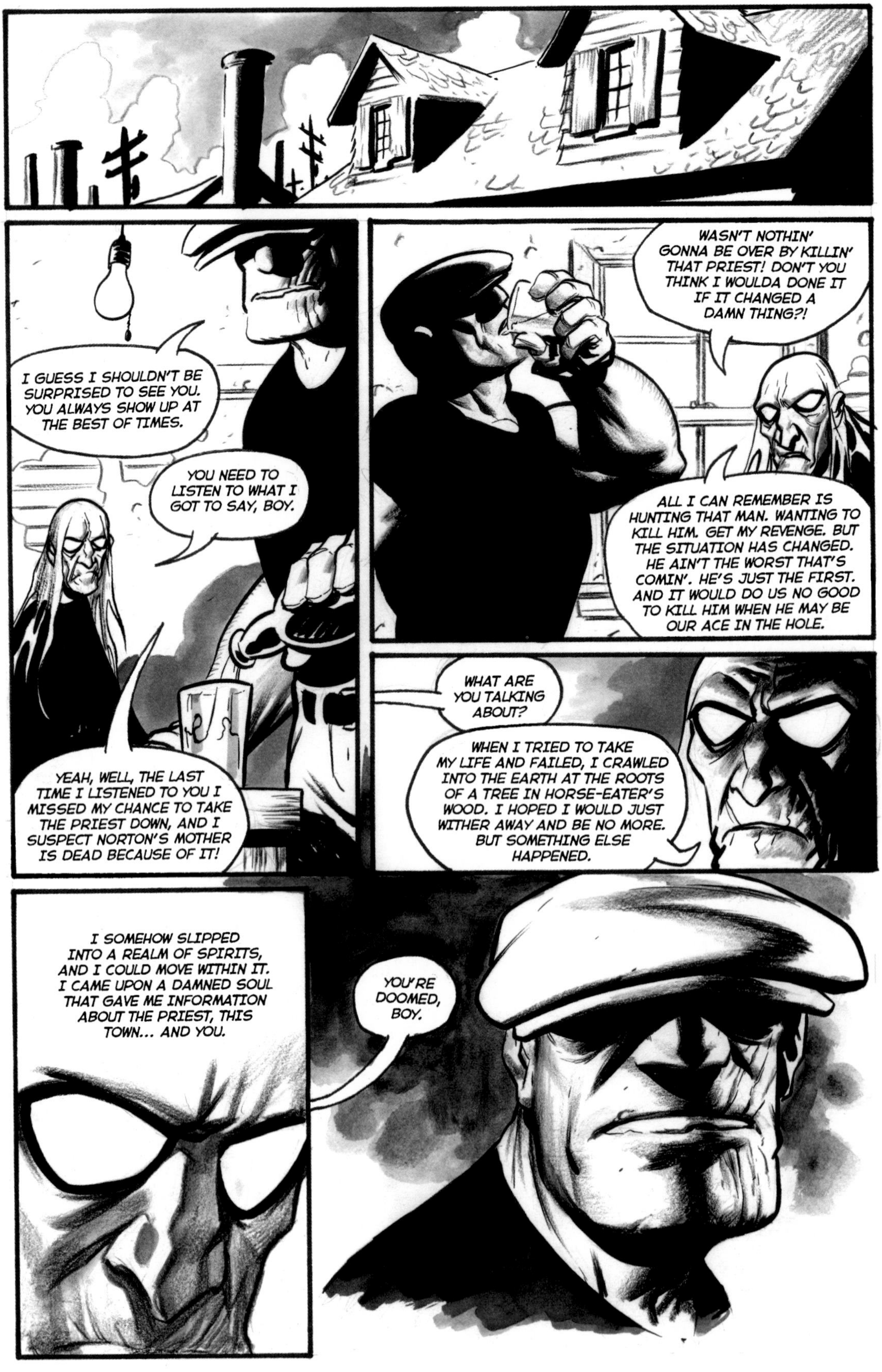
I GUESS I SHOULDN'T BE SURPRISED TO SEE YOU. YOU ALWAYS SHOW UP AT THE BEST OF TIMES.
YOU NEED TO LISTEN TO WHAT I GOT TO SAY, BOY.
YEAH, WELL, THE LAST TIME I LISTENED TO YOU I MISSED MY CHANCE TO TAKE THE PRIEST DOWN, AND I SUSPECT NORTON'S MOTHER IS DEAD BECAUSE OF IT!
WASN'T NOTHIN' GONNA BE OVER BY KILLIN' THAT PRIEST! DON'T YOU THINK I WOULDA DONE IT IF IT CHANGED A DAMN THING?!
ALL I CAN REMEMBER IS HUNTING THAT MAN. WANTING TO KILL HIM. GET MY REVENGE. BUT THE SITUATION HAS CHANGED. HE AIN'T THE WORST THAT'S COMIN'. HE'S JUST THE FIRST. AND IT WOULD DO US NO GOOD TO KILL HIM WHEN HE MAY BE OUR ACE IN THE HOLE.
WHAT ARE YOU TALKING ABOUT?
WHEN I TRIED TO TAKE MY LIFE AND FAILED, I CRAWLED INTO THE EARTH AT THE ROOTS OF A TREE IN HORSE-EATER'S WOOD. I HOPED I WOULD JUST WITHER AWAY AND BE NO MORE. BUT SOMETHING ELSE HAPPENED.
I SOMEHOW SLIPPED INTO A REALM OF SPIRITS, AND I COULD MOVE WITHIN IT. I CAME UPON A DAMNED SOUL THAT GAVE ME INFORMATION ABOUT THE PRIEST, THIS TOWN... AND YOU.
YOU'RE DOOMED, BOY.

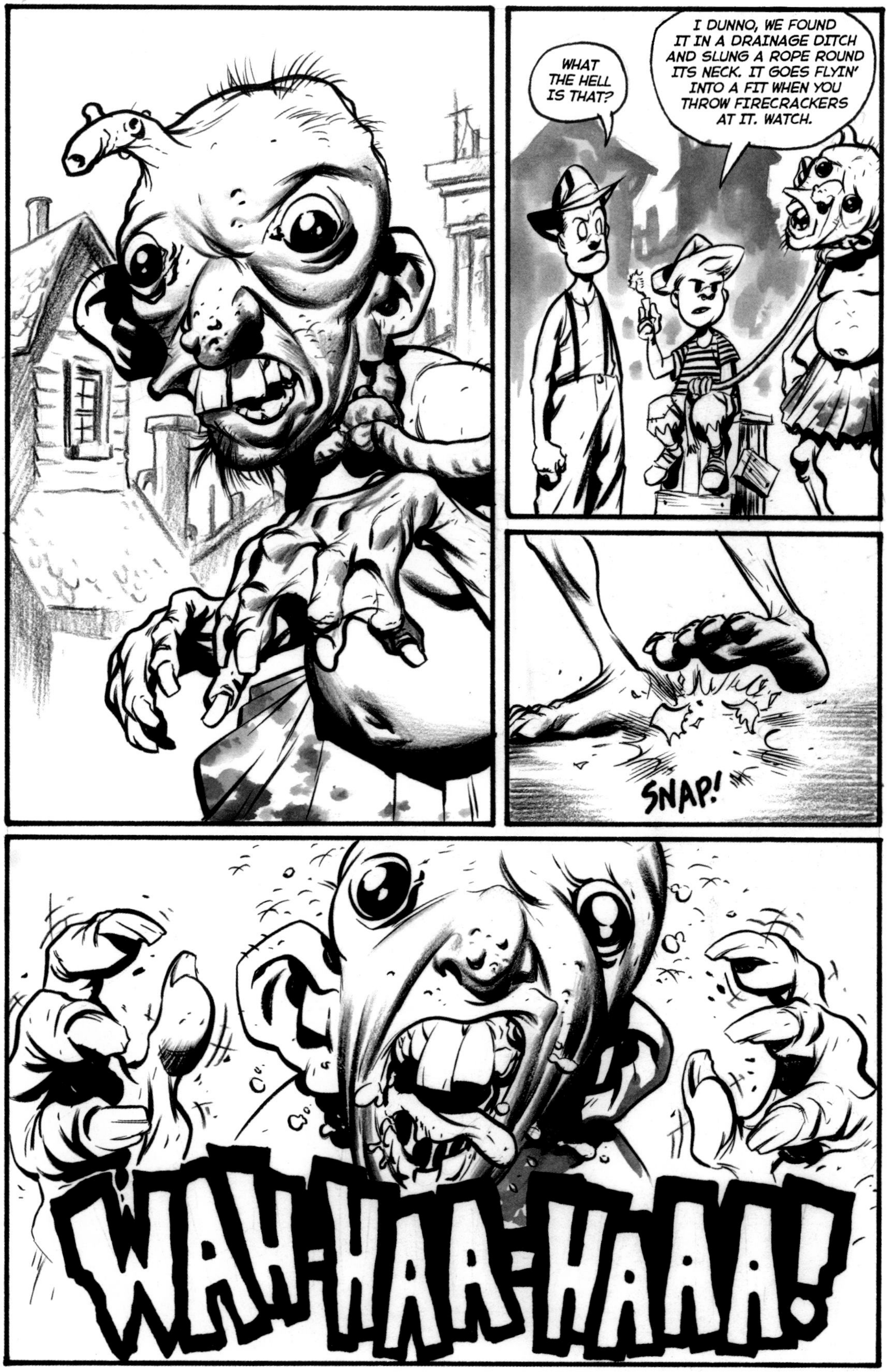
WHAT THE HELL IS THAT?
I DUNNO, WE FOUND IT IN A DRAINAGE DITCH AND SLUNG A ROPE ROUND ITS NECK. IT GOES FLYIN' INTO A FIT WHEN YOU THROW FIRECRACKERS AT IT. WATCH.
SNAP!
WAH-HAA-HAAA!

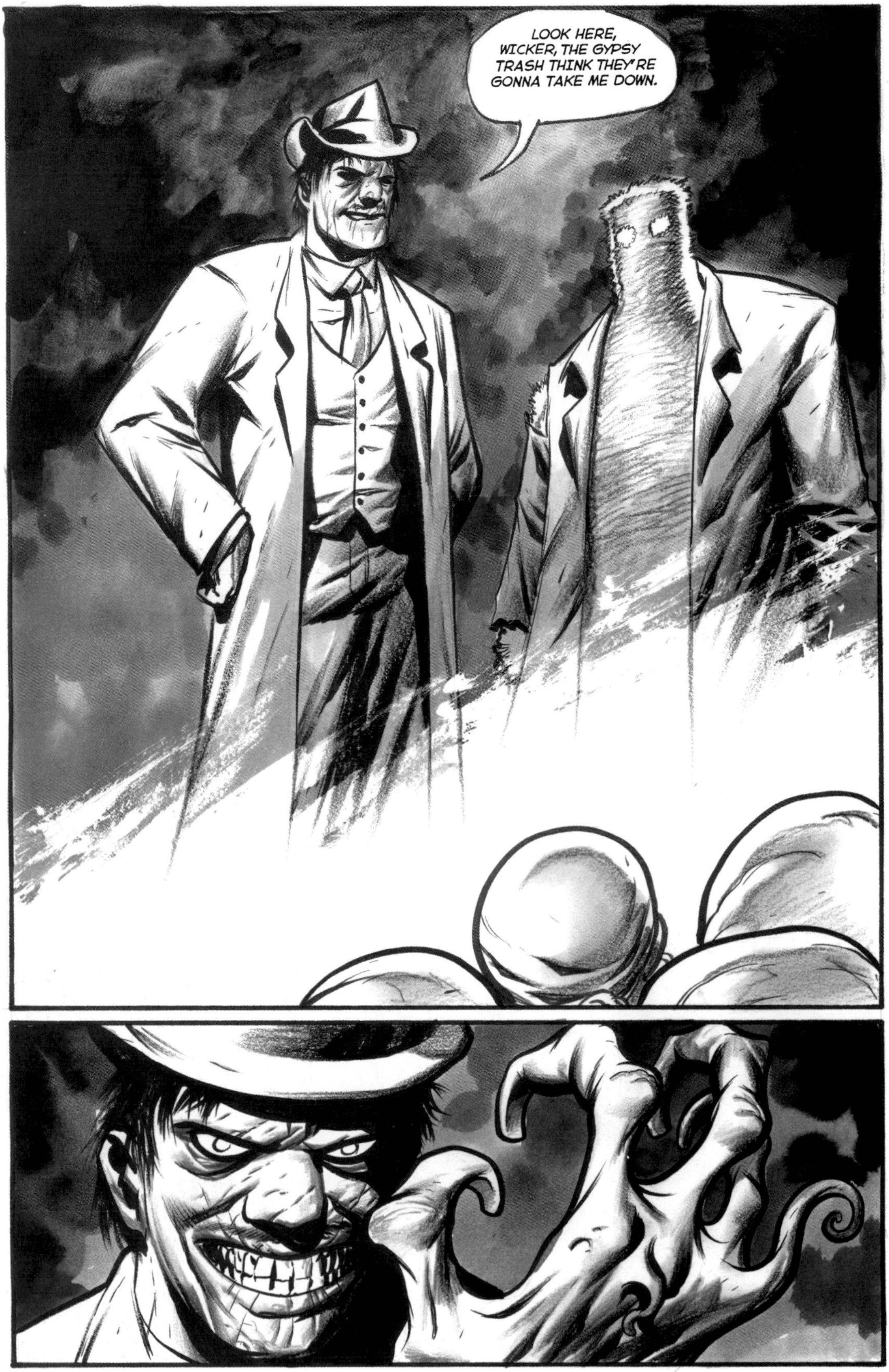
LOOK HERE, WICKER, THE GYPSY TRASH THINK THEY'RE GONNA TAKE ME DOWN.

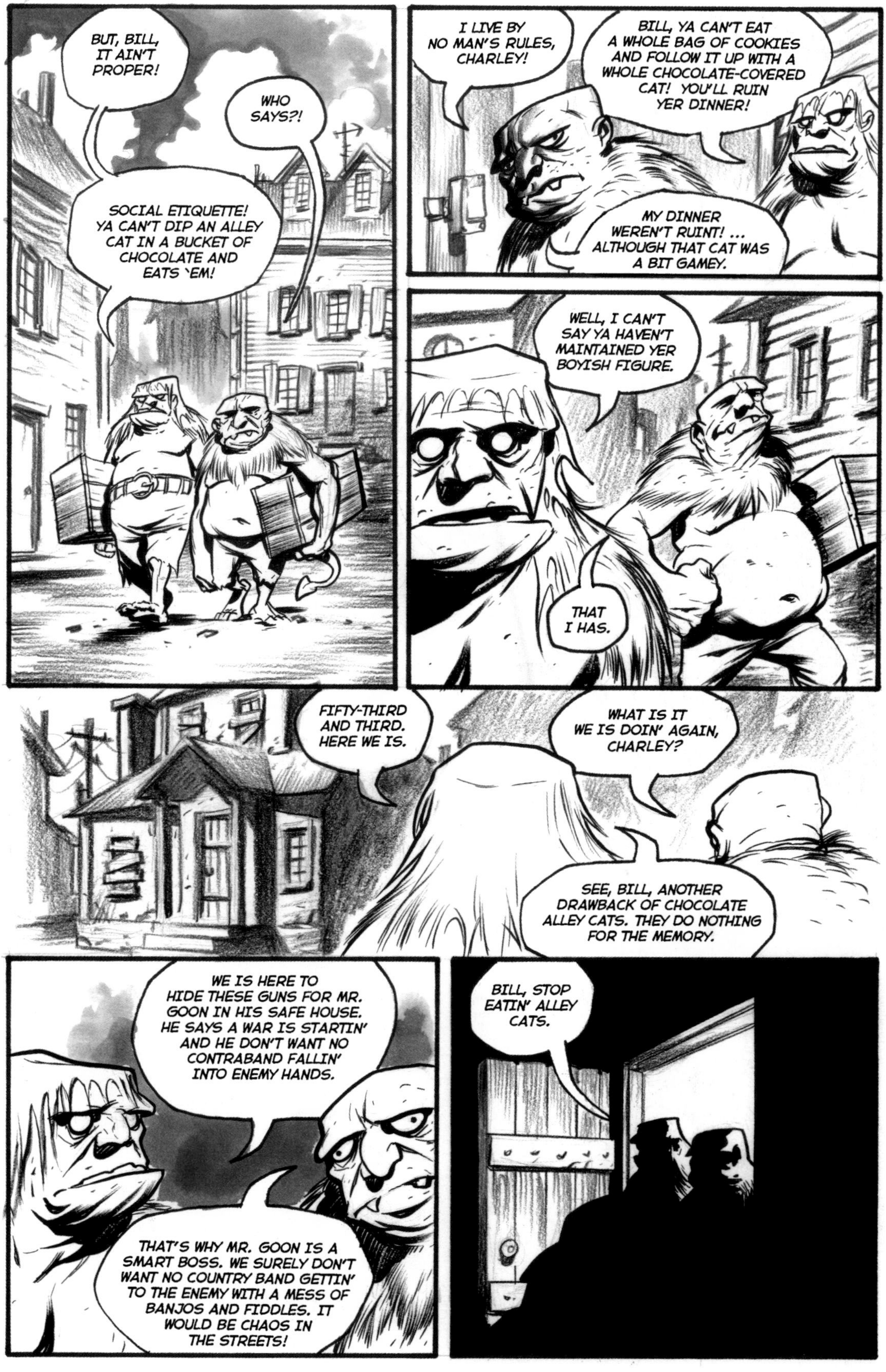
BUT, BILL, IT AIN'T PROPER!
WHO SAYS?!
SOCIAL ETIQUETTE! YA CAN'T DIP AN ALLEY CAT IN A BUCKET OF CHOCOLATE AND EATS 'EM!
I LIVE BY NO MAN'S RULES, CHARLEY!
BILL, YA CAN'T EAT A WHOLE BAG OF COOKIES AND FOLLOW IT UP WITH A WHOLE CHOCOLATE-COVERED CAT! YOU'LL RUIN YER DINNER!
MY DINNER WEREN'T RUINT! ... ALTHOUGH THAT CAT WAS A BIT GAMEY.
WELL, I CAN'T SAY YA HAVEN'T MAINTAINED YER BOYISH FIGURE.
THAT I HAS.
FIFTY-THIRD AND THIRD. HERE WE IS.
WHAT IS IT WE IS DOIN' AGAIN, CHARLEY?
SEE, BILL, ANOTHER DRAWBACK OF CHOCOLATE ALLEY CATS. THEY DO NOTHING FOR THE MEMORY.
WE IS HERE TO HIDE THESE GUNS FOR MR. GOON IN HIS SAFE HOUSE. HE SAYS A WAR IS STARTIN' AND HE DON'T WANT NO CONTRABAND FALLIN' INTO ENEMY HANDS.
THAT'S WHY MR. GOON IS A SMART BOSS. WE SURELY DON'T WANT NO COUNTRY BAND GETTIN' TO THE ENEMY WITH A MESS OF BANJOS AND FIDDLES. IT WOULD BE CHAOS IN THE STREETS!
BILL, STOP EATIN' ALLEY CATS.

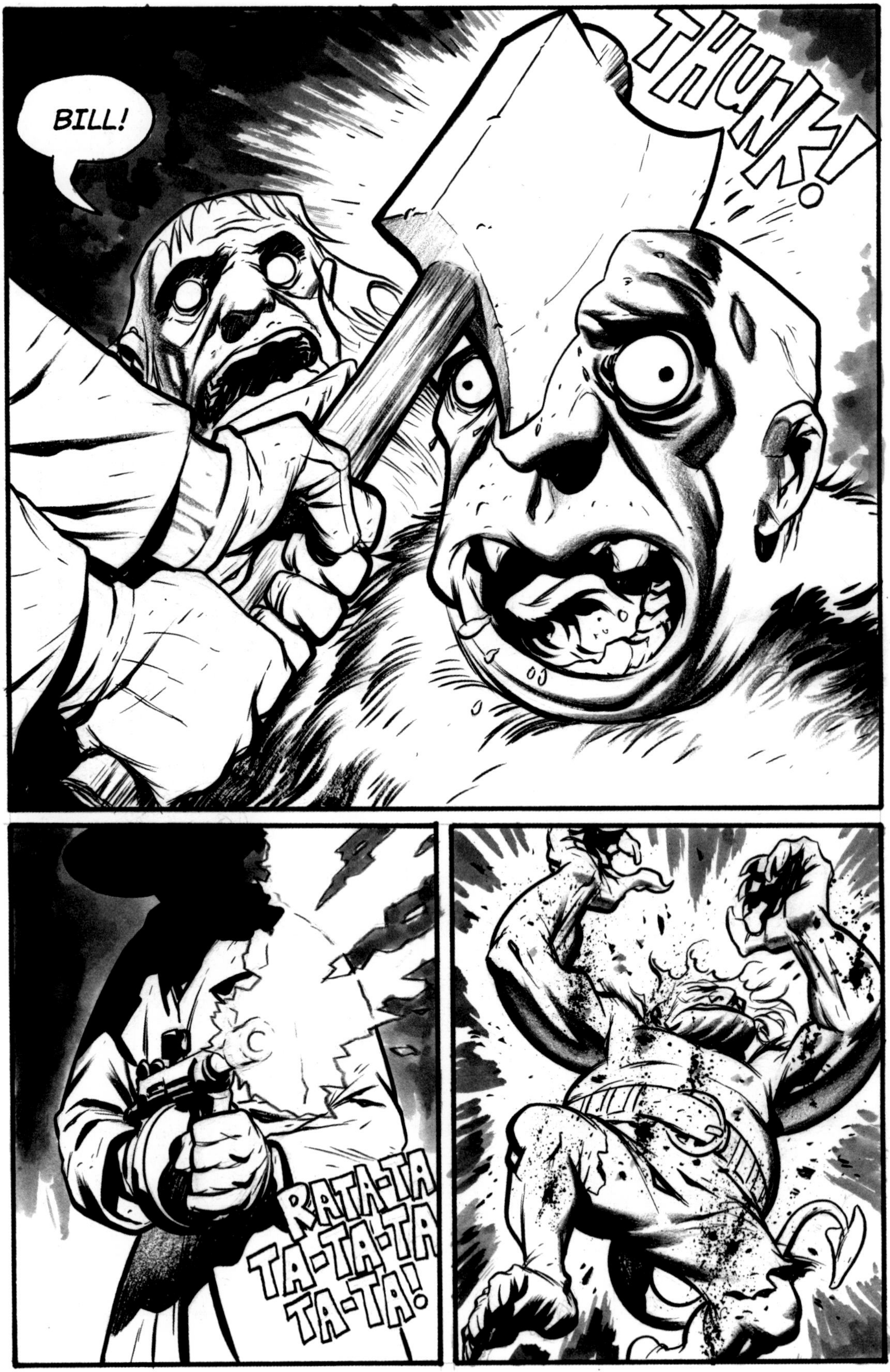
BILL!
THUNK!
RATA-TA
TA-TA-TA
TA-TA!

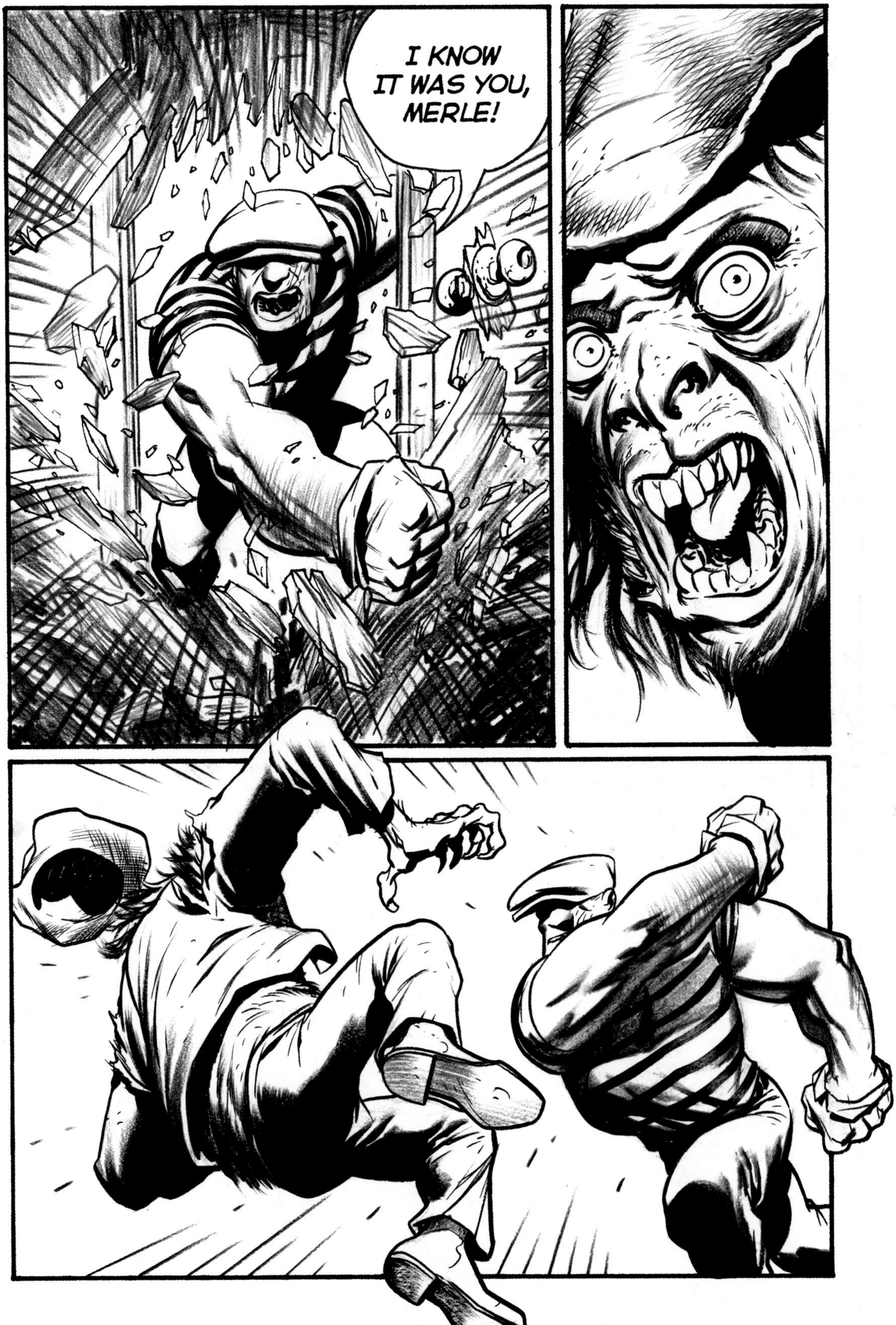
I KNOW IT WAS YOU, MERLE!

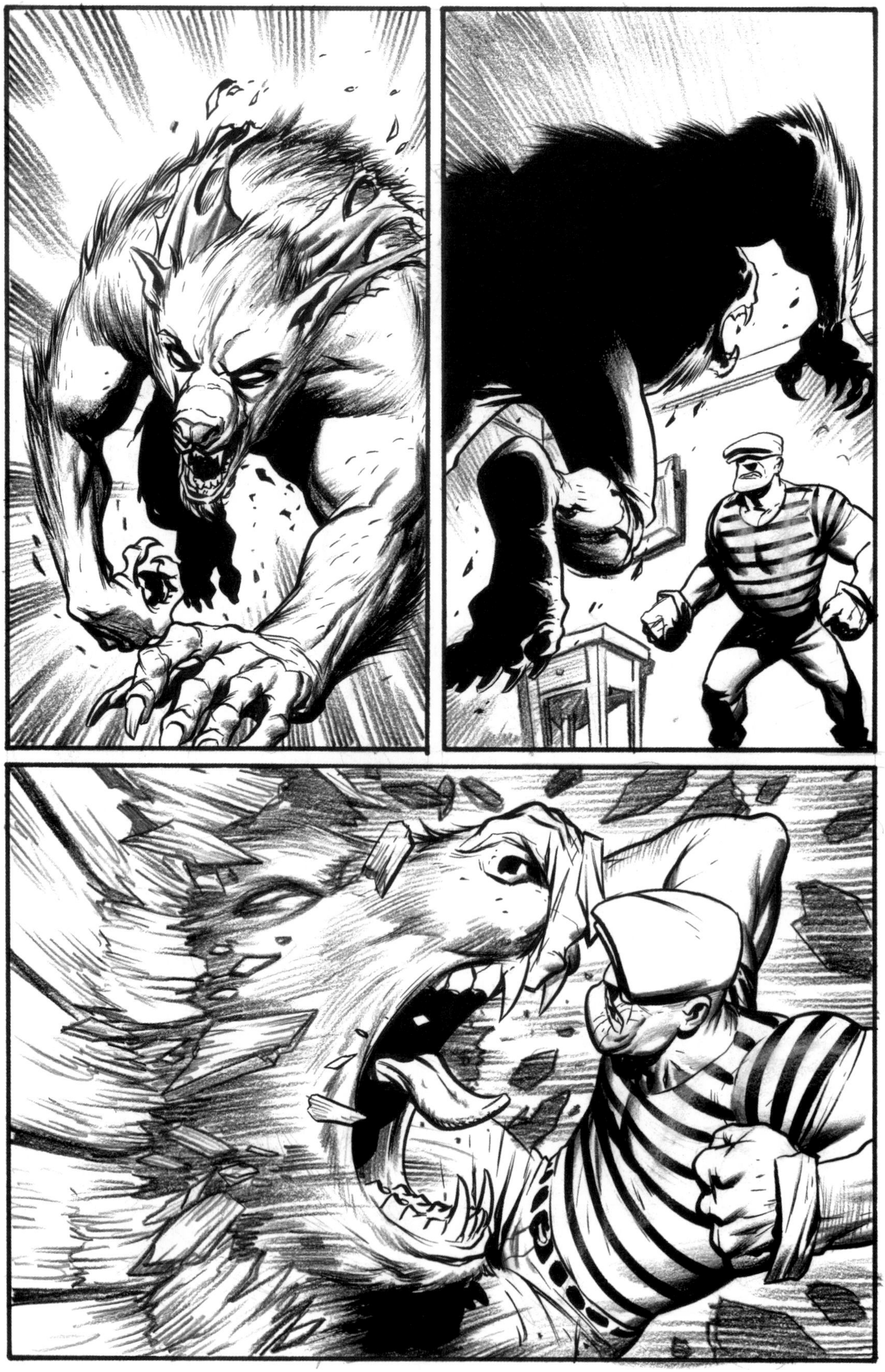

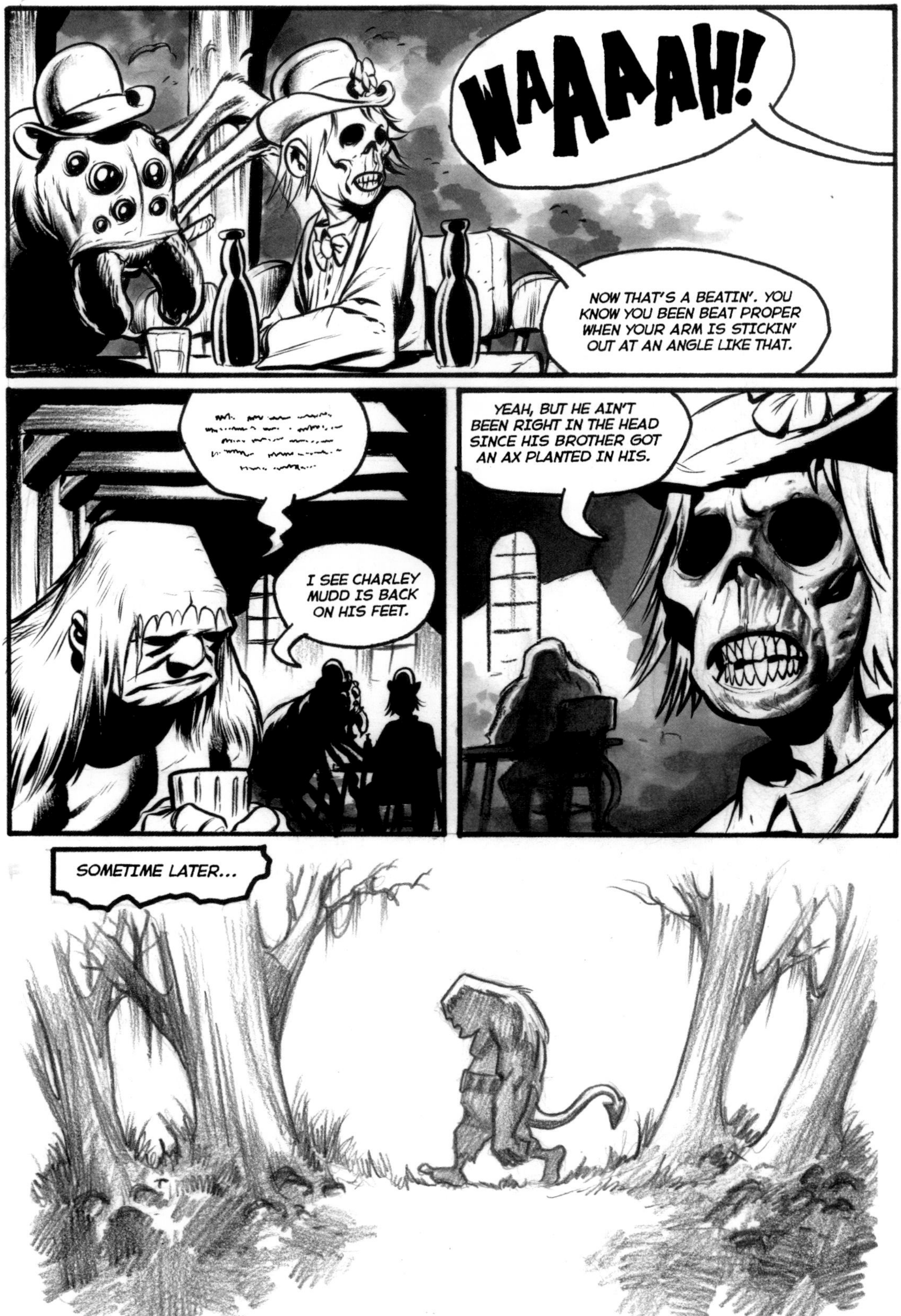
WAAAAH!
NOW THAT'S A BEATIN'. YOU KNOW YOU BEEN BEAT PROPER WHEN YOUR ARM IS STICKIN' OUT AT AN ANGLE LIKE THAT.
I SEE CHARLEY MUDD IS BACK ON HIS FEET.
YEAH, BUT HE AIN'T BEEN RIGHT IN THE HEAD SINCE HIS BROTHER GOT AN AX PLANTED IN HIS.
SOMETIME LATER...

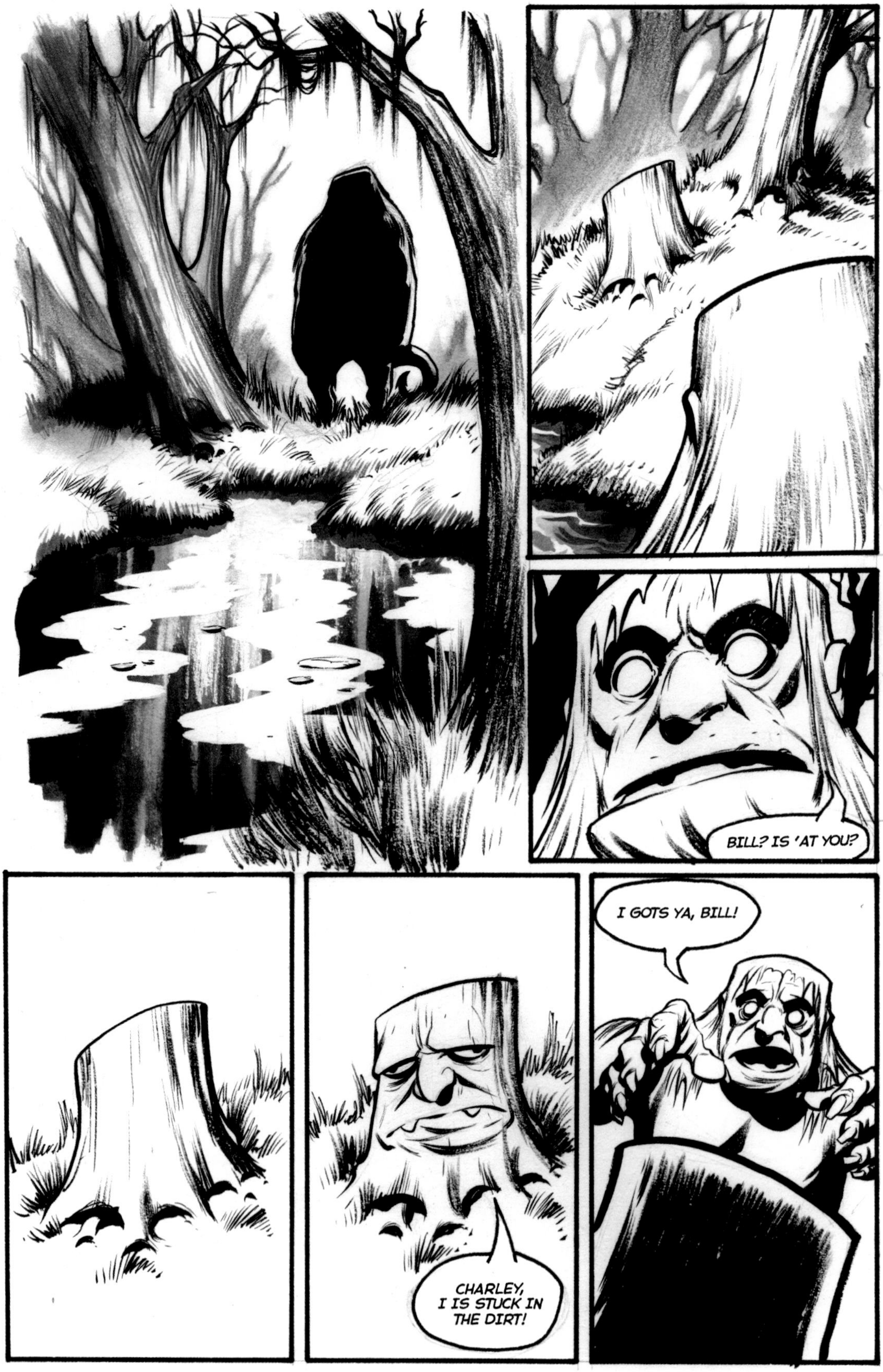
BILL? IS 'AT YOU?
CHARLEY, I IS STUCK IN THE DIRT!
I GOTS YA, BILL!

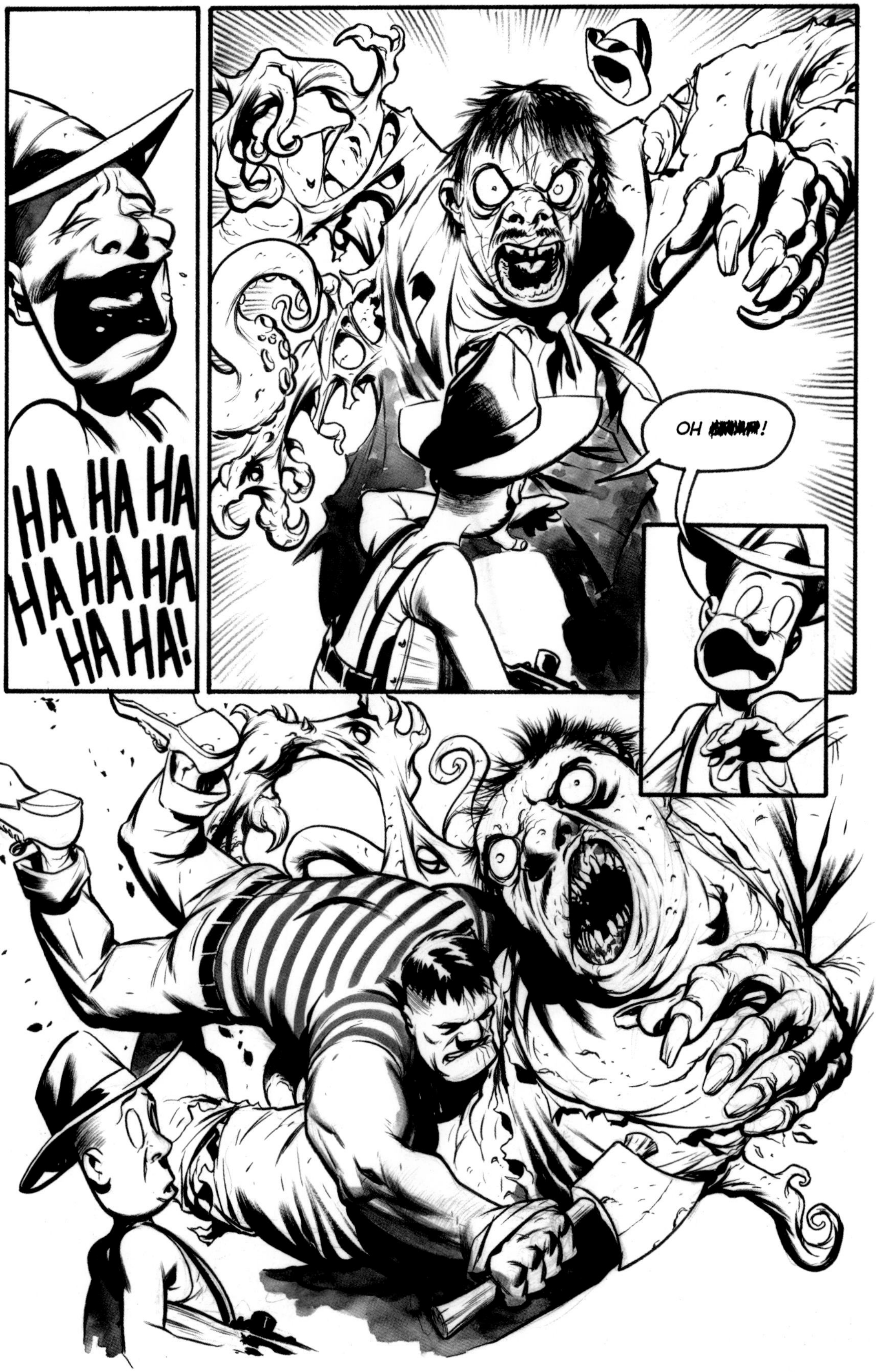
HA HA HA
HA HA HA
HA HA!
OH [redacted]!

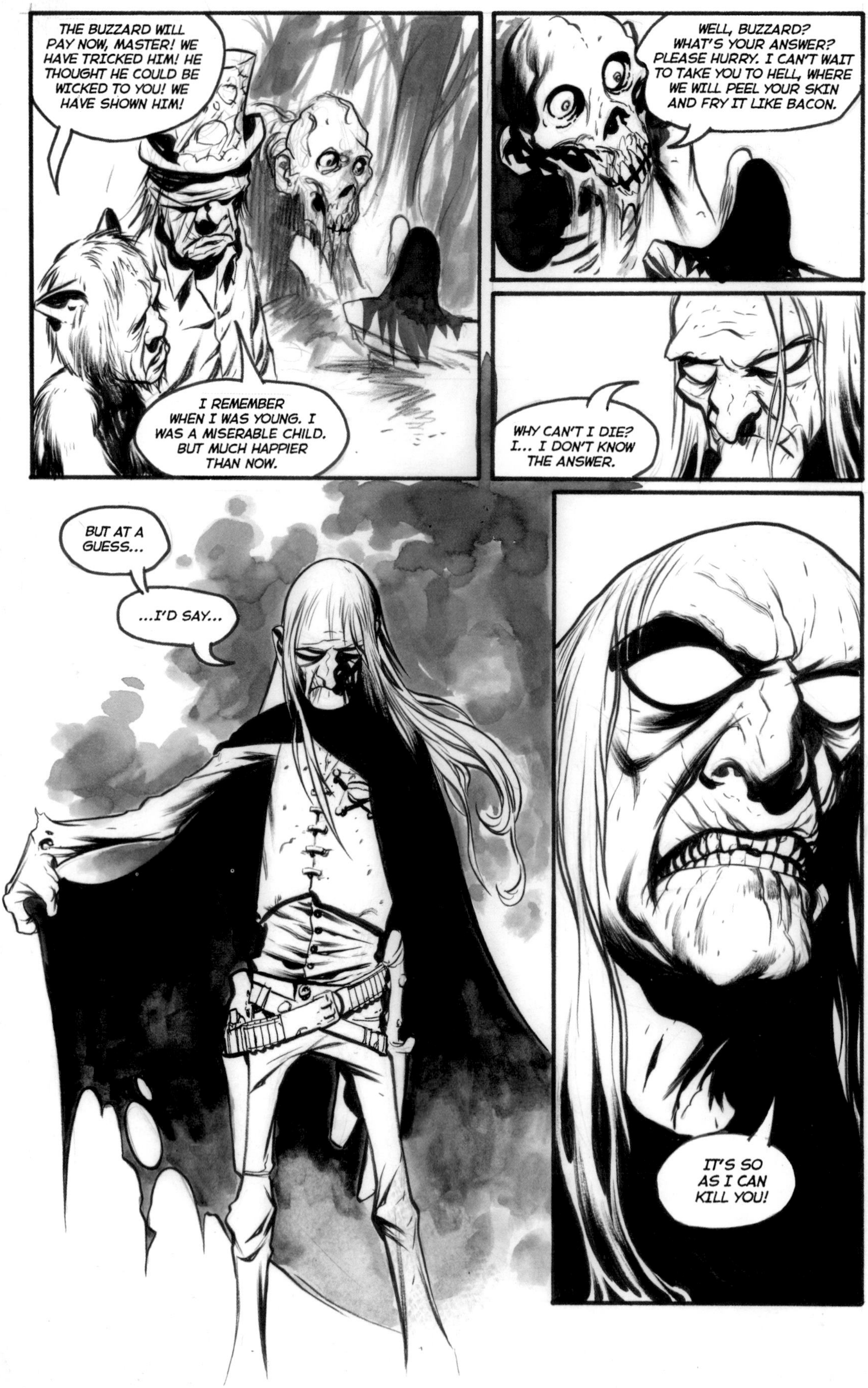
THE BUZZARD WILL PAY NOW, MASTER! WE HAVE TRICKED HIM! HE THOUGHT HE COULD BE WICKED TO YOU! WE HAVE SHOWN HIM!
I REMEMBER WHEN I WAS YOUNG. I WAS A MISERABLE CHILD. BUT MUCH HAPPIER THAN NOW.
WELL, BUZZARD? WHAT'S YOUR ANSWER? PLEASE HURRY. I CAN'T WAIT TO TAKE YOU TO HELL, WHERE WE WILL PEEL YOUR SKIN AND FRY IT LIKE BACON.
WHY CAN'T I DIE? I... I DON'T KNOW THE ANSWER.
BUT AT A GUESS...
...I'D SAY...
IT'S SO AS I CAN KILL YOU!

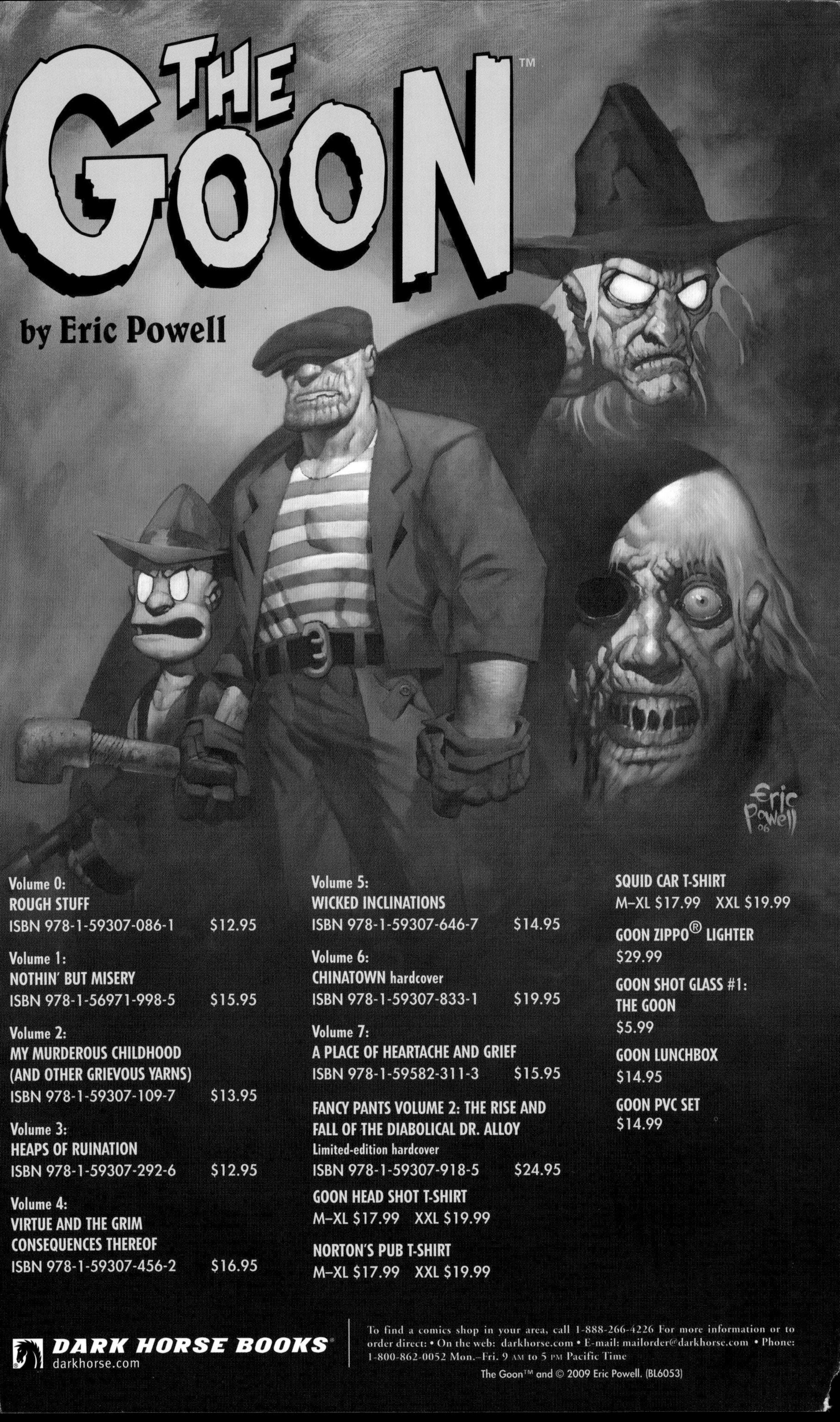
THE GOON™
by Eric Powell
Eric Powell '06

Volume 0:
ROUGH STUFF
ISBN 978-1-59307-086-1 $12.95

Volume 1:
NOTHIN' BUT MISERY
ISBN 978-1-56971-998-5 $15.95

Volume 2:
MY MURDEROUS CHILDHOOD (AND OTHER GRIEVOUS YARNS)
ISBN 978-1-59307-109-7 $13.95

Volume 3:
HEAPS OF RUINATION
ISBN 978-1-59307-292-6 $12.95

Volume 4:
VIRTUE AND THE GRIM CONSEQUENCES THEREOF
ISBN 978-1-59307-456-2 $16.95

Volume 5:
WICKED INCLINATIONS
ISBN 978-1-59307-646-7 $14.95

Volume 6:
CHINATOWN hardcover
ISBN 978-1-59307-833-1 $19.95

Volume 7:
A PLACE OF HEARTACHE AND GRIEF
ISBN 978-1-59582-311-3 $15.95

FANCY PANTS VOLUME 2: THE RISE AND FALL OF THE DIABOLICAL DR. ALLOY
Limited-edition hardcover
ISBN 978-1-59307-918-5 $24.95

GOON HEAD SHOT T-SHIRT
M–XL $17.99 XXL $19.99

NORTON'S PUB T-SHIRT
M–XL $17.99 XXL $19.99

SQUID CAR T-SHIRT
M–XL $17.99 XXL $19.99

GOON ZIPPO® LIGHTER
$29.99

GOON SHOT GLASS #1: THE GOON
$5.99

GOON LUNCHBOX
$14.95

GOON PVC SET
$14.99

DARK HORSE BOOKS
darkhorse.com

To find a comics shop in your area, call 1-888-266-4226 For more information or to order direct: • On the web: darkhorse.com • E-mail: mailorder@darkhorse.com • Phone: 1-800-862-0052 Mon.–Fri. 9 AM to 5 PM Pacific Time

ALSO FROM DARK HORSE BOOKS

REX MUNDI
BOOK ONE
The Guardian of the Temple
ARVID NELSON • ERICJ
JEROMY COX

REX MUNDI VOLUME 1: THE GUARDIAN OF THE TEMPLE

Arvid Nelson, EricJ, Juan Ferreyra, and Jeromy Cox

A quest for the Holy Grail unlike any you've ever seen begins here—in a world where the American Civil War ended in a stalemate, the Catholic Church controls Europe, and sorcery determines political power!

ISBN 978-1-59307-652-8

$16.95

ARVID NELSON
ERICJ
JEROMY COX
JIM DI BARTOLO
JUAN FERREYRA
REX MUNDI
BOOK THREE
The Lost Kings

REX MUNDI VOLUME 3: THE LOST KINGS

Arvid Nelson, EricJ, Jim Di Bartolo, and Juan Ferreyra

Julien furthers his investigation, only dimly aware of the forces tugging him down the trail of clues that lead to the doorstep, literally, of the Duke of Lorraine—a powerful man who seeks to provoke a massive, globe-spanning war that will soak the world in blood.

ISBN 978-1-59307-651-1

$16.95

a cal mcdonald mystery
CRIMINAL MACABRE
my demon baby
steve NILES
nick STAKAL
michelle MADSEN

CRIMINAL MACABRE: MY DEMON BABY

Steve Niles and Nick Stakal

To say that paranormal investigator Cal McDonald has been through hell and back would be a misstatement. He's been to hell, all right, and he seems to be stuck there for good. Devil worshipers in sunny SoCal are doing their best to bring Satan into the world, and by the looks of things, Cal's already too late. What does one feed a bouncing baby Beelzebub, anyway?

ISBN 978-1-59307-908-6

$12.95

BOB FINGERMAN'S
RECESS PIECES

RECESS PIECES

Bob Fingerman

Bad things are brewing in the halls of The Ben Turpin School. When a science project goes wrong, only the prepubescent children are spared the fate of zombification . . . but can they escape being eaten alive? George Romero covered night, dawn, and day, but how about recess?

ISBN 978-1-59307-450-0

$14.95

AVAILABLE AT YOUR LOCAL COMICS SHOP OR BOOKSTORE! • To find a comics shop in your area, call 1-888-266-4226.
For more information or to order direct visit darkhorse.com or call 1-800-862-0052 Mon.-Fri. 9 A.M. to 5 P.M. Pacific Time. Prices and availability subject to change without notice

DARK HORSE BOOKS® *drawing on your nightmares*
darkhorse.com

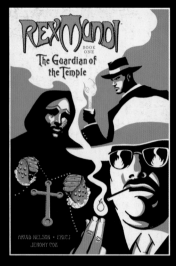

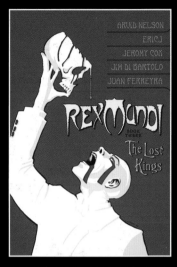

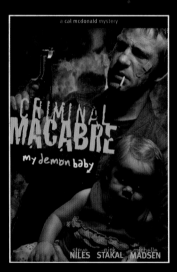

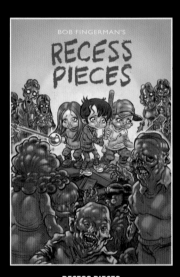